GRANGER, QUILTER, GRANDMA, MATRIARCH

Life on the Reiss Family Farm 1944–1948 in
St. Clair County, Illinois

BY STEPHEN W. REISS

Granger, Quilter, Grandma, Matriarch
Copyright © 2025 by Stephen W. Reiss

ISBN: 979-8894792187 (hc)
ISBN: 979-8894792163 (sc)
ISBN: 979-8894792170 (e)

The Reading Glass Books
1-888-420-3050
www.readingglassbooks.com
fulfillment@readingglassbooks.com

Dedication

This book is dedicated first to Catherine "Katie" Luetzelschwab Reiss because she wrote it, a day at a time over five years as her personal diary. Secondly, along with his photo on the next page, this book is also dedicated to Richard Reiss, the first of Katie's six adult grandchildren to pass to his greater reward.

Katie's love of family, neighbors, service, and rural life become evident to the reader as these days go by in her diary. Her character as matriarch to children, grandchildren, relatives, and friends is genuine because she lived her life that way never knowing that these five years of it would be published. She was my grandmother, my dad's mom. Our lives overlapped by 42 years. She was a major role model for two generations.

The following paragraph appeared in the Yale University Alumni magazine: Richard Franklin Reiss was born on November 21, 1944 and raised in Urbana, Illinois. Upon graduating from Yale in 1966 with a degree in economics, he accepted a Fulbright scholarship to study in Berlin. Following this he attended Oxford University where he received a bachelor's degree in philosophy. He was studying for his PhD in philosophy at Rockefeller University in New York when he discovered and began to study the scriptures and religious philosophy of the Church of Scientology. In 1973 he decided to devote himself full time to this ministry, eventually becoming a senior minister of the church's largest and most advanced organization in Clearwater Florida, a position he held for a quarter of a century. His primary duty was to oversee the precise application and technical quality of the spiritual counseling of the church by ministers all over the world. He was personally known and loved by tens of thousands. Richard is survived by his wife Cala, son Jesse, and daughter Rebecca.

Acknowledgements

Proofreading and adding elaborations (*in italics*) to make parts of Katie's diary a bit more self-explanatory were assisted by granddaughter June Ann Reiss McBrayer and great grandson Jesse Reiss. Actually, Richard Reiss to whom this book is dually dedicated also helped with this process because his son Jesse read it to him during his final days in hospice care.

Pay special attention to all the family photographs in this book and then thank grandson Ken Reiss who put that part of this project together. Ken is our self-appointed family photo archivist. He has digitized literally thousands of family photos from old black and white prints, old negatives, color slides and prints, plus new digital pictures he has taken himself.

We are greatly indebted to these relatives for their contributions but most importantly for their love, affection, and appreciation for Katie Luetzelschwab Reiss.

1

The Stage and Cast of Characters

Leading Lady: Catherine "Katie" Luetzelschwab was born on 3/25/1890 in St. Clair County, Illinois of Swiss parents. She had about six years of formal education and eventually worked as a domestic servant in the household of Frank and Anna Syvilla Reiss in 1910 where she met their oldest surviving son George Reiss and married him on 4/16/1911. She wrote the 5-year diary which appears below. It starts January 1944 when she is age 54 and her husband is age 71. She enjoyed quilting and volunteering at several area Grange halls, but never learned to drive an automobile. Her first language was German. Their three children were bi-lingual. Her diary is written in English.

Leading Man: George "Geo" or "Pop" Reiss was born on 4/22/1873 in St. Clair County, Illinois of German parents. He had about four years of formal education and worked for/with his parents on the family farm. He married his parents' domestic servant, Katie Luetzelschwab, on 4/16/1911. She was 17 years his junior. He and Katie eventually bought the family farm established by his grandfather Adam Reiss in 1838. George retired from farming in 1948 having farmed only with horses. He never owned a tractor. His vehicles were a 1925 Ford coupe and a 1930's pickup truck. His first language was German.

Supporting Cast One: Their first son is William "Bill" or "Willie" Reiss born 5/6/1912 on the family farm. He married Anita Hesse and had one surviving child, June Ann Reiss. They lived half an hour north in Maplewood, Illinois where he was a maintenance foreman with Socony Oil. They alternated visits for most Sunday evening meals with his Reiss parents and her Hesse parents who lived five miles apart.

Supporting Cast Two: Their second son is Franklin "Frank" Reiss born 10/31/1915 on the family farm. He married Gerry Hulet and had two sons, George Reiss and Richard Reiss. They lived two hours northeast in Urbana, Illinois where he was a professor of Agricultural Economics at the University of Illinois. They visited every three or four months.

Supporting Cast Three: Their third son is Irwin "Irv" Reiss born 9/18/1917 on the family farm. He married Mary Stephenson and had three children, Stephen "Steve" or "Stevie" Reiss, Kenneth "Ken" Reiss, and Mary Kay "Mickey" Reiss. They lived four hours east in Sullivan, Indiana where he was a professional farm manager with Meadowlark Farms which owned farm clusters near Denmark and Canton, both in Illinois, Chinook in Indiana, and other locations. They visited every three or four months. Irv often tied a visit home with a business visit to the Denmark farm which his mother often calls the "south" farm.

Other Cast – Her Relatives: Katie was the fifth of eleven Luetzelschwab children. Her sisters and their husbands who often visited were: Mary and Jacob Weihl, Minnie and John Sponemann, Lottie and Edward Sander, Lena and Joseph Speichinger, Caroline and Elmer Gummersheimer, and Edna and Henry Lang. Her brothers and their wives who often visited and occasionally helped with odd jobs were: Johnny and Katie, bachelor Herman, Jacob "Jaky" and Cora, and bachelor Frank. Other visitors were her married niece Elsie Weihl Hoffman and husband Albert.

Other Cast – His Relatives: George was the fourth of eleven Reiss children and the oldest of seven to reach adulthood. His sisters and their husbands who often visited were: Anna and George Dintelmann and widowed Katie Petry. His brothers and their wives who often visited were: John and Mary Etta from Sikeston, Henry and Bertha from St. Louis, Louis and Hattie from Texas, and Will and Rose from Belleville.

Other Cast – Neighbors: Katie and George could walk a quarter mile south to the farm of Frank and Clara Schilling or they could walk a quarter mile west to the farm of Ignatius "Boobie" and Marcella Klein. Marcella Klein is the Schilling's daughter which made the neighborhood even more friendly. "Boobie" is the German word for "boy" which was his childhood name that stuck. Katie and George had private telephone lines with those families that used old wooden wall-mounted crank telephones. They could also walk or drive 1.7 miles west to the village of Floraville for church or meetings at the Floraville Grange. Other neighbors like the Metzgers, Koerbers, and Roushes often provided transportation help because Katie did not drive and George's vehicles were old and small. When Katie writes, for example, that Oscar Koerbers were here in the evening, she means both husband and wife.

Smithton Sportsmen's Club: This is a 40-acre parcel on the east edge of the Reiss Farm which Katie and George leased to this group of mostly fishermen since mid-1951. The Sportsmen built a clubhouse and put in three lakes which cover 11 acres. They have about 150 members and have been very supportive and partnering with the extended Reiss family for well over 70 years.

St. Paul United Church of Christ in Floraville: Katie and George were 50+ year members here. All three of their children were confirmed here. They attended regularly but were sometimes limited by weather and lack of transportation. Also in Floraville is a one-room brick school which all three of their sons attended.

Quilting and Patching: Katie found great relaxation and community in quilting. "Patching" is her word for making designs about a foot square which were then sewn together to create the overall quilt. Her second diary of 1949 - 53 shows her quilting on 31 days in 1949, 58 days in 1950, 93 days in 1951, 61 days in 1952, and 43 days in 1953.

Grange Work: Katie found great satisfaction and accomplishment in volunteering at ten different Granges. She and George were founder members of the Floraville Grange from 3/8/1948. Her second diary shows her working at or working for various Granges on 31 days in 1949, 39 days in 1950, 29 days in 1951, 35 days in 1952, and 46 days in 1953. The National Grange was founded in 1867 in the aftermath of the Civil War. Peak national membership was 600,000. Illinois had 34 active Granges in 2008.

Farm Work: Katie's kitchen stove burned wood or corn cobs. In 1952 they upgraded to a new stove which was half electric and half solid fuel. One of George's major jobs was cutting firewood. They bought mail order baby chickens two or three times a year to raise and eventually sell meat and eggs in nearby communities. Those chicks started in the brooder house and were moved to a chicken house when old enough. A "brooder" is a sheet metal shelter about a foot tall and five feet in diameter with a central heat lamp which kept baby chicks warm. George and Katie also raised hogs and sold or butchered them as needed. They also received crop share income in renting out their farm after 1948. First tenant was the Howertons, second was the Josephs, and third was Lavern and Lucille Lang who started in April 1954. Lavern is Katie's nephew as the son of her sister Lena.

The Reiss Family Farm: Adam Reiss purchased 120 acres in 1838 for $2.50 per acre. Adjacent 40- and 20-acre parcels were purchased in 1854 and 1868, respectively, by Adam's widow Margaret and her second husband Conrad Ebert. Margaret's oldest son Frank Reiss and his wife Anne bought the 180-acre family farm from his mother and siblings in 1869. Their oldest son George Reiss and his wife Katie bought the family farm from his parents in 1920. George and Katie had previously bought 180 adjacent acres in 1917 from the Schaefer family. They continued to refer to those fields by the Schaefer name. The Reiss Family Farm continues to this day as 360 acres in Sections 7 and 8 of Prairie du Long Township in St. Clair County, Illinois.

Reiss Farm Buildings: Adam Reiss built a log cabin and a log granary in 1838. The cabin was home for his family of wife Margaret and five children. Then it was the home for his son Frank's family of wife Anne and ten children until 1889 when they built a modern six-room home. The new house was then home for his son George's family of wife Katie and three sons until they built another modern seven-room home in 1940. During these diary years, the two log buildings were used for farm storage. The farm tenants lived in the 1889 home and Katie and George lived in the 1940 home. The log granary continues to this day but sadly the log cabin was removed about 1957.

Explanation – How Katie Wrote

Instead of writing "We went to church," Katie would write "We were at church." And instead of writing "Gus and Alma Metzger visited," she would write "The Gus Metzgers visited." For space reasons there are also lots of phrases and partial sentences. Some of Katie's word and phrase choices may relate to German being her first language and to her formal education being limited to just six years. Anyway, you'll quickly get used to Katie's style after just a few weeks of her diary.

Katie's word choices would have been a big problem for the proofreading service which is normally provided by book publishers. But, we turned that service off so Katie's real character was preserved. Consequently, you'll never know whether a few spelling errors that still appear in this book are my transcription "typos" or Katie's actual spellings!!!

Granddad's Mondays

These stories are what make this book a "Second Edition." I was sitting in the First United Methodist Church of Peoria on Palm Sunday 2012 which was March 31. During a long hymn by the choir, I realized that I was already 67 years older than our first two grands in diapers and that we may not have many years together for heavy adult conversations on family history, fun times, travel, etc. So, I resolved to write two stories with photos and documents every Monday as emails to their parents and occasional relatives. I called them "Granddad's Mondays." Every December I further resolved to take the stories for that year to PIP Printing in Peoria who would bind them into Christmas books for each of our now four grands, their parents, and ourselves. Those seven copies would survive me and be useful for occasional reference or updates. In 13 years there have been over 1,600 Granddad's Mondays stories. **I am thrilled with this addiction and consider myself incredibly blessed!!! You should think about doing this for your progeny.**

Stephen W. Reiss
Peoria, Illinois

Table of Contents

Matriarch #3 – Catherine Charlotte Luetzelschwab Reiss

Dear Will, Kayla, and Ava,   August 25, 2014

Last Monday you learned about Matriarch #1 who was my great great grandmother Margaret Basler Reiss Ebert and about Matriarch #2 who was my great grandmother Anna Antonia Sybilla Feder Reiss. Today you can learn about Matriarch #3 who is my grandmother Catherine Charlotte Luetzelschwab Reiss. She is the only one of these three women that I actually knew because our times on earth overlapped by 42 years with about 37 of those years being on the Reiss family farm.

Grandma Katie was born on 3/25/1890 on the Luetzelschwab family farm in St. Clair County. She was baptized at Zion United Church of Christ in Millstadt (renamed Zion Evangelical in 2005) on 5/8/1890 and confirmed there on Palm Sunday 4/5/1903. She married George William Reiss at St. Paul's United Church of Christ in Floraville on 4/16/1911. All three sacraments and the local church documents were in German. The St. Clair County wedding document was in English. Three of those four documents are framed and displayed in our home.

Catherine Luetzelschwab Reiss wedding Picture

One of the wedding gifts which Katie and George received was this porcelain bowl which is also on display in our home. It probably had a pitcher with it originally and was a bedroom set for washing faces and hands before the times of indoor bathrooms and running water. There is a note on the bottom of this bowl from my Aunt Gerry Reiss saying it was a wedding gift to Katie and George that was given by her mother Catherine Hoelscher who had received it as a wedding gift when she married Jacob Luetzelschwab on 5/26/1881. So as a double wedding gift, this bowl is really very special.

When Katie married George in 1911, he was living with his parents, Frank age 70 and Anna Sybilla ages 67, on the family farm. He was farming those 180 acres and was doing quite well. He farmed with horses and raised crops, hogs, sheep, and chickens. He also owned 160 acres of farmland in Lamb County, Texas which he had bought sight-unseen on 10/18/1907 for $15 per acre or a total of $2,400.

Katie's first ten years of marriage were exciting to say the least. Here are the major details –

- Son William George was born on 5/6/1912.

- Son Franklin Jacob was born on Halloween night 10/31/1915. Trick or treat!!!

- Katie and George bought 140 adjacent acres on 4/12/1917 from the Schaefer family for $4,000. They paid $1,000 down and signed two $500 mortgages and a $2,000 mortgage held by the Schaefers, all with different due dates.

- Katie and George bought 40 acres on 10/20/1917 from the Chamberlin family for $800. That corner has been leased to the Smithton Sportsman's Club since 7/20/1951. Initial rent was $25 per year which is only a 3.1% return on investment.

- Son Irwin Henry was born on 9/18/1918.

- Katie and George bought the 180-acre family farm from his parents on 4/12/1920 for $7,700. Parts of that deed appear on the next page. George's father died 1.5 years later on 11/21/1921.

I remember Grandma Katie telling me several times how she cried and cried over how much debt they were accumulating in buying 160 acres in Texas and 360 acres in Illinois. They did all this while raising three very young sons which meant all the farm labor fell on her husband with occasional help from hired hands. To further underscore the challenge, their farm did not get electricity until 11/17/1945 and George did all his field work by hand or with horses. He never owned a tractor. I find the first 30 years of their married life absolutely amazing.

12

WARRANTY DEED.—Statutory Form.

This Indenture Witnesseth, That the Grantors _Frank J. Reiss and Anna S. Reiss his wife_

of the _Prairie du Long Township_ County of _St. Clair_ and State of _Illinois,_ for and in consideration of the sum of _Seventy seven Hundred (7700 00/100)_ DOLLARS, in hand paid, **Convey** and **Warrant** to _George W. Reiss and Catherine Charlotte Reiss his wife_

of the _Prairie du Long Township_ County of _St. Clair_ and State of _Illinois_

Dated this _12th_ day of _April,_ A. D. 19_20_.

Frank J Reiss SEAL

Anna S Reiss SEAL

SEAL

Here's Katie with her handsome family about 1935.

On the next page is a photo from about 1943 of all eleven Luetzelschwab siblings and one niece. From left to right in back are Lena Becker, Mary Weihl, Katie Reiss, Herman, Lottie Sander, John, Jacob, and Frank. Minnie Sponemann is in the wheelchair. Front row is Edna Lang, niece Janet Pauketat, and Caroline Gummersheimer. Brother John is the carpenter-contractor who built Katie and George's new home in 1940.

George and Katie Reiss with sons Irwin, Bill, and Franklin

Grandma Katie kept two five-year daily diaries – 1944 through 1948 and 1949 through 1953. I transcribed both diaries, added old photos, inserted elaborations in italics where needed, and submitted both galleys to Author House for publishing. Both books appear below.

Katie's entries for ten days in July 1949 made me laugh out loud as she recounts babysitting for us three grandchildren. I was six months older than you, Will. My brother Ken was six months older than you, Kayla, and my sister Mickey was a year older than you, Ava. It was fun to draw comparisons between 1949 and the three five-day babysits we just finished with you three. Will and Ava, your folks enjoyed a July vacation in Las Vegas and an August vacation in New York. Kayla, your mom had a business trip to Rhode Island and your dad was working second shift.

Here are Katie's words from July 1949 –

Fri 1 – 85 degrees at 8 o'clock a.m., fair. I had my work with the children. Pop mixed feed. We mailed 3 dollars to the Successful Farmers paper for renewal for 3 years.

Sat 2 – Fair hot. I couldn't do more than take care of the children.

Sun 3 – Fair hot. Bill, Anita, and June came in the evening. They brought fireworks. June stayed here for the week.

Mon 4 – Fair hot. We did only our cooking and cared for the children. Irwin called up in the evening from Montana.

Tues 5 – Fair hot. We washed and ironed. Taxes for 1948 were $280.31 for our land and everything.

Wed 6 – Fair hot. We canned apple sauce and took care of the children.

Thurs 7 – Partly cloudy, hot. I washed and peeled apples. By five o'clock we got the hardest rain ever. Creeks were out.

Fri 8 – Hot. We baked cookies and washed and picked blackberries, and took care of the children.

Sat 9 – Fair. June Ann & I canned apple sauce and made jelly. Bill & Anita came and took June along home.

Sun 10 – Fair cooler. Mary & Irv came back from their trip to Montana. We all went to the Turner picnic in the evening.

As the titles of these two books suggest, Katie was an avid quilter and Grange member. She and George were even co-founders of the Floraville Grange in 1948. They were also active in their church in Floraville. These two books will thoroughly amaze and impress all readers.

Here's Katie with her first great granddaughter, Tammy McBrayer, who was born on 9/28/1968.

Will, Kayla, and Ava, you can see that quilting, Grange, church, farming, family, and friends all combined very well for Katie and George Reiss. You have to also include hugs, smiles, walks through the woods to the mailbox, gathering eggs, making pies, playing with kittens, and many other fun farm activities in that list. It's obvious to me that grandmas always know best.

Grandma Katie lived to age 96 and George to age 91. But now all their siblings and spouses, their three sons and spouses, a grandchild, and a great grandchild have passed on to a greater reward. That's the way life works. The challenge is to create, shape, and foster what we leave behind for others.

Love, Granddad

Your Grandfather's Grandmother's Grandfather

Dear Will, Kayla, Ava, and Blake,   November 24, 2025

The man at the left is John Baptiste Luetzelschwab who was born 201 years ago this Thursday. This photo is from 1890 and is the oldest of thousands in our family collection. That's my grandmother Katie on her mom's lap. She was born March 25, 1890 and baptized two months later on May 25 per the certificate we have below in German. This photo was probably taken on John's 66th birthday of November 27, 1890, so it's 135 years old. There's a note on the backside.

This picture was taken in fall of 1890
Grandpa - John Baptiste Luetzelschwab,
his son Jacob, and his wife Charlotte nee
Hoelscher, and their first five Children
back row - Mary and John B. L.
Front row - Minnie, Katie and Herman L.

Here's my Grandma's baptism certificate from May 28, 1890 which was written in German.

Here are notes from my family tree for John and his granddaughter Katie Luetzelschwab Reiss. Notice how various census takers really misssspelled their last name with my underlines. **John Baptiste Luetzelschwab** (11/27/1824 – 4/26/1916) was born in Magden, Switzerland and married Maria Anna Stuber (11/12/1828 – 2/26/1878) in 1849 and had four children. They left Magden, Aargau, Switzerland and arrived in the port of New York on the ship "Energie" on 8/3/1865. <mark>I now have their immigrant trunk.</mark> The family consisted of Johann age 39, Anna Maria age 35, Rosalia age 14, Johann Arnold age 7, and Jacob age 6. They settled first in Missouri and later moved to Granite City, Illinois where Maria Anna is buried in St. John's Cemetery. She was born in Canton Berne, Switzerland. He is buried in Freivogel Cemetery in Millstadt. The **1870 Census** shows

John <u>Litzilshaw</u> age 46 working as a farmer, Mary age 42, Rosie age 26, Arnold age 14, Jacob age 12, and laborer Chas. Stanger age 35 living on a farm near Collinsville in Madison County at Township 3, Range 9. Living nearby is the Herman Hoelscher family which includes daughter Charlotte age 7 who will become Jacob's wife 11 years later. The **1880 Census** shows John <u>Litxelschaup</u> age 58 working as a farmer, daughter Rosa Dogita age 30, granddaughter Anna Dogita age 9, and Jacob <u>Litxelschaup</u> age 22 working as a farmer living in Nameoki, Madison County, Illinois. The **1900 Census** shows widowed John B. <u>Litzelschwaab</u> age 75 living with his son Jacob and family near Millstadt. The **1910 Census** shows widowed John B. Luetzelschwab age 85 living with his son Jacob and family near Millstadt.

Catherine (Katie) Charlotte Luetzelschwab (3/25/1890 – 10/17/1986) married George William Reiss (4/22/1873 – 8/16/1964) on 4/16/1911 at home. Witnesses were Herman F. and Lottie H. Luetzelschwab. They are buried in Franklin Cemetery in Smithton. The **1910 Census** shows George 37 as head, his parents Frank age 68 married 44 years and Anna age 65 with 7 of 11 children still living, and servant Katie <u>Lueteelschwab</u> age 20 who he married in 1911. A 1919 auto-owners directory shows him driving a Ford. George's **9/12/1918 World War I Draft Registration Card** shows him as a self-employed farmer with height "tall", build "medium", eyes "hazel", and hair "dark brown". The **1920 Census** shows George age 46, Katherine age 29, William age 7, Franklin age 4, Irwin age 2, father Frank age 78, and mother Anna Syvilla age 75 living on the home farm. The **1930 Census** shows George age 56 owning his own farm, Katy C. age 40 married 19 years, William age 17, Franklin age 14, and Irwin age 12 living in Prairie du Long Township. George and Katie hosted the **1934 Reiss Centennial**.

Our family visited the Luetzelschwab home in Magden, Switzerland on June 18, 1962 and met a lady who might be my seventh cousin. Here's the immigrant trunk my great great grandparents used in coming to America in 1865. Did they bring clothes, dishes, a pendulum wall clock, a family Bible, cell phones, and a laptop computer?

Will, Kayla, Ava, and Blake, we are truly blessed with old family photos, a significant trunk, memories, our 187-year-old family farm, and someone who thoroughly enjoys writing all this stuff into Granddad's Mondays stories for his four grands.

Love, Granddad

Katie's Diary

January 1944

Sat 1 – We have about 3 inches of last year's snow on the ground. It was 15 above this morning, warmed up to 35. We were at Bill & Anita's for dinner.

Sun 2 – 32 degrees, very cloudy, snow towards evening. I canned some meat and wrote a letter to Irwin to Camp Reynolds, Penn.

Mon 3 – 34 degrees, thawing snow. We butchered a 450 lb hog, made summer sausage. Boobe, Romuald, and Clara helped.

Tues 4 – 30 degrees, cloudy, and thawing during the day. We rendered the lard today. It made 10 gals. I canned 7 quarts of liver sausage.

Wed 5 – 35 degrees but getting colder, 30 by six o'clock evening. I helped butcher at Klein's.

Thurs 6 – 20 degrees, fair, warmed up to 40 by noon. I worked with taking care of the meat. Pop shelled corn.

Fri 7 – 25 degrees, cloudy, getting colder. We were in Belleville today.

Sat 8 – 14 degrees, cloudy to fair. Bill and Anita and June Ann were here in the evening.

Sun 9 – 16 above, fair. Sanders were to get some roosters.

Mon 10 – 24 degrees, fair, warmed up to 44 by noon. I washed in the evening. We visited with Grandma and Emil Morhmans.

Tues 11 – 25 degrees, fair, getting colder. I fried in 6 pints of pork sausage.

Wed 12 – 15 above, stayed cold all day, didn't get above 24. We were at Belleville to producers meeting.

Thurs 13 – 10 above, fair. I was at Schillings today, we patched.

Fri 14 – 10 above, fair, warmed up a lot during the day. Franklin talked on the radio today.

Sat 15 – 20 above, fair. I baked bread & cookies. Geo is making firewood.

Sun 16 – 22 above, fair. We were at Klein's in the evening.

Mon 17 – 22 above, fair. I fried down bacon and we went to the home bureau meeting at Carr's. Dorothy had a shower.

Tues 18 – 26 above, fair. Fried in more bacon. We have been getting around 6 doz eggs every day so far.

Wed 19 – 38 degrees, fair.

Thurs 20 – 35 degrees, fair. We were to the funeral of Mrs. Stuel at Smithton. She was 98 years. In evening we were at the Grange.

Fri 21 – 38 degrees, fair. John & Katie were here and we played cards.

Sat 22 – 35 degrees, fair, warmed up to 64 by noon.

Sun 23 – 30 degrees, fair. We were at church. Then Hesses came over for dinner. Bill & Anita and June Ann came in afternoon.

Mon 24 – 45 degrees, fair. Took our first hatching eggs to Smithton today. Were at Margret Merhman's in evening.

Tues 25 – 45 degrees to 65 by noon, fair. We were at Herman's to help butcher. I'm quilting a baby quilt.

Wed 26 – 46 degrees, cloudy, 65 by noon. We and Kleins and Schilling boys were to the family night at Turkey Hill Grange.

Thurs 27 – 61 degrees, showers in the morning, 68 by noon and fair.

Fri 28 – 45 degrees, fair. I helped Schillings with wallpapering. Getting colder.

Sat 29 – 30 degrees, fair. We butchered. John & Katie were here to help. Irwin called from Penn.

Sun 30 – 30 degrees, fair to warmer. We were at Schilling's.

Mon 31 – 28 degrees, fair. Pop made logs. I worked on Gerry's quilt. Evening John & Katie were here, we played cards.

February 1944

Tues 1 – 23 degrees, fair. We were at Belleville today. In the evening we were at Dintelmann's for Geo Birthday.

Wed 2 – 28 degrees, raining. I was at the ladies aid meeting. We planned to have a card party on the 20th of Feb. I'll have to help buy prizes.

Thurs 3 – Fair, colder, but only 40 degrees. I worked on Gerry's quilt. Pop shelled & crushed corn and made firewood.

Fri 4 – 30 degrees. We butchered a 300 lb hog.

Sat 5 – 44 degrees, fair. We helped Bill & Anita move to Edgar's house. Turned colder by night.

Sun 6 – 22 degrees, fair. We were at church and then at John Rapp's. Bill & Anita & June Ann and Uncle Wills were here in evening.

Mon 7 – 40 degrees, very pretty day. I salted and wrapped up the 2 hams and 2 shoulders. I was at Schilling's in afternoon.

Tues 8 – 35 degrees. Mrs. Gasser, Mrs. Orlando Skare, and I were at Belleville to buy card party prizes.

Wed 9 – 28 degrees, cloudy all day. I was quilting at the church hall. Fried in sausage and canned ribs in evening.

Thurs 10 – 35 degrees, sleeting, turning to rain all day, turning much colder by night. I was at Schilling's quilting.

Fri 11 – 20 degrees, snow flurries all day, strong winds.

Sat 12 – Zero, warmed up to 20 by noon. I washed and cleaned the wash house. It was 10 above again by 10 p.m.

Sun 13 – 10 above, very cloudy all day. We were at Willie's house to move more things. Peter Neffs were here in the evening.

Mon 14 – 22 above. We got 150 starter chicks at Luhr's today. We had a 7 inch snow last night, drifted some.

Tues 15 – 18 degrees, fair, warmed up to 40 by noon.

Wed 16 – 35 degrees, fair, and warm snow melted quite a bit. Geo started to work on the brooder house.

Thurs 17 – 35 degrees, raining. Uncle Henry & Aunt Bertha brought Mary out here from the station. Colder in evening.

Fri 18 – 20 degrees, fair. Geo worked on the brooder house. Mary & I worked on Gerry's quilt.

Sat 19 – 20 degrees, fair. Mary, Geo, and I were at Johnny & Katie's in the evening to their card party.

Sun 20 – 33 degrees, partly cloudy. We were at church, then Bill, Anita, June Ann, Mary, Pop, and I went to Henry Langs.

Mon 21 – 35 degrees, cloudy. We were to the home bureau meeting at L. Koche's. Mary went along home with Bill & Anita yesterday.

Tues 22 – 65 degrees, rained hard thru the night. Fair & stormy today. We got 400 chicks at Mascoutah, 300 week olds and 100 three-week olds.

Wed 23 – 30 degrees, fair. We were at Smithton to get feed. Then we worked with the chickens and brooder house.

Thurs 24 – 35 degrees, fair, much warmer by noon, 70 degrees. We let our chicks in outside shed for the first time. Boobe, Marcella & Ludger were here evening.

Fri 25 – 48 degrees, cloudy, light rain.

Sat 26 – 55 degrees, very pretty day. We worked outside cleaning up around the brooder house. Were at Brandenburgers in evening.

Sun 27 – 40 degrees, cloudy. Bill & Anita brought Mary home. Vernon Alberts and Aunt Katies were here, also Oscar Koerbers.

Mon 28 – 35 degrees, raining hard, turned to snow by noon. Mr. & Mrs. F. Klein and Margaret M. were here in evening.

Tues 29 – 4 inch snow on the ground, fair, thawing, 27 degrees in morning. Mary & I worked on the quilt.

March 1944

Wed 1 – 32 degrees, fair, warmed up nicely.

Thurs 2 – 40 degrees, fair. Mary finished sewing the patches on Gerry's quilt. Pop & Orville Koerber took hogs to yards.

Fri 3 – 45 degrees, cloudy, rain by night. We loaded the first sycamore log but could not move it. Horses could not pull it.

Sat 4 – 60 degrees, cloudy, strong west wind blew up by noon, came down to 40. Mary & I baked cakes.

Sun 5 – 34 degrees, cloudy to fair. Herman & Frankie were here, also Bill & Anita & June Ann. Mary went along with them. She will leave for home.

Mon 6 – Rain, thundering & lightning, then turned much colder, strong winds from the west. We were at Belleville.

Tues 7 – 24 degrees, very stormy and some snow flurries. Geo and Walter Brandenburgers hauled our sycamore logs.

Wed 8 – 18 degrees, fair, very stormy, too ugly to do much work.

Thurs 9 – 18 degrees, fair. I helped Mrs. Schilling with her washing. Romuald & Leo are sick with mumps. We got our first letters from Irwin since he left for overseas.

Fri 10 – 23 degrees, fair, got much warmer during the day. We butchered for Willie's hog. Henry Lang helped.

Sat 11 – Very cloudy and much warmer, no frost. Mr. & Mrs. Gus Metzger took me along to New Athens to church for Clement Mueth who was killed in Italy.

Sun 12 – 42 degrees, fair. We were at Frieda & Vernon Albert's for dinner.

Mon 13 – 31 degrees, cloudy, cold east wind. Bill, Anita, and June Ann were here for supper.

Tues 14 – 37 degrees, fair, warmed to 77 degrees by 2 p.m. I salted meat for Bill today and we put windows in brooder house.

Wed 15 – 57 degrees, partly cloudy. We worked on the brooder house. It's just about finished. Were at church in evening.

Thurs 16 – 53 degrees, NW winds, getting colder. We finished the brooder house and set up the new wood burning brooder.

Fri 17 – 42 degrees, fair. We moved our chickens into the new brooder house. Then I pruned grapes. Pop ground corn.

Sat 18 – 42 degrees, rained all day and all night. Couldn't do any work outside.

Sun 19 – 30 degrees, sleeting, getting colder, 24 by 4 p.m., still sleeting. Pop & I were at Schillings to get the quilt frame.

Mon 20 – 24 degrees, 6 inch snow on the ground, warmed up to 40 by noon. We were at Ed Groth's for my home bureau meeting.

Tues 21 – 22 degrees, cloudy all day. We were at Mascoutah first then we got 8 pigs at Herman's. Snow is thawing fast.

Wed 22 – 35 degrees. We cleaned the brooder house in morning, then I went to a quilting at church hall. Were at Klein's in evening.

Thurs 23 – 40 degrees, warmed up to 60 by noon, fair. We cleaned the brooder house. Pop shelled and ground corn.

Fri 24 – 50 degrees, fair, very pretty day, warmed up to 70 by noon. I washed. I got a telegram from Irwin.

Sat 25 – 45 degrees, fair. I cleaned everything and baked bread and coffee cake. Boobe Kleins, Ludger, and Mrs. Mary Klein came for my birthday.

Sun 26 – Very cloudy, 40 degrees, east wind. We were at church at Millstadt, then we went to Gus Metzgers. Bill & Anita also were here.

Mon 27 – Very cloudy and colder. We took the hatching eggs to Belleville. Then I sewed some in evening. F. Kleins & Margaret Merhman, John & Katie were here.

Tues 28 – 36 degrees, rained. Clara was over to put the quilt in frame and we started to quilt.

Wed 29 – 26 degrees, snow flurries, very stormy. Clara was over to help quilt. Romuald fixed the washer. We were at church in evening.

Thurs 30 – 25 degrees, fair, strong winds. Had my quilting in the evening. Metzgers took us along to the card party at Grange.

Fri 31 – 25 degrees, strong winds, fair. Alma, Elisa, and Clara were here to help me quilt.

April 1944

Sat 1 – 25 degrees, fair, warmed up to 50 by afternoon. Mrs. Mary Klein was over to help me quilt. In evening we were at R. Frank's.

Sun 2 – 50 degrees, fair to partly cloudy. Mr. Keim brought us two loads of road rock @ $21.00. We cleaned the brooder houses.

Mon 3 – 25 degrees, fair but storm. We took hatching eggs to Belleville. Schillings sewed oats on our land today.

Tues 4 – 30 degrees, fair. I washed. Geo husked corn. Margret Merhman came in the evening to help quilt.

Wed 5 – 25 degrees, fair. We got a cablegram from Irwin. Geo disked corn land. I quilted.

Thurs 6 – 32 degrees, strong south winds. Geo plowed and I finished Gerry's quilt.

Fri 7 – 50 degrees, partly cloudy, some thundering, shower at night. We were at church in evening. Sold our first spring chickens today.

Sat 8 – 40 degrees, very foggy in the morning, cloudy all day. Geo plowed the truck patch. I made garden and cleaned brooder house.

Sun 9 – Easter day. 60 degrees, rained mostly all day. Henry & Bertha were here.

Mon 10 – 65 degrees, raining all day. We got our first letters from Irwin today. He arrived in India.

Tues 11 – 55 degrees, cloudy, shower by evening. We cleaned chicken house and ground corn. We got 3 letters again from Irwin.

Wed 12 – Fair 50 degrees. Moved our first chickens into the house by the lane.

Thurs 13 – Jack frost 32 degrees. I spaded some garden and raked and cleaned yard. Mowed lawn first time.

Fri 14 – Cloudy, showers all day. Planted onions and beets & carrots. Sold 20 spring chickens again. Rain hard by night.

Sat 15 – 50 degrees, cloudy, light rain in evening. Geo got Franklin, Gerry and Georgie at the bus station at Millstadt. Edgar & Toddy and boys, Aunt Katie & Bill & Anita & June Ann were here.

Sun 16 – 38 degrees, very cloudy. Romuald took us all to Bill & Anita's. Had dinner there. Bill took Frank, Gerry & Georgie to the station in evening.

Mon 17 – 40 degrees, very cloudy. We were at our home bureau meeting at Margie Skare's, also stopped in at Dintelmann's.

Tues 18 – 47 degrees, cloudy, light rain early in morning. Geo plowed and I worked around the house.

Wed 19 – 42 degrees, fair but foggy. Pop plowed and I washed.

Thurs 20 – 55 degrees, fair. Pop plowed. I worked in the garden all day.

Fri 21 – 62 degrees, fair. We got 300 red chickens at Belleville. Then Pop plowed while I worked with the chickens.

Sat 22 – Rained all day, thundered. Schillings, Frank Kleins and Margret Merhman & boys were here in evening for Pop's birthday.

Sun 23 – 58 degrees, fair, awful stormy. We were at church. Then Henry & Bertha took us along to Hesse's for Anita's & Pop's birthdays.

Mon 24 – 42 degrees, awful stormy. Pop shelled corn. We were at Westerheide's in evening.

Tues 25 – 42 degrees, fair. I worked in the garden, set out first cabbage, mowed lawn. Geo crushed corn, mixed feed. Planted first tomatoes.

Wed 26 – 57 degrees, cloudy, planted canna bulbs & flower seed and beans.

Thurs 27 – 48 degrees, fair. We got some feed at Smithton. Then Geo dug up brush along the road. I worked in the lawn & garden.

Fri 28 – 43 degrees, fair. I washed. Then we planted our first potatoes, first 11 rows of Wolf's cobblers. Then almost 5 rows of his snowflakes. Then our own seed. These potatoes are in the lower patch, started planting at the south end.

Sat 29 – 44 degrees, fair. We planted last potatoes. Bill and Anita & June Ann were here in the afternoon.

Sun 30 – 56 degrees, light rain, then fair. Metzgers and we went to Mrs. Dora Mueth's. It was very windy. We saw the high water at New Athens.

May 1944

Mon 1 – 60 degrees, rained hard all day, creeks were out. I patched. George ground corn.

Tues 2 – 64 degrees, very cloudy to fair, strong light rain by night. We finished our rock walk thru the gate by brooder house.

Wed 3 – 60 degrees, very stormy, fair to cooler by evening. We moved the west yard fence in and moved shrubs.

Thurs 4 – 48 degrees. Geo got corn land ready. I went to Belleville with Marcella and Ludger to see the remains of Mrs. Meng.

Fri 5 – 40 degrees. Geo planted first corn in Schaeffer's place. I worked with my flower bed. Were at O. Koerber's in evening.

Sat 6 – 35 degrees. Geo plowed in back of barn for corn. I worked in garden. In evening we were at the Grange.

Sun 7 – 32 degrees, hoar frost ice on water bucket out on walk. We were at Aunt Katie's for dinner. Then at Bill & Anita's. Also at Belleville.

Mon 8 – 52 degrees, rained hard all day. Pop went to East St. Louis with Schillings. I patched and wrote letters.

Tues 9 – 52 degrees, more rain. We worked around the house, too wet outside.

Wed 10 – 59 degrees, fair. We were at our home bureau meeting at Turkey Hill. Bill, Anita & June were here for supper.

Thurs 11 – 60 degrees, fair, hot during day. I got cabbage plants at Schilling's. Gus Metzgers were here in evening.

Fri 12 – 65 degrees, fair, hot during the day. We cleaned chicken house. Katie & John were here in evening.

Sat 13 – 62 degrees in morning, 80 later in day. We were at Aunt Katie's for supper. It was Toddy's birthday. Shower in afternoon.

Sun 14 – 65 degrees, very hot later, 85 by afternoon. Bill, Anita, June Ann, and the Hesse family were here for Mother's Day dinner. We were at Frank Klein's in evening.

Mon 15 – 60 degrees, very hot later, rained hard by 5 o'clock p.m. We were to our home bureau meeting at Mrs. Seibert's. Planted first sweet potatoes.

Tues 16 – 62 degrees early, later it got very hot. We worked around the yard.

Wed 17 – 62 degrees. Geo crushed corn and mixed feed. I worked in my yard.

Thurs 18 – 62 degrees, hot later. Geo disked the bottom land. I worked in the garden, planted butter beans.

Fri 19 – 64 degrees, very hot and thundering. During the day we worked the potatoes and chopped weeds.

Sat 20 – 62 degrees. We were at Smithton. Then I mowed the lawn. Geo plowed in the bottom.

Sun 21 – 64 degrees, cloudy to fair. We were in church. Then Alma came, Bill & Anita also came. Had a good shower.

Mon 22 – 64 degrees. I cleaned the old brooder house and moved the red chicks in it. Geo plowed in the bottom.

Tues 23 – 65 degrees. It always got hot during the day, 85 to 90 at noon. I picked 3 quarts strawberries.

Wed 24 – 65 degrees. Geo planted the long bottom in corn and harrowed it. I worked in my garden.

Thurs 25 – 68 degrees, later it went up to 90. Geo plowed the truck patch for second time. I spaded flower beds. In the evening we were at Armbruster's & Schilling's.

Fri 26 – 65 degrees early, by noon it was 95, by evening it lightninged and thundered. We took eggs to Smithton, got groceries.

Sat 27 – 89 at noon, had a good rain by 5 p.m. I butchered chickens and prepared for Sunday dinner.

Sun 28 – 89 at noon. Aunt Katie's & Aunt Edna's families, Aunt Lena & Ed, Bill & Anita & June, and Uncle Wills were here.

Mon 29 – 89 at noon. Schillings baled our alfalfa today, 156 bales in all.

Tues 30 – 99 at noon. I washed. We got an awful hard rain & storm.

Wed 31 – 89 degrees at noon. It thundered but didn't rain. I transplanted flowers. Dad worked the potatoes.

June 1944

Thurs 1 – 89 degrees at noon. I got my permanent today at Kathryn Smith's.

Fri 2 – 90 degrees at noon. Dad finished planting corn. I was at Klein's a little while and Mrs. Westerheide was here.

Sat 3 – Fair, hot like always. Dad harrowed his corn. I mowed the lawn. Got letter from Irwin and from Mary.

Sun 4 – Not so hot but very stormy. We were at church in the evening. We were at Alma Metzger's birthday party.

Mon 5 – Cloudy, cool, showers. We were at Belleville in morning. Then Dad cut the clover here in front of the house. I chopped weeds.

Tues 6 – Very cool, stormy, NW winds. Dad is mowing again. I chopped weeds and hoed the garden. Planted the last sweet potatoes.

Wed 7 – 46 degrees, fair. I ironed and patched. Clara came over for the afternoon. Dad mowed again.

Thurs 8 – 70 degrees, drizzle rain. Pop replanted corn in long bottom. I cleaned the wash house and chopped weeds.

Fri 9 – 80 degrees, partly cloudy. Pop replanted corn. I planted beans then did some patching and cleaning. Got 3 letters from Irv and 1 from Mary. Johnny & Katie were here in evening.

Sat 10 – Getting hot again, 85. Dad hoed corn. I sewed and cleaned upstairs. Then we shelled & ground corn. Got a letter from Frank and Mrs. Hulet.

Sun 11 – 70 early, about 85 at noon. We were at New Athens church and then went to Belleville to Will Feder's for dinner.

Mon 12 – Several showers. Geo worked in corn. I transplanted flowers and chopped weeds. Henry Lang got his combine to start combining barley. Stephen William Reiss was born today in California.

Tues 13 – Cloudy to fair, cool winds. Pop worked in corn. I also replanted some in the truck patch, also planted sugar melons. Got a letter from Mary, also got word that little Stephen was born.

Wed 14 – 90 degrees by noon. We were at Belleville today.

Thurs 15 – 95 by noon, hot winds. State men were here to measure and outline the pond or lake. Got 500 stamped envelopes today. Got a letter from Irwin today. He is still in India.

Fri 16 – 95 at noon, hot winds. We took eggs and chickens to Millstadt. Then Pop went to get wheat crushed. I cut the lawn.

Sat 17 – Hottest day so far, 98 at noon. Got a letter from Mary and one from Irwin.

Sun 18 – Very hot, 95 at noon. Mary & Lillian Weihl were here. We were at church in the morning. Bill & Anita & June Ann were here too.

Mon 19 – We were to our home bureau meeting at Mrs. Frank Joseph's. Schillings & Westerheide started combining today.

Tues 20 – Very cool and nice. Pop helped the boys unload wheat at the granary. I chopped weeds. Got a card from Mary.

Wed 21 – Very cool, down to 57, got a good rain. Stopped combining for a day & half. Got a letter from Mary, one from Irwin, and one from Franklin & Gerry.

Thurs 22 – Getting very hot again, 95 by noon. Elsie Glades and Harvey were here to get peaches. I picked beans for canning.

Fri 23 – It was very hot today, 97, hot winds. Schillings finished combining. We got about 500 bu, one third. Got a letter from Irwin. He is in a new place in India and is teaching now.

Sat 24 – 85 the highest of the day. I washed and picked peaches and then we cleaned a chicken house.

Sun 25 – 97 degrees. We visited with Herman, Frank & Minnie. In evening Bill, Anita & June Ann came. June stayed for the week. Rained hard in the nite.

Mon 26 – 96 degrees. We worked in the garden and we picked peaches. Got a letter from Louis.

Tues 27 – 98 degrees. June and I were at Schillings. We also were at Smithton to get ice & milk. Got a letter from Irwin.

Wed 28 – Hottest day so far, 100 degrees by 5 p.m. I canned peaches. Geo hoed in the corn. June fed the small chickens. Got letters from Mary & Franklin today.

Thurs 29 – Cooler. We were at Belleville to get our gas stamps. Bill & Anita were here in evening. Light shower in morning. Schillings combined oats. Picked the last of the early peaches.

Fri 30 – Very cool in morning, 65. I picked and canned beans. We helped Geo shell corn. Aunt Katie & Johnny, Barbara & Nancy were here.

July 1944

Sat 1 – 85 degrees. We shelled corn. Geo got some wheat ground and he crushed corn. We were at Klein's in evening. Second peaches ripening.

Sun 2 – 84 degrees at noon. We took June to Sunday School, then we went to Dintelmann's with Bill & Anita for dinner.

Mon 3 – 90 degrees at noon. Geo is mixing feed all day. I am cleaning cupboards in the basement. In the evening, we visited Westerheides. Got a letter from Irwin of June 19 and from Mary too.

Tues 4 – 60 degrees at 6:00 a.m. and 90 by late afternoon. Westerheide started combining oats on our place.

Wed 5 – 90 degrees at noon. We took 33 old hens to Millstadt. We got 2 letters from Irwin, one from Mary, one from Franklin.

Thurs 6 – 94 degrees at noon. We cleaned the chicken house and then moved the red chickens in it. Schillings bailed hay here.

Fri 7 – 95 degrees at noon. I cleaned the old brooder house. Pop worked in the corn. I also picked some peaches.

Sat 8 – Cloudy, very warm, light showers. I was at Koerber's. They want to thresh, but it rained too much. Had our first ripe tomatoes.

Sun 9 – Fair, hot. We were at Elsie and Albert's for dinner today. Aunt Ednas were there also. Bill & Anita came in the evening to our house.

Mon 10 – Very hot. I helped cook for threshers at Koerber's.

Tues 11 – Hot again, still threshing at Koerber's. A small tornado blew up by 2 o'clock p.m. Broke a lot of our peach trees and shade trees.

Wed 12 – Some cooler. Pop and I cleaned away the broken up peach trees. Jakie & Cora and Janet were here.

Thurs 13 – 85 at noon, fair. Geo cleaned weeds out of the corn. I also worked about the yard. Got a letter from Franklin.

Fri 14 – Pop plowed. I cleaned the living room and hoed some weeds.

Sat 15 – 90 degrees at noon. We finished thresher cooking at Koerber's. Pop plowed. We were at Millstadt in the morning.

Sun 16 – 85 degrees at noon. We were in church then I baked for my meeting. Bill & Anita & June Ann and Schillings were here in evening. Got a letter from Irwin.

Mon 17 – 89 degrees. Had the home bureau meeting here today, 22 ladies with the 2 visitors.

Tues 18 – 85 degrees at noon. Henry & Bertha and Hazel & girls were here.

Wed 19 – 88 degrees at noon. I helped cook at Alma's for the thresher. This was the last job. Pop plowed. Got a letter from Franklin.

Thurs 20 – 60 early in morning, fair. Dad plowed and I worked about the house. Got a letter from Irwin.

Fri 21 – 50 degrees, fair. We got 8 feeder pigs at Oliver Mueller's @ $4.00 a piece. Then Schilling boys helped us put up straw for litter. Got a letter from Mary and one from Franklin.

Sat 22 – 55 degrees. Pop mowed grass and then we went to Smithton with eggs.

Sun 23 – Sunday, getting much warmer. In the evening, we fenced up the hogs to take them away in morning. Metzgers took us along to picnic at Smithton.

Mon 24 – 99 at noon, thunder shower in afternoon. Pop cut brush along the road. I worked around the house & yard. Orville Koerber & Pop took the 8 red hogs to the yards. We got $13.95 for them, weight 243 lbs. Got a letter from Frank & Gerry.

Tues 25 – Cloudy, sultry hot. We were at the Ronnenburg sale. Hard rain in the night. We got one old radio at Waterloo in morning.

Wed 26 – 95 at noon, sticky hot. I washed. Pop mixed feed. I sowed celery cabbage and turnips and Swiss chard & endive. Got a letter from Irwin.

Thurs 27 – 70 at sunrise, fair. We went to a sale at Metzger's.

Fri 28 – We went to Belleville to meet Franklin, Gerry and Georgie at the bus station and then we all went to the fair.

Sat 29 – Still hot. We have lots of fun playing with Georgie.

Sun 30 – Hot. Bill, Anita & June were here for Sunday dinner.

Mon 31 – Hot. Frank, Gerry, and Georgie and Pop & I went to Seibert's for supper.

August 1944

Tues 1 – Hot. Emil Heidenreich and wife & baby were here for supper. Pop & Franklin were at Rau's sale.

Wed 2 – Hot. We ironed and cooked catsup.

Thurs 3 – Hot winds. We didn't work much while Franklin & Gerry were here.

Fri 4 – Today we took Franklin, Gerry & Georgie to Bill & Anita's.

Sat 5 – Hot. It was around 98 all week.

Sun 6 – Franklin, Gerry & Georgie left for home with the early morning train. Rapp's were here in evening.

Mon 7 – I went to help Clara patch, we had hot winds.

Tues 8 – Hot. Pop chopped weeds along the road. I canned peaches.

Wed 9 – Too hot to work.

Thurs 10 – Hot. Henry Lang plowed in the eight acres.

Fri 11 – Hot. I helped Clara peel peaches.

Sat 12 – Hot. We had a 2 inch rain from 9:30 to 11:00 a.m. Then we went to Bill's to go to Uncle John's in the afternoon.

Sun 13 – Hot. We came back from Uncle John's at 7:30 p.m. Then we went to Clara Schilling's birthday party.

Mon 14 – Hot. I helped Clara cook peach butter.

Tues 15 – Hot, thundering. We went to Bill & Anita's to get our truck, also got fertilizer. Got a letter from Franklin.

Wed 16 – 100 degrees, thundering. Clara was here to help me peel peaches. In evening Aunt Katies were here.

Thurs 17 – Shower and much cooler. We dug our first potatoes today. Were at Klein's in evening.

Fri 18 – Fair, cool. I washed. Pop disked the pasture. Got a letter and pictures of Stevie from Mary.

Sat 19 – 55 in early morning. I canned 14 quarts of peaches. Pop disked his wheat land. Got a letter from Franklin.

Sun 20 – Fair. We went to Hecker to cook for the picnic.

Mon 21 – Rain slowly all morning. We got 2 letters from Irwin today. We went to my home bureau meeting at Mrs. H. Stahlmann's.

Tues 22 – Fair. We were at Waterloo and in the afternoon I canned peaches. Got a letter & pictures from Mary.

Wed 23 – Fair, cooler. Pop disked Henry's wheat land. I canned peaches.

Thurs 24 – Fair to cloudy, cool. Schillings harrowed our wheat land. Pop disked again. I canned peaches & grapes.

Fri 25 – Very cool. I cleaned flower beds and lawn. Pop disked again. We got a letter from Irwin.

Sat 26 – Rain all day. We were at Henry Lang's and then went to Millstadt to get tile for our well.

Sun 27 – Cloudy & cold all day. Johnny & Katie and Kleins & Schillings helped us drill our well. It's 31 feet deep. Had 13 feet of water the next day.

Mon 28 – Fair & cold. We went to Belleville today and to Millstadt to get more tile.

Tues 29 – Fair, warmer. Schillings and I went to East St. Louis shopping and then we got a load of fertilizer. Johnny & Katie came in evening to put on the pump.

Wed 30 – Cold and raining all day. I set up Etta's quilt and started quilting.

Thurs 31 – Fair, cool. I helped Clara cook peach butter. Pop mixed feed. Herman & Frank brought us a bu of damson plums.

September 1944

Fri 1 – Fair, warmer. I canned 19 quarts of damsons and then mowed lawn. Pop sowed fertilizer.

Sat 2 – Fair, hot. Geo sowed fertilizer and I mowed the lawn. We got a letter from Irwin.

Sun 3 – Fair, hot. We were at Millstadt picnic.

Mon 4 – Fair, hot. We were at Smithton church picnic. John & Katie were here in evening. They got some poulets.

Tues 5 – Partly cloudy, cooler. I washed and worked in the yard. Geo chopped weeds. Got a letter from Franklin today.

Wed 6 – Fair, very cool. Pop mowed weeds in the pasture and I cleaned the lawn and picked grapes and peaches.

Thurs 7 – Clara came over and helped me set up the quilt for Etta and we quilted till evening. Then I ironed.

Fri 8 – Worked on Etta's quilt and also canned some peaches. Geo ground corn.

Sat 9 – We both helped dress chicken at Floraville for the picnic and baked cakes for the picnic at home here.

Sun 10 – We worked at our picnic all day, had a very large picnic.

Mon 11 – We cleaned up at Floraville after the big chicken dinner and picnic. Then it rained hard all day.

Tues 12 – Canned peaches and worked on Etta's quilt. Clara helped me. Geo mixed feed.

Wed 13 – I quilted all day. Geo chopped hedge fence. Got letters from Irwin and Franklin.

Thurs 14 – Fair. Canned peaches and worked about the yard. Geo chopped hedge. Got a letter form Irwin.

Fri 15 – Fair. I canned peaches and baked two cakes for Pearl's wedding. Got a letter from Mary.

Sat 16 – Nice day. Mary Weihl and I went to Millstadt to cook for Pearl's wedding. We came home with Gus Metzgers.

Sun 17 – Very pretty day. We were at church. Then we went to visit the Hesses. Bill & Anita and June Ann came in the evening.

Mon 18 – Very warm. I canned peaches. Geo cut hedge fence. Got a letter from Franklin. Irwin's birthday today.

Tues 19 – Very hot, 90 degrees. Geo cut hedge fence. I baked bread and coffee cake and cleaned the house. Got a letter from Irwin.

Wed 20 – Very hot, 94 degrees. John, Etta, and Audrey were here. John & Katie were here in evening. Got a present from Irwin from India.

Thurs 21 – Rain thru the night, much cooler. Geo and I worked on cutting brush along the wheat fields. Cleaned wheat for Schillings. Mrs. Westerheide was here.

Fri 22 – Very cool in morning. We chopped brush along the wheat field. In the afternoon, we went to home bureau meeting.

Sat 23 – Rained light all night and day, very cool. I cooked elderberry and grape jelly and canned 3 quarts of beans. Geo crushed corn.

Sun 24 – Very pretty day. We and Johnny & Katie were at Irma Gummersheimer Borcharding's at Fultz. In evening Bill & Anita & June Ann were here.

Mon 25 – Fair, warmer. Schillings combined the alfalfa seed. Geo sowed wheat in the hog pasture.

Tues 26 – Very warm. Schillings started to sow wheat on our land. Geo & I finished cleaning and burning the hedge fence. Were at card party in evening. Got a letter from Franklin.

Wed 27 – Rained all afternoon. In morning Bertha Etling was here to get chickens. In evening we peeled apples at Koerber's. Got a letter from Irwin.

Thurs 28 – Rained all day. Pop & I and Romuald & Ludger Schilling filled out AAA papers at Grange. Then I helped Koerber's cook apple butter.

Fri 29 – Cloudy all day. We went to the Grange for Booster nite. Had the man-less wedding play that evening.

Sat 30 – Cloudy, light rain in morning. Geo & I got Frank and Georgie at Bill & Anita's. Johnny & Katie were here in evening.

October 1944

Sun 1 – Very pretty day, warm. Franklin, Georgie, Pop, and I went to Bill & Anita's for dinner. Then we went to Forest Park.

Mon 2 – Cloudy, rain by evening. Geo sowed wheat. I cooked catsup and potted flowers. Got a letter from Mary.

Tues 3 – Very cloudy. Geo & Henry Lang got fertilizer. I was at Schilling's. Geo sowed wheat in afternoon. I planted potted flowers.

Wed 4 – Cloudy to fair, warm, 70 degrees in early morning. We and Johnny & Katie were at Lena Feder's birthday party in evening.

Thurs 5 – Hard rain in early morning, 70 degrees. We were at Margret Merhman's birthday party.

Fri 6 – Fair. Geo sowed wheat for Uncle Henry. I sewed on the quilt.

Sat 7 – Fair and much cooler. I baked cake and butchered chickens for the chicken supper at the Grange. Finished sowing wheat. Westerheides took us to the show, seeing "Going My Way."

Sun 8 – Very cool, fair. Henry & Bertha were here for dinner. Then we all went to the Grange chicken supper.

Mon 9 – Cloudy, very cold. John Rapp, Mrs. Schilling, and Geo & I picked our pears today. There were about 30 bu.

Tues 10 – Fair, cold, 43 degrees. We were at Mrs. Frank Klein's birthday party. I sorted pears. Geo made firewood.

Wed 11 – Fair, cold. I helped Clara peel pears for pear butter. Geo mixed feed and shelled corn. Got a letter form Irwin.

Thurs 12 – Fair, cold, 38 degrees, no frost yet. I helped Clara cook pear butter. We got some honey at Frank Helfrich's in evening. Got 2 letters from Irwin.

Fri 13 – Fair, light frost. I quilted. We were at Belleville in morning.

Sat 14 – Fair, some warmer. Geo shucked corn. I finished Etta's second quilt. I baked bread & coffee cake.

Sun 15 – Fair, very pretty day. Beulah, Edwin, George, and Marge & George Dintelmann were here. Sold the last pears today.

Mon 16 – Fair. We shelled corn in morning. Then we went to home bureau meeting in New Athens. Got a letter from Irwin.

Tues 17 – Fair, frost. I washed. Pop husked corn. We were to the ladies aid meeting in the evening.

Wed 18 – We were at Smithton in morning. Then Clara came and helped me set up a quilt. Bill, Anita & June Ann were here.

Thurs 19 – Fair. We were at Millstadt to have truck tested. Mrs. Westerheide helped me quilt in the afternoon.

Fri 20 – Fair, light frost every morning. Geo husked corn. Clara came to help me quilt. We were at the Grange meeting.

Sat 21 – Fair, frost. We were to the wedding dance at the Grange of Glenn Brandenburger.

Sun 22 – A very pretty day. We and Mrs. Hesse and Elsie were at Bill & Anita's all day. Brandenburger brought us corn.

Mon 23 – Fair, warmer. Geo husked corn. I worked about the house & yard. Westerheide brought us some of our third of the corn. We got a letter and pictures from Mary.

Tues 24 – Very pretty day, no frost. We were at home with the boys with Westerheides. In evening we visited with Westerheides.

Wed 25 – Very pretty day, no frost. We and Gus and Alma visited with Emil Fredricks. Edgar Kellers were there too.

Thurs 26 – Very pretty day, no frost. We were at Waterloo to the doctor for my arm. Then Geo husked corn and I carried in my flowers.

Fri 27 – Very pretty day. I hemmed the quilts. And we blood tested all of our chickens. Geo mixed feed.

Sat 28 – Very pretty day. Geo and I were at Millstadt and we also got some cider. Then we moved some chickens.

Sun 29 – Very pretty day. We were at church harvest festival and missions in evening church. Carlena & Elmer came and we had dinner at Hecker.

Mon 30 – Partly cloudy, warm. I cleaned the hen house in the yard over there. Geo husked corn. Bill & Anita were here for dinner. We got a letter from Irwin and one from Mary.

Tues 31 – Very warm day. We were at Waterloo to the chiropractic doctor for my arm. It was awful windy all day. We got a letter from Franklin.

November 1944

Wed 1 – Very warm day, 80 degrees, windy, awful dry. Geo husked corn. I worked around the house. We got a letter from Irwin.

Thurs 2 – Very warm. I brushed Irwin's suits, also Pop's, and cleaned up in the house. Geo husked corn.

Fri 3 – Rained mostly all day. I baked bread, coffee cake, and birthday cake for Gus. Geo mixed feed.

Sat 4 – Fair, cold, light frost. We were to the funeral of Mrs. Jacob Schaeffer, Jr. In evening, we were at Gus Metzger's birthday party. We got a letter from Irwin.

Sun 5 – Partly cloudy and cold. Ed and Willie Feder, John & Katie, and Bill, Anita & June Ann were here. In the evening we were at Mrs. Westerheide's birthday.

Mon 6 – Cloudy, cold, no frost tho. Geo husked corn. I raked the lawn and put ground along the foundation. We got a letter from Irwin today.

Tues 7 – Partly cloudy. We went voting. Then I went to Belleville with Schillings. Geo crushed corn and mixed feed. Got a letter from Franklin.

Wed 8 – Fair to cloudy. We were at Waterloo in morning. Then we went to Bill & Anita's. Bill was very sick, high fever, and head cold. Shower at night.

Thurs 9 – Cloudy and cold. We were at Millstadt to have truck fixed and tested.

Fri 10 – Cloudy, 50 degrees. I washed in the morning. Then I took the rug out and cleaned it. Pop husked corn.

Sat 11 – Cloudy, warmer. We were at the chiropractic doctor at Waterloo. Then we went to Bill & Anita's. Bill was feeling some better.

Sun 12 – Fair & warm. We were to the turkey dinner at Herman & Minnie & Frankie's. Were at church in the evening.

Mon 13 – Fair & warmer. Romuald Schilling and Geo took 7 fat hogs to the yards today. Then we went to Herman's. Got 7 pigs.

Tues 14 – Fair, awful warm 80 degrees. We were to the farm bureau dinner at Belleville. In evening we were at Klein's. Had a rain at night. We got a letter from Mary and one from Franklin.

Wed 15 – Cloudy, cold west winds, no frost. I planted my tulip bulbs and dug up canna bulbs. Geo husked corn. We got a letter from Irwin.

Thurs 16 – Cloudy, cold. I washed and raked weeds outside the yard. Geo husked corn and brought in the pumpkins. We were to the birthday party of Margaret Mehrman's father.

Fri 17 – Cloudy & misty all day. We were at Boobe Klein's birthday in evening.

Sat 18 – Partly cloudy, cold but no frost. We cleaned a hen house. Then Geo husked corn and I cleaned the house over there.

Sun 19 – 33 degrees, snowing all day, but it all melted. Bill & Anita and June Ann were here.

Mon 20 – Cloudy and cold. Geo husked corn and I cleaned part of the old house. We were to Frank Klein's birthday in evening.

Tues 21 – Franklin called up early in morning for me to come as the baby son Richard Franklin was born at eleven o'clock a.m.

Wed 22 – Cloudy. This was my first day with Georgie alone while Franklin went to his office. We got along fine.

Thurs 23 – Cloudy. Georgie and I had a nice day together. In the evening Mrs. Hulet and Marge and I went to see Gerry. Had Thanksgiving dinner at the Hulet home.

Fri 24 – Cloudy. Georgie and I had another nice day. We played together.

Sat 25 – Partly cloudy. We were to the hospital to see Gerry & baby Richard.

Sun 26 – Cloudy, light rain. Franklin, Georgie & I went to Sunday School. Afternoon we went to visit Gerry.

Mon 27 – Cloudy, getting colder. I washed Georgie's clothes. Then Georgie & I took a walk around the block.

Tues 28 – Cloudy, cold. Today I ironed, then Georgie and I went to the store.

Wed 29 – Cloudy, some snow, quite cold but Georgie and I took our daily walk.

Thurs 30 – Snowed slowly all day, getting much colder. I think it was down to 16. Gerry & baby came home today.

December 1944

Fri 1 – Cloudy, cold. We all were very happy to have Gerry & Richard home. Franklin left for LaSalle Co. tonight.

Sat 2 – Fair and cold. I washed the baby's things. Franklin came back from his convention at 10:30 p.m.

Sun 3 – Fair. Franklin & I washed all the clothes with their washer. Mrs. Hulet was over and cooked the dinner.

Mon 4 – Cloudy, south wind. Franklin took me to the bus station at 5 o'clock a.m. I got to Bill & Anita's at 12 o'clock noon. Pop got me at Bill & Anita's.

Tues 5 – Rained all day. Geo & I went to Smithton to pay our taxes. Then we went to Waterloo to see Mary and Melba.

Wed 6 – Cloudy. We got a letter from Irwin. I cleaned in the basement.

Thurs 7 – Rain all day, colder by night.

Fri 8 – 30 degrees, fair. I washed today and then quilted. Pop husked corn and fixed chicken house roofs.

Sat 9 – Very cloudy, snow by night. We were to the Husto funeral in evening. We were at Johnny's birthday at Millstadt. I paid Mrs. Pockter 2 dollars for cleaning our lot on cemetery.

Sun 10 – 6 in. snow, cold 28 all day. Schillings were here in afternoon. I wrote Xmas cards and letters in evening. Got a letter from Franklin.

Mon 11 – 25 degrees, snowstorm all day. I quilted. Geo did the feeding and brought in wood. Got a Xmas package from Mary.

Tues 12 – 18 degrees, fair getting colder by night. Geo got some wood in. I washed windows inside. Mail carrier couldn't get thru the snowdrifts today.

Wed 13 – 22 degrees, light snow all day. I was at Marcella's. We baked cookies. Got a Xmas card from Irwin.

Thurs 14 – 8 above, fair. I went to Belleville with Metzgers. Got a letter from Franklin.

Fri 15 – 24 degrees, fair. I ironed and patched and swept the basement. Geo crushed corn. It warmed up to 44 by noon.

Sat 16 – 22 degrees, fair to cloudy. I baked cookies. Geo made firewood.

Sun 17 – 24 degrees, very pretty day. We went to see Peter Wachtel at Freeburg. Bill & Anita were here in evening.

Mon 18 – 21 degrees. We were to the Peter Wachtel funeral, then at our home bureau meeting at Ed Barthel's.

Tues 19 – 20 degrees, fair, warmed up nice during noon. I helped Marcella bake cookies. Larney is sick yet. Got 2 letters from Irwin.

Wed 20 – Very pretty day, thawing, got colder by nite. John & Katie were here a little while. I helped at Schilling's in afternoon. We went to O. Koerber's birthday in evening.

Thurs 21 – 24 degrees, snow flurries. We were at Waterloo today. It's getting very cold tonight, 16 at 8 p.m. Got a letter from Irwin and one from Franklin.

Fri 22 – 10 above, fair. Pop is mixing feed and making firewood. I worked about the house.

Sat 23 – 20 degrees, partly cloudy. We prepared to go to Franklin's tomorrow. It didn't thaw much today. We got a letter from Irwin and one from Franklin.

Sun 24 – 25 at 6 a.m. Geo & I left for Urbana to spend Christmas with Franklin and family. It was partly cloudy.

Mon 25 – 27 degrees at Urbana, snowing all day, got very much colder in the nite. 5 below at 5 a.m. on the morning of 26 Dec.

Tues 26 – 5 below at 5 a.m. Franklin took us to the bus station. Got to Belleville by 12:45 noon. Got home by 3:30 p.m.

Wed 27 – 26 degrees. It rained thru the nite and froze into slick ice. I was at Schilling's butchering. It's very slick to walk.

Thurs 28 – 21 degrees all day, heavy slick ice all over. Clara & I walked to Marcella's to do her washing. In evening John Rapps were here.

Fri 29 – 26 degrees, went up to 32 by noon, still very icy. I washed and Geo made firewood.

Sat 30 – 33 degrees, very foggy all day and night. Geo made firewood and I patched and ironed and worked on income report.

Sun 31 – 33 degrees, very foggy all day, colder by night. Geo & I visited with Bill, Anita, and June Ann. In the evening we stayed home.

January 1945

Mon 1 – We have about 3 inches of last year's snow on the ground. It was 15 above this morning, warmed up to 35. We were at Bill & Anita's for dinner.

Tues 2 – 10 above, cloudy. It got up to 20 by noon, snow flurries. Geo made firewood. I baked cookies. We got a letter from Irwin of Nov. 27.

Wed 3 – 17 above, got quite a bit warmer by noon. Geo & I went to Waterloo and then to Columbia and to Schilling's in the evening. Got a letter from Irwin and one from Mary.

Thurs 4 – 20 above, warmed up to 30 by noon. Geo & Schillings made telephone poles. In evening we were at George Neff's. We got a letter from Irwin.

Fri 5 – 20 degrees, warmed up nicely by noon. I baked cookies. Geo and Frank S. hauled telephone posts. Got a letter from Hattie.

Sat 6 – 34 degrees, light rain, foggy. Geo & I went to Belleville with Schillings to make out our income tax report. The boys set telephone posts.

Sun 7 – 25 degrees, cloudy. We were at Herman's today and stopped in by Edna's. Bill & Anita were here in the evening.

Mon 8 – 32 degrees, light rain. We were in Belleville with Leo Wachtel. In the evening Margret & Sylvester and Frank Kleins were here. Snowed, colder. A letter from Irwin.

Tues 9 – 4 inch snow, 1 below zero, fair. Didn't get above 12 all day. We were at Boobe & Marcella's in evening to play cards. Got 2 letter from Irwin.

Wed 10 – 10 above, fair, warmed up to 28 by noon. Johnny & Katie were here for dinner. Geo crushed corn and I patched.

Thurs 11 – 10 above, warmed up very much during the day. Clara came over and helped me set up a quilt.

Fri 12 – 35 degrees, thawing, got very muddy, 50 by noon, fair. I was along to Belleville with Schillings.

Sat 13 – 25 degrees, fair to cloudy. I quilted all day. Geo made firewood and was to the telephone meeting after noon.

Sun 14 – 34 degrees. We were in church and then it rained all day.

Mon 15 – 30 degrees, getting colder, snow flurries. I quilted all day. Geo tried to chop off a tree. Got a letter from Irwin.

Tues 16 – 22 degrees, fair. Clara came over to help me quilt. Pop worked on the wood. Got a letter from Franklin.

Wed 17 – 24 degrees. We were at Millstadt today. We got 2 letters from Irwin. He is in the hospital at Assam. Also got a letter from Franklin.

Thurs 18 – 30 degrees, cloudy. Geo downed the big maple tree by the house over there. I helped Clara dress chickens for market.

Fri 19 – 34 degrees, sorta raining all day. I quilted. Geo did the feeding.

Sat 20 – 30 degrees. We were to the Speichinger funeral. In evening we were to the Grange birthday dance. Very cloudy.

Sun 21 – 31 degrees, very cloudy, rain by night. We were at Aunt Edna's for dinner. In evening Bill, Anita, and June Ann were here.

Mon 22 – Very cloudy. I washed then I quilted. Geo worked on the big tree. Got a letter from Irwin.

Tues 23 – 30 degrees, fair. We were at Belleville with hatching eggs. Ordered my chicks for the 27 Feb. Got a letter from Franklin.

Wed 24 – 30 degrees, fair. We raked leaves and burned brush in the yard over there. Were to 4H play in evening. Got a letter from Mary.

Thurs 25 – 32 degrees, light rain to fair, warmer. I raked more leaves. Finished the star quilt yesterday.

Fri 26 – 32 degrees, cloudy, 65 by noon. We and Kleins and Schilling boys were to the family night at Turkey Hill Grange.

Sat 27 – 30 degrees, very cloudy, snow by noon. We brought in a lot of wood. Geo went to have corn crushed.

Sun 28 – 20 degrees, snowing, didn't get above 24 all day, 4 in. snow. Fred Wachtels were here in evening. It cleared up in afternoon.

Mon 29 – 10 above, fair to cloudy, light snow. I was quilting at Schilling's. Geo had a cold so he stayed in the house.

Tues 30 – 7 above, fair. We were to the funeral of Grandpa Luetzelschwab and also went to Belleville from there to take eggs in.

Wed 31 – 5 above, fair, did not get above 19 all day. Geo did the feeding. I was sewing all day. Had letter from Franklin.

February 1945

Thurs 1 – 5 above, clear, not stormy, didn't get above 19 all day. I sewed. Geo had a cold so he didn't do much.

Fri 2 – 15 above, cloudy all day. I helped Marcella bake cookies. Geo made firewood.

Sat 3 – 22 above, very cloudy. We were at Electric meeting at Waterloo. Bill & Anita, June Ann came here for supper.

Sun 4 – 32 above, very cloudy, light drizzle, frost but all thawed later. Irma & Albert and Mr. & Mrs. H. Borcharding were here to get radio.

Mon 5 – 20 above, very cloudy. I helped Clara wash. In evening we were at Margret's to quilt.

Tues 6 – 25 degrees, mostly fair. I was at Brandenburger's today to cook for Leona's wedding. We all had a nice time. Got 4 letters from Irwin.

Wed 7 – 35 degrees. We took hatch eggs to Belleville today. Also got 2 bu apples at Eckert's. It's getting colder.

Thurs 8 – 22 degrees, very cloudy. Clara Schilling was operated on today. I stayed with Marcella's children. Got a letter from Franklin.

Fri 9 – 32 degrees, fair, got very warm today. I washed. Then we burned brush and cleaned the yard over there.

Sat 10 – 35 degrees. We worked on the firewood and burned brush. It was nice sunshine all day.

Sun 11 – 30 degrees, fair. We were at Jakie & Cora's today.

Mon 12 – 30 degrees, white frost, fair to very cloudy. I helped Marcella a while in afternoon. Got a letter from Irwin.

Tues 13 – 40 above, fair. I was at Schilling's. Clara came home from the hospital. Henry & Lavern Lang were here in afternoon.

Wed 14 – 45 above, fair, very pretty day. We were at Belleville to file income report. Got a letter from Irwin saying he is coming back to the States.

Thurs 15 – 50 degrees, fair, windy. Got a Valentine box of candy from Franklin & Gerry. We were working outside.

Fri 16 – 32 degrees, sleeting and snowing, getting colder. Geo and Schillings moved a bee hive to our orchard.

Sat 17 – 23 degrees with a 6 in. snow, some drifted. I set up a quilt today. Geo did the feeding.

Sun 18 – 8 above, fair. This was Sunday. We stayed home all day. Bill, Anita & June Ann came in evening.

Mon 19 – 18 above, cloudy, thawed by noon. We were to the home bureau meeting at Mrs. Gerhold's at New Athens.

Tues 20 – 32 degrees, cloudy, misty. We took the hatching eggs to Belleville. In evening we were at Marcella's birthday party. It rained then.

Wed 21 – 40 degrees, getting warmer, rained hard all morning, cleared in evening. Marcella & Alma were here to help quilt.

Thurs 22 – 33 degrees, cloudy to fair. Geo & I were at Bill & Anita's for a quilting. Mrs. Hesse & Mrs. Seibert were there also.

Fri 23 – 32 degrees, very pretty day. Johnny & Katie came and we butchered. We got a letter from Mary.

Sat 24 – 32 degrees, white frost, but warmed up nice during the day. Geo was at Krupp's sale. Elmer Gummersheimer was operated on.

Sun 25 – 35 degrees, fair to cloudy. Johnny was here a while and Herman & Frank were here for dinner. We were at Rapp's toward evening.

Mon 26 – 25 degrees, sleeting & snowing, getting colder, 20 by noon. I washed and canned some apple sauce. Geo shelled corn.

Tues 27 – 22 degrees, fair. We got 325 started white rock chicks. I also went quilting to Marcella's. Geo Dintelmann died.

Wed 28 – 31 degrees, fair, thawing. We took eggs to Belleville, then we went to Dintelmann's.

March 1945

Thurs 1 – 32 degrees, later in day warmer and rain by night. I was to a quilting at Margaret's all day. Geo made firewood.

Fri 2 – Rained all day. We were at the funeral of George Dintelmann.

Sat 3 – Fair. We worked around the house.

Sun 4 – Fair. John & Katie were here to move our basement pump up in the kitchen.

Mon 5 – Rained very hard, creeks were out.

Tues 6 – Rained in morning, then turned colder. Romuald & Leo came over to fix the car. In evening we all were at Koerber's birthday.

Wed 7 – Light frost, cloudy all day. We worked around the house. Were at church in evening.

Thurs 8 – 31 degrees. I helped Schillings quilt all day and evening. Geo fixed roofs and shelled corn.

Fri 9 – 31 degrees, fair. I raked some of the yard here and we cleaned the brooder house and were at Smithton to get feed.

Sat 10 – 33 degrees, fair, very pretty day. Leo dug the septic tank hole. Mary Klein helped me mark a quilt.

Sun 11 – Fair, John & Katie were here to set our septic tank. Annie Wachtel helped set up her quilt.

Mon 12 – Fair, warm, very pretty day. Irwin called up from Miami, Florida. He had just arrived from overseas. Franklin also called.

Tues 13 – Fair, very pretty day. I had a quilting party for Annie Wachtel's quilt. Geo mixed feed.

Wed 14 – Partly cloudy, cooler. Alma and I were at Rapp's quilting. We were at church in evening.

Thurs 15 – Showers to fair and warm. It was 78 by 4:30 o'clock. We were at Belleville to take my lesson on wardrobe selection.

Fri 16 – Fair, hot, it was 85 at 4:00 o'clock. I raked in the garden. Geo plowed for oats. We got a letter from Irwin.

Sat 17 – Fair, somewhat cooler. Geo is plowing again and I washed.

Sun 18 – Fair to cloudy, rain by afternoon. We were at Waterloo church for Gladys Hoffman's confirmation. Then went to Hoffman's for dinner.

Mon 19 – Rained hard mostly all day. Pop & I were to my home bureau meeting at Brandenburgers.

Tues 20 – Light drizzle all day and colder, down to 40. Geo and I moved the chicks into the old brooder house and cleaned the new house.

Wed 21 – Fair. I went to a quilting at Jack Wachtel's. In the evening we were at Floraville. Got a letter from Irwin. He is on his way to Calif.

Thurs 22 – Fair warm. Geo and I were at Millstadt to the doctor for myself. In afternoon Geo plowed his oats patch. I worked with the chicks.

Fri 23 – Fair, very pretty day. Geo is working on his oats field. I'm starting the 300 red chicks which we got today.

Sat 24 – Fair. We got Franklin and Georgie at the bus station at Belleville. Then stopped at Seibert's a while. Bill & Anita came in evening.

Sun 25 – Rained hard all day. We were at Bill & Anita's for dinner. Irwin & Mary called by phone in evening. The neighbors were here in evening.

Mon 26 – Fair and windy. Too wet to work outside. Was to a quilting at church in evening.

Tues 27 – Took our eggs to Smithton. It's fair to hot today, 89. We got the baby bed today.

Wed 28 – Fair, hot 80 degrees, windy. I mowed the lawn and hooked on screens. Irma & Alfred were here.

Thurs 29 – Rain all morning. We were to see the doctor at Millstadt in afternoon. I sewed. Pop made firewood.

Fri 30 – Rain all day, 50 degrees. I sewed. Pop did the feeding. Creeks were out.

Sat 31 – 45 degrees, fair. We got a letter from Irwin from Birmingham Hospital today.

April 1945

Sun 1 – 45 degrees. Easter Sunday. We were at Hesse's all day. Rained all afternoon and evening.

Mon 2 – Cloudy, 60 degrees. I sewed. Geo crushed corn.

Tues 3 – 65 degrees, fair. We took eggs to Belleville and then went to Mrs. Ed Groth's to fix up our lesson for the April 16 meeting.

Wed 4 – 45 degrees in morning, 38 by night, very strong NW winds. John & Katie were here in evening.

Thurs 5 – 28 degrees, heavy frost, ice on water troughs, fair. I helped Marcella quilt. Geo made firewood.

Fri 6 – Fair. We started on the yard fence.

Sat 7 – Fair, warm. We worked on the back yard fence. We got a letter from Irwin. He saw his son on Easter.

Sun 8 – Fair, very pretty day. We were at Elmer & Carlena's for dinner. In evening we were at Frank Klein's.

Mon 9 – Fair. We worked about the yard and crushed corn. Got a letter & pictures from Mary.

Tues 10 – Fair. We were at Grange to help clean & paint. In evening we were at Millstadt. Got my hair curled at Katie Besse's.

Wed 11 – I worked in the garden. Geo plowed on Schaeffer's place for corn. Light rain by nite. We got a letter from Irwin & Franklin.

Thurs 12 – Partly cloudy, warm 80, rain by night. I worked in the garden, planted spinach, onions, peas, beans, lettuce, radishes. Pop plowed for corn.

Fri 13 – Clearing after an all night heavy rain, very warm. We worked about the house.

Sat 14 – Fair to cloudy. Pop shelled corn and I worked about the house.

Sun 15 – Rained all day. We were at church. Then in the afternoon Fred Wachtels came.

Mon 16 – Very cool to warmer. We were to our home bureau meeting at Margie Skare's. I and Mrs. Groth gave the lesson.

Tues 17 – Cool, fair to cloudy. We were to visit at home with Herman and Minnie and Frank.

Wed 18 – Very cool, fair. We took the eggs to Belleville. Then Geo & Boobe worked on our road.

Thurs 19 – Heavy frost. We butchered today. Henry & Lavern Lang helped.

Fri 20 – Getting warmer. We took our meat to the locker. In afternoon we worked around the house.

Sat 21 – Fair. I prepared for Pop's birthday. Pop worked in the field.

Sun 22 – Fair. A large crowd came to celebrate Pop's birthday. Also Anita's. Neighbors were here in evening.

Mon 23 – Light rain, then fair. I spaded in the flower beds. Geo shelled corn. We got a letter from Mary & Irwin.

Tues 24 – Light rain, cooler by nite. We took eggs to Smithton, stopped in at Mrs. P. Wachtel's a while. Then cleaned hen house.

Wed 25 – Cloudy, cool rain by night. I was to a women's guild meeting at Waterloo. Geo worked in the orchard.

Thurs 26 – Fair, cool. We moved the white spring chickens into Pop's hen house, 317. We sold 10 last week. Got a letter from Gerry.

Fri 27 – Very pretty day, warm. Geo plowed and I spaded in the garden. We also cleaned the brooder house. Got a letter from Irwin.

Sat 28 – Cloudy to fair. I prepared for Sunday dinner.

Sun 29 – Cloudy to fair, getting warmer. John & Katie, Lottie & Ed, Mary & Lillian, Elsie, Albert, Gladys and Harvey Hoffman were here.

Mon 30 – Rain mostly all day. I worked in the house.

May 1945

Tues 1 – Cloudy & cold, some rain. We took eggs to Belleville.

Wed 2 – Very cloudy & cold. We cleaned the brooder house.

Thurs 3 – Rain. Couldn't do much.

Fri 4 – Showers. We worked around the house. Henry came to get some dressed chickens.

Sat 5 – Fair. We were at Dintelmann's in evening to see Louis & Katie, Bob & Syvilla.

Sun 6 – Fair, very pretty day. We were to church at Smithton to go to the church Sunday for Grange. Then went to Dintelmann's for dinner.

Mon 7 – Rained mostly all day. We worked around the house.

Tues 8 – Rained some today. I cut some lawn. Geo shelled corn. Johnny & Katie came in evening.

Wed 9 – Rained mostly all day. We took the eggs to Belleville.

Thurs 10 – Fair, cold 40 degrees. I was in Belleville with Harry Frankes, also were at Philip Ettling's.

Fri 11 – Fair, 41 in morning. We were at Belleville and Millstadt. Got the truck fixed. Got a letter from Irwin & Mary.

Sat 12 – Cloudy to fair, much warmer, got up to 75 degrees by afternoon. We got 9 pigs at Herman's. Then I worked in garden. Geo plowed.

Sun 13 – Fair, very warm 83. This was Mother's Day and we and Hesses were at Bill & Anita's. In evening I went to Millstadt church.

Mon 14 – Fair, very warm 85. Geo planted a few rows of corn on the Schaeffer place. I planted beans.

Tues 15 – Very hard rain thru the night, storm & some hail, creeks were out. Got a letter from Franklin.

Wed 16 – Rain & cooler. We were in Belleville with the hatching eggs. Got a letter from Irwin.

Thurs 17 – Rain all day. I cleaned the basement. John & Etta came in the evening and stayed over night.

Fri 18 – Fair, cooler. O. Koerber & Geo took 7 hogs to the stockyard. Beulah & Robin came over. John & Etta left after dinner for St. Louis.

Sat 19 – Fair. I felt so sick, so we went to the doctor. Geo also went to have corn crushed.

Sun 20 – Fair. We were at Belleville first, then went to Aunt Katie's for dinner. Bill, Anita, & June Ann & Feders were there too.

Mon 21 – Fair to cloudy. We were at Belleville hospital to have x-ray taken. Then we went to home bureau meeting at Fred Herr's.

Tues 22 – Fair. Knab was here to rent our house for his hired man.

Wed 23 – Fair. Our new renters moved in today, so we helped along. They moved in on the 24th.

Thurs 24 – Fair to cloudy. Schillings bailed our alfalfa today. Geo planted corn by the north chicken house.

Fri 25 – Rain in morning. Henry came to get chickens so I went along to bake the wedding cake at Bertha Ettling's.

Sat 26 – Fair. Orville & Marie came to get flowers for their wedding.

Sun 27 – Fair, very pretty day. Orville & Marie's wedding was beautiful.

Mon 28 – Rain all day. Couldn't do much of anything. Got a letter and pictures from Franklin.

Tues 29 – Rain mostly all day. Clara came over and helped me clean the living room.

Wed 30 – Rain, then fair. We cleaned the brooder house and moved some chickens. Also washed.

Thurs 31 – Fair, hot. We were at Belleville to get an electric motor. Were at Klein's in the evening to get strawberries.

June 1945

Fri 1 – Fair, hot. We took 12 qt for us and 6 qt of strawberries for Boobe & Marcella to the locker. John & Katie came in evening.

Sat 2 – Very stormy & cooler. Geo plowed. I mowed lawn and cleaned sun porch.

Sun 3 – Cold, very cloudy. We were at Koerber's in afternoon. In evening we were at Alma Metzger's birthday party.

Mon 4 – Cold, rain. I cooked strawberry jelly. Pop plowed until it started to rain. Got a letter from Irwin.

Tues 5 – Cold 49, light rain, cloudy all day. We worked on backyard fence between rains. Got a letter from Gerry.

Wed 6 – Cold 49, light drizzle. We worked on the backyard fence. Got a letter from Louis.

Thurs 7 – Warmer, rain mostly all day.

Fri 8 – Rain all day. We got a letter from Irwin.

Sat 9 – Rained all morning. Afternoon Johnny came to put stool in bathroom. Got a letter from Irwin.

Sun 10 – John, Katie, Edna and Henry Lang and family were here. In evening we were at Walter Brandenburger's.

Mon 11 – Showers. Cleaned part of the brooder house.

Tues 12 – We washed. Had a few showers. Geo mixed feed. Got a letter from Franklin.

Wed 13 – Shower. I ironed. Pop spread fertilizer on corn. In afternoon I helped Clara patch.

Thurs 14 – Showers. Pop & I were at Belleville. Then we worked around the house. Sold our first peaches today.

Fri 15 – No entry.

Sat 16 – Fair, some showers. I cleaned the whole house. Emil Merhman worked on some lights.

Sun 17 – Rain all day and colder. Henry got the 15 chickens for the wedding.

Mon 18 – Very cold, cloudy and rainy all day. Got a letter from Irwin.

Tues 19 – Fair, very pretty day. We washed. Geo mixed feed.

Wed 20 – No entry.

Thurs 21 – No entry.

Fri 22 – Fair. Sold 25 red spring chickens. Lottie and Al and Edna were here.

Sat 23 – Fair, getting hot. We were at Millstadt in morning, then George worked in the corn. I cleaned.

Sun 24 – Fair, hot. I was at church and in the afternoon Mrs. Dora Meuth and family were here.

Mon 25 – Very warm, fair to showers. I canned apricots and beans. Geo worked in the corn.

Tues 26 – Very warm, showers. Geo worked on the corn land. I worked in the yard.

Wed 27 – Getting very hot. Mrs. Wachtel got some peaches. Jakie & Cora were here also. I cut weeds. Geo planted corn east of hog pen.

Thurs 28 – Hot winds all day. I cooked soap for Mrs. Johnson. Then I worked in the yard. Geo planted corn back of barn.

Fri 29 – Hot winds all day. I cooked soap and picked apricots. Geo worked in the corn. Frank & Gerry & boys came.

Sat 30 – Fair, cool. Mary & Irwin and Stevie came today. We hadn't seen Irwin for one and one half years.

July 1945

Sun 1 – It rained hard last night. Our children and grandchildren were all here today. We also were to the funeral for Delbert Seibert who was killed in the war.

Mon 2 – Fair. We are enjoying ourselves with Mary, Irwin, and Stevie.

Tues 3 – We washed today. Mrs. Schilling was here. Henry Lang is combining.

Wed 4 – Mary & Irwin went to Bill & Anita's, also to Forest Park Highlands.

Thurs 5 – Mary & Irwin went to Bill & Anita's to go to the show at St. Louis.

Fri 6 – Henry Lang finished combining.

Sat 7 – Bill & Anita were here.

Sun 8 – Fair, getting warmer, some rain. Uncle Henry, Uncle Wills, and the Cooks and Mrs. Golden were here.

Mon 9 – No entry.

Tues 10 – Fair to partly cloudy. Mary, Irwin, Stevie, and I were at Belleville today.

Wed 11 – We washed today.

Thurs 12 – Fair & cool. We worked around outside.

Fri 13 – Fair, cool. Geo worked in the corn. I cleaned flower beds. Mary & Irwin are at Urbana.

Sat 14 – Fair, cool. Threshed wheat. Bill & Anita were here in the evening. Irwin & Mary came back from Urbana.

Sun 15 – Cool all day. We were at Aunt Mary's, then at Carlena's for dinner, then at Lottie's and then we went home.

Mon 16 – Cool all day. I helped cook for threshing at Koerber's. Frank & Boobe Kleins were here last night.

Tues 17 – Cool all day. Mary & Irwin were at St. Louis shopping. Stevie stayed with us. I cooked plum jelly.

Wed 18 – Cool all day. Mary & Irwin were at Belleville shopping. Stevie stayed with us. Pop worked in the corn.

Thurs 19 – Very hot all day. Mary, Irwin & Stevie went to Bill & Anita's this afternoon to go to the park opera this evening.

Fri 20 – No entry.

Sat 21 – No entry.

Sun 22 – No entry.

Mon 23 – No entry.

Tues 24 – No entry.

Wed 25 – No entry.

Thurs 26 – No entry.

Fri 27 – No entry.

Sat 28 – Fair. Mary, Irwin and Stevie, Pop & I and Bill, Anita and June Ann all went to the Paderborn picnic for supper.

Sun 29 – Fair. Bill & Anita & June Ann were here.

Mon 30 – We washed today. Irwin worked on his car and they started packing.

Tues 31 – No entry.

August 1945

Wed 1 – Fair, very hot 99.

Thurs 2 – Fair, very hot up to 102, shower towards evening & cooler. Mary, Irwin & Stevie left for California today.

Fri 3 – Fair, somewhat cool.

Sat 4 – Fair, hot.

Sun 5 – Fair, very hot all day. We were at church, then we went home to Herman's for dinner.

Mon 6 – Very cloudy, cool. I worked in the house. Geo worked in his corn.

Tues 7 – Cool, 62 in morning, NE winds. I washed. Geo shelled and crushed corn.

Wed 8 – No entry.

Thurs 9 – No entry.

Fri 10 – No entry.

Sat 11 – No entry.

Sun 12 – No entry.

Mon 13 – No entry.

Tues 14 – No entry.

Wed 15 – No entry.

Thurs 16 – No entry.

Fri 17 – No entry.

Sat 18 – Fair, warm.

Sun 19 – Fair, getting hot. We were at church in morning, then in the evening we were at the Hecker picnic.

Mon 20 – Very hot all day. Bill & Anita & June Ann were here in evening.

Tues 21 – Very hot all day, a light shower at night & cooler. I was at Margret's & Robert's wedding. Geo & Frank Klein came in evening.

Wed 22 – Cloudy & cool all day. I was at Schilling's a short while. We rested up after the wedding.

Thurs 23 – Cold, 54 degrees. Romuald came and hauled manure. We also got 2 loads of lime dust from Kern.

Fri 24 – Very cool, 59 degrees, fair. We cleaned about the other place. Irwin called from St. Louis airport. Is going back to Calif.

Sat 25 – Very cool in morning. We made firewood.

Sun 26 – Very cool all day. We were to the Grange basket picnic. John & Katie were here in the evening.

Mon 27 – 60 degrees in morning, no rain yet. We made firewood and then I ironed.

Tues 28 – Hot winds. We were to the Ed Reiss funeral. Were at Belleville in the morning, at Koerber's in the evening.

Wed 29 – Very hot, 95 degrees, hot winds. Bill & Anita and June Ann were here in evening.

Thurs 30 – Hottest day, 100 degrees. I canned grapes in the morning, then I went to help Clara. She is sick.

Fri 31 – Very hot, 100 degrees. We were at Hesse's towards evening. Stopped at Schilling's on way back. Canned grapes.

September 1945

Sat 1 – Hot winds all day, cooler towards evening. Couldn't work much.

Sun 2 – Fair, cool all day. We were at church then at the Millstadt picnic.

Mon 3 – Fair, hot. We were to the picnic at Smithton. We ate supper at a dollar each.

Tues 4 – We worked around the place.

Wed 5 – Fair, cool. We were to the ladies aid meeting at Floraville in the evening.

Thurs 6 – Fair, hot. We helped clean up for the picnic at Floraville. I also potted flowers for the winter.

Fri 7 – Fair, very hot. The Schilling boys wired our basement today. I potted more flowers.

Sat 8 – Light rain early in morning, then fair. We helped butcher chickens for the picnic.

Sun 9 – Fair, hot. We had our big picnic at Floraville today with a very large crowd.

Mon 10 – Cold, rainy in morning, then fair. We helped clean up after the Floraville picnic. They took in $2,800.

Tues 11 – Cold, 54 degrees in morning, very pretty day. I washed, then we went to New Athens. Westerheides started to plow in the sheep pasture.

Wed 12 – Cold, 58 in morning, very cloudy with light rain. I helped Clara with patching. Geo mixed feed. Schillings started to plow.

Thurs 13 – Rained all day and so cold. I sewed. Geo shelled corn.

Fri 14 – Rained all day and it was so cold. I was to the show with Boobe & Marcella to see the picture "Mom & Dad."

Sat 15 – Very pretty day. We were at Mrs. Wm. Probst's birthday party with Metzgers.

Sun 16 – Very pretty day. We were at church. Then we went to Edna's. In the evening Phillip Ettling and Bill & Anita & June were here.

Mon 17 – Very pretty day. We were at New Athens. Then went to the district meeting of the home bureau at the Grange.

Tues 18 – Very pretty day, 80 degrees by noon. We worked around the yard. Got a letter from Franklin and 2 from Irwin & Mary.

Wed 19 – Very warm and cloudy. Ludger was here all day to put in switch box and wire basement and tested all lights. Alex broke his leg at school today.

Thurs 20 – Cool, very pretty day. I sewed. Geo worked in the orchard.

Fri 21 – Rained mostly all day. I worked on the quilt patches. Geo shelled & crushed corn.

Sat 22 – Very warm, fair. We were at Aunt Katie's birthday in the evening. Feders were there also.

Sun 23 – Partly cloudy, very warm. We were to the Grange chicken supper. Rained some during the night.

Mon 24 – Cloudy with some showers thru the day. I sewed quilt patches in the morning & afternoon Geo & I trimmed peach trees & made firewood.

Tues 25 – Partly cloudy. Geo and Romuald got fertilizer and I helped Clara patch & iron.

Wed 26 – Rainy all day. We were at Waterloo to take care of the milk stock.

Thurs 27 – I helped Schillings butcher chickens. We had bad thundershowers all afternoon. I drove with Kleins to their house, then walked home from there.

Fri 28 – Cold, rain by afternoon, lightning killed Schilling's heifer. Geo crushed corn. I sewed quilt patches.

Sat 29 – Cold, rainy all day. I finished sewing together the patch quilt. Geo made firewood & mixed feed.

Sun 30 – Rain all day. Bill, Anita & June Ann were here.

October 1945

Mon 1 – Rain. We couldn't do much of anything. Ludger got the truck rear end and the porch.

Tues 2 – Fair. We got a letter from Franklin. Bill & Anita were here. We paid our taxes at Smithton, $166.20.

Wed 3 – Fair. John Rapp and Geo picked our pears. I was at Marcella's a while.

Thurs 4 – Fair. I cooked soap. Geo fixed his disk.

Fri 5 – Cloudy. I cooked soap. Geo husked corn.

Sat 6 – 48 degrees, fair to cloudy. Bill & Anita and June Ann came to stay overnight.

Sun 7 – Fair, cold, 45 in morning, very pretty day. Bill & Anita and June Ann were here and in evening Kleins & Kempfs were here.

Mon 8 – Windy, getting much colder around 52 all day. I took my flowers in on the porch. Geo husked corn.

Tues 9 – Jack frost, 34 degrees, cold all day. I put a lot of wood in the basement and cleaned the porch and kitchen. Got letters from Irwin & Franklin.

Wed 10 – Fair, cold. I helped Clara patch and iron today. Geo crushed corn.

Thurs 11 – Fair, cool. I helped Clara butcher chickens today. Geo husked corn and mixed feed.

Fri 12 – Fair, cool. We went to Millstadt in evening to see Rollie, Barbara and Nancy. This is wrong. We were there Saturday eve Oct. 13.

Sat 13 – Fair warmer. I cooked a kettle-ful of soap. Geo worked on his wheat land.

Sun 14 – Cold, cloudy, light rain in morning. We got some honey and sweet potatoes at Edna's, also went to Mrs. F. Klein's birthday.

Mon 15 – Fair, light frost, cold all day. We were at Mrs. Nick Englert's in morning. Afternoon to the home bureau meeting at L. Koch's. Clara Marie died today.

Tues 16 – Fair, cool. I was at Klein's all day or afternoon. We were at Mrs. Nick Englert's in morning. In evening we were at Waterloo with Metzgers.

Wed 17 – Fair, warm. Clara Marie Klein was buried today. I helped cook the dinner. It was also Ludger's 21st birthday.

Thurs 18 – Fair, warm. Geo sowed wheat on the Schaeffer place. I helped Clara cook pear butter. We got 8 dozen eggs today.

Fri 19 – Fair, very pretty day. I worked around the yard and house. Geo mixed feed. John & Katie were here in evening.

Sat 20 – Very pretty day. We were at Columbia to get feed.

Sun 21 – Rainy all day and a very hard rain by 5 o'clock till about 7, rained about 4 inches. We were at Willie & Anita's. Willie went to the hospital.

Mon 22 – Fair, very muddy. We shelled corn and worked around the other place.

Tues 23 – Fair, cold. We were at Belleville, got some feed. Brandenburgers were here in the evening.

Wed 24 – Rainy and cold all day. We brought in some firewood. Then I started on the baby pad for Mary.

Thurs 25 – Fair, cold about 37 degrees. We took eggs to Anita's for Mrs. Golden.

Fri 26 – Very pretty day, 35 degrees. I washed. In the afternoon Oscar Probst trimmed our pigs.

Sat 27 – Very pretty day, so warm. I washed. Geo husked corn.

Sun 28 – Very pretty day, so warm. We were at church. Then at John Rapp's and in the evening at Gus Metzger's.

Mon 29 – Very pretty day. We worked about the place. The Illinois Power men staked off our line today.

Tues 30 – Fair, very windy. I helped Clara patch in the afternoon. In morning we were at Mrs. Nick Englert's.

Wed 31 – Very pretty day. I cut some lawn. Geo mixed feed. Then we hauled some manure.

November 1945

Thurs 1 – Partly cloudy, awful windy, warm. Geo mowed the roadside to Klein's till the rain shower. I pulled weeds in flower bed. In evening Schillings were all here.

Fri 2 – Rained some during the night. Geo cleaned some in the hen house. He and O. J. Probst trimmed the last of our pigs. I baked coffee cake and pies.

Sat 3 – Very pretty day, cold 35. Franklin & Georgie came last night. Katie & Johnny were here for supper.

Sun 4 – Cold, 25 degrees, ice on water and ground frozen. Franklin and Georgie went to Sunday School. Then we went to Bill & Anita's.

Mon 5 – Warmer, very pretty day. We worked around yard and so on.

Tues 6 – Very warm, 60 in morning, very windy, a light shower. We were at the card party in evening at Paderborn.

Wed 7 – 62 degrees, still very windy, fair. Geo husked corn. The poles for our electric line came today.

Thurs 8 – Partly cloudy, 65 degrees, very stormy all day, rain by night. The electric men brought the hole digger and things.

Fri 9 – Fair, cold, ice on water. Geo & Orville took 6 hogs to the yards. Then we went to New Athens. The electric men dug the hole for the pole.

Sat 10 – Cloudy, very windy. We worked around the place.

Sun 11 – Cloudy & cold all day and foggy. We were at Pearl & Melvin's in the evening. We were at church, saw pictures of India & Japan.

Mon 12 – Fair to cloudy, very windy, warmer, rain by nite & colder. We were at Mrs. Mary Klein's birthday party.

Tues 13 – Fair, cold, no frost tho. We were to the farm bureau meeting & dinner.

Wed 14 – Fair, cold, 34 degrees. Geo husked corn and I washed windows and brought the flowers in from the porch.

Thurs 15 – Fair, cold, 25 in morning. We went to the Farmer's Institute at Freeburg in the afternoon. In evening, we went to Millstadt with Clara & Romuald.

Fri 16 – Partly cloudy, strong SW winds, warmer. I helped Clara patch a little while. In evening we went to Institute at Freeburg with Boobe Kleins. The men finished our electric today.

Sat 17 – Fair, very pretty day. Mr. Lane hooked up our electric this morning. Lights are fine. In evening was Boobie's birthday.

Sun 18 – Fair, very pretty day. Uncle Henry and Bertha were here.

Mon 19 – Partly cloudy. We worked around the place.

Tues 20 – Fair, warm. We were at Smithton at Nick Englert's and in the evening at Frank Klein's birthday. It lightninged and hailed as we went home.

Wed 21 – Very strong NW winds and much colder. We couldn't work outside.

Thurs 22 – 20 degrees, still very stormy. Bill, Anita & June came and we had Thanksgiving dinner together. In evening Harry Frankes were here.

Fri 23 – 20 degrees, very stormy, yet fair.

Sat 24 – 27 degrees, getting warmer. I helped Clara today iron and paint.

Sun 25 – 30 degrees, fair. Henry and Bertha came and took us along to Viola & Ralph's for dinner.

Mon 26 – Fair to cloudy, 35 degrees. I washed. Geo took wood in the basement. In evening, we were at Brandenburger's. It lightninged & rained by 10 o'clock.

Tues 27 – Fair, colder, very cloudy by night. We were at Orville's birthday party. We were at Smithton and Millstadt. 35 degrees.

Wed 28 – Very cloudy all day, 35 degrees. We worked around the place. I also ironed. NW winds.

Thurs 29 – Very cloudy, 37 degrees, NW winds. We opened the sewer. I carried in corn cobs.

Fri 30 – Cloudy to fair, 35 degrees. Oscar Koerber took our 7 hogs to the yards. I went along to Millstadt. Got my hair fixed at Katie Southby's.

December 1945

Sat 1 – 30 degrees, fair to cloudy, light rain by night. We went to St. Louis Union Station with Brandenburgers to go to Urbana.

Sun 2 – Fair to cloudy, some warmer. We had a nice visit with Franklin, Gerry, and the boys.

Mon 3 – Very cloudy, misty. Franklin took us to the station early in the morning. We got home by one o'clock.

Tues 4 – Cloudy, getting much colder. We were at Smithton in morning. At Schilling's in evening. Was down to 25 by then.

Wed 5 – 22 degrees, fair. Henry Lang was here for hunting. I baked cookies. Geo made firewood.

Thurs 6 – 32 degrees, partly cloudy. Baked cookies and afternoon I went to a brush party to Mrs. Glauber with Marcella & Clara.

Fri 7 – 35 degrees, very pretty day. I baked cookies. In afternoon we went to Millstadt. Were to Grange potluck in evening.

Sat 8 – 36 degrees, fair, very pretty. We got a load of cinders at Millstadt. Johnson got some of their furniture.

Sun 9 – Fair, wind turned to NW, getting much colder. Bill, Anita, and June Ann were here for supper.

Mon 10 – Cold, fair, 14 degrees. I finished baking cookies. Geo made firewood and mixed feed.

Tues 11 – Cold, 12 degrees above, fair to cloudy. We mailed Mary & Irwin Xmas box. We were at Smithton also at Mrs. Englert's.

Wed 12 – Cloudy, cold southeast wind. Brandenburger brought the last of our third of the corn. Geo & I made firewood for butchering and for basement.

Thurs 13 – Cloudy to fair, snowed 2 inches over night, 25 degrees. We butchered one 400-lb hog. Henry & Lavern Lang helped. Schillings brought fertilizer.

Fri 14 – Cold NW winds, 25 degrees. I canned 12 qts liver sausage and rendered the lard. Geo mixed feed.

Sat 15 – Colder 17 degrees, getting colder, 14 degrees by 2:00 o'clock in afternoon. I washed in the basement. Geo did the feeding & made some firewood.

Sun 16 – 2 above, snow, stayed cold all day. Boobe and Marcella were here for supper, then we played cards.

Mon 17 – 20 above, warmed up to 25 by noon. We were to the home bureau meeting at Seibert's, had potluck dinner.

Tues 18 – 12 above, snowed heavy all day, started drifting by nite.

Wed 19 – 3 above, didn't warm up much during the day. I washed and worked around the house.

Thurs 20 – 7 above, warmed up to 32. We brought in a lot of wood. In the evening Boobe & Marcella took us along to Oscar Koerber's birthday.

Fri 21 – 7 above, warmed up to 22. I fried in 3 gals. of pork sausage. In evening, I wrote the rest of the Xmas cards.

Sat 22 – 7 above, warmed up to 25. I helped Clara bake cookies. Westerheides brought us the first third of our corn.

Sun 23 – 20 above, cold northeast wind, very cloudy. Lawrence was here while Marcella went to church. Franklin and family phoned to us today.

Mon 24 – 32 degrees, raining and very foggy, cloudy, rain by night. We brought in some wood. We got Mary & Irwin's package today.

Tues 25 – 25 degrees, strong NW winds, very cloudy, a lot of ice on the ground. Bill called up. We were home all day.

Wed 26 – Fair, 20 degrees, warmed up to 32. O. Koerber brought us a load of coal today. We were to Elisa's birthday party in evening.

Thurs 27 – 25 degrees, cloudy all day, light drizzle in afternoon which froze ice. We got a ¼ beef at W. Brandenburger's and took it to the locker today.

Fri 28 – 32 degrees, fair, warmed up to 47 by noon. We worked around the house.

Sat 29 – 32 cloudy, light rain by evening, then fair again. Bill, Anita, and June Ann were here.

Sun 30 – 29 degrees, snow flurries to drizzle rain. We were to the Fred Daab funeral at Smithton, also stopped at Mrs. Wachtel's.

Mon 31 – 26 degrees, snow all afternoon. We were at Schilling's to get wheat ground. Also were to Floraville to pay electric bill.

January 1946

Tues 1 – 9 above with a 3 inch snow on the ground, fair. We were at church, then we went to Herman's for dinner, also stopped at Edna's.

Wed 2 – 15 above, fair to cloudy. I set up a quilt, Marcella and Clara helped me quilt in evening. The men folk played cards.

Thurs 3 – 35 degrees, thawing. I quilted. Geo mixed feed.

Fri 4 – Very warm, 48, rainy all day, thundershowers by night. We and Kleins were to Robert Probst's birthday party.

Sat 5 – Showers all day, 52 degrees. Katie Petry came today. I finished the quilt.

Sun 6 – 50 degrees, 60 by noon, fair to cloudy, rain by night. We were at Sander's today.

Mon 7 – Warm, rainy all day. We set up a quilt. Romuald was here to put in our front porch light.

Tues 8 – Very cloudy, light to heavy rain. We quilted all day.

Wed 9 – Very cloudy. I went along to Belleville with Schillings to make out income report. In evening we and Katie Petry were at Koerber's.

Thurs 10 – Cloudy, 33 degrees. Katie Petry and I were to a quilting at Schilling's. Geo made firewood.

Fri 11 – 33 degrees, rain and snow but it all melted. Katie and I hemmed the 2 quilts. Geo did the feeding.

Sat 12 – 33 degrees, fair, getting colder. We took Aunt Katie Petry to New Athens. Yesterday we sold 16 ½ doz eggs @ $.40 = $6.60.

Sun 13 – 20 degrees, fair. We were at church and in the evening John Rapps were here.

Mon 14 – 30 degrees, fair. We cleaned one hen house and brought in some wood.

Tues 15 – 27 degrees. I was at Clara's in the afternoon. In evening I set up a quilt. Geo made firewood.

Wed 16 – 18 degrees, fair. We took our first hatching eggs to Belleville and then I sewed on the quilt.

Thurs 17 – 22 degrees, fair. I worked on my quilt & Pop shucked corn. We got a letter from Mary & Irwin and one from Franklin & Gerry.

Fri 18 – Henry Reiss came to get some chickens. It was a very pretty day, so warm.

Sat 19 – 33 degrees, cloudy. Clara came over and helped me quilt. Willie called up. Geo chopped off hedge along the road.

Sun 20 – 31 degrees, rained, turned to snow and snowed all day. I finished my quilt today.

Mon 21 – 11 degrees above, fair. We were to the home bureau meeting at Mrs. Kayson's.

Tues 22 – Zero for the first time this winter, but warmed up to 25 by noon. I sewed. Geo did the feeding.

Wed 23 – 15 above, fair. We went to Belleville with the hatching eggs.

Thurs 24 – 25 degrees, fair. Geo mixed feed. I sewed on the quilt.

Fri 25 – 35 degrees, warmed up to 48. I sewed on the quilt. Geo shucked corn and made wood.

Sat 26 – 10 above, fair, strong winds. I finished the fourth quilt.

Sun 27 – 5 above but warmed up nicely. We went to O'Fallon with Uncle Henry and Bertha. Gus and Alma were here in the evening.

Mon 28 – 30 degrees, fair. I was at Marcella's to set up the quilt.

Tues 29 – Rainy all day. We were at Belleville and then at the 4H play at Floraville in the evening.

Wed 30 – Fair, 37 degrees, stormy. I was at Marcella's quilting. In evening we were at Westerheide's. It turned much colder.

Thurs 31 – 18 above, fair, very stormy. I helped Marcella finish her quilt. Geo and Tommy shucked corn.

February 1946

Fri 1 – Fair and warmer. I cleaned the basement. Geo mixed feed.

Sat 2 – Fair, very pretty day. Geo & the Westerheide boys hauled corn home. Then we got the washer and I washed yet.

Sun 3 – Fair and warm. Johnny & Katie and Bill, Anita & June Ann were here. They put our new washer into the basement.

Mon 4 – Very cloudy all day, 45 degrees, light rain by night. I washed for Mrs. Westerheide for the first time. Ludger was here in the evening.

Tues 5 – Thunder & lightning mostly all day. We took the eggs to Belleville. In evening we were at Schilling's quilting. Turned colder then.

Wed 6 – Fair, very stormy, west winds, 32 degrees. I was at Clara's quilting all day. In evening I was on the program at the women's guild meeting.

Thurs 7 – Fair, 25 early in morning but warmed up nicely. Geo shucked corn. I cleaned up the house. Were at the card party in evening.

Fri 8 – 38 degrees, warmed up a lot. We got a load of cinders at Millstadt and then worked around the place.

Sat 9 – 24 degrees, partly cloudy. I baked and did my Saturday work. Geo worked on the road and hauled hedge away.

Sun 10 – Fair, 32 in morning. Herman and Frank were here for dinner.

Mon 11 – Fair, warm, very pretty day. I washed Westerheide's wash.

Tues 12 – Cloudy, colder but no frost, rain by night. We were at Belleville. Made out AAA papers and income tax papers. Afternoon I was quilting at Frank Klein's. Irwin called in the night. The baby boy was born.

Wed 13 – Rained hard all day, creeks were out. Geo pulled Geo Hoelscher out of ditch. We got a Valentine box of candy from Franklin.

Thurs 14 – 20 degrees, light snow flurries, strong winds all day. We and Metzgers were to the quilting party at Rapp's in the evening.

Fri 15 – Fair, 15 above. Geo shucked corn for a little while.

Sat 16 – Fair, 32 degrees, warmed up to 62 by afternoon. Geo went grinding. I moved my potted flowers out on the sun porch.

Sun 17 – Fair. I was to the women's guild meeting at Floraville in afternoon.

Mon 18 – Cloudy, warmer. We were at New Athens at my home bureau meeting at Mrs. Gerhold's. It started to rain in the evening.

Tues 19 – Rain in morning. Afternoon we took the eggs to Belleville and brought some blue seal feed home.

Wed 20 – Cloudy to fair. We got more feed at Smithton. Then we cleaned the brooder house. In evening we were at Marcella's birthday party.

Thurs 21 – Cloudy. Geo brought straw into the brooder house. I got the brooder in running order and we put in more wood.

Fri 22 – Fair, very pretty and warm, 65 at noon. We got 345 two-week old chicks today, all reds. I raked the back lawn and sowed lettuce seed in flower bed.

Sat 23 – Cloudy, drizzle rain to fair, colder. Last night Boobe & Marcella took us along to Progressive Grange for a picture show. Today we worked around the place.

Sun 24 – Fair. Bill, Anita, and June Ann were here for dinner.

Mon 25 – Fair, very pretty and warm. I washed for Mrs. Westerheide. Then we went to Uncle Johnny's to get ashes and wood boards and so on.

Tues 26 – Very cloudy, colder, rain afternoon. We were at Belleville. In the evening we were at Paderborn card party with Boobe and Marcella.

Wed 27 – Fair, cold, 30 degrees, strong NW winds. I was to the quilting at Annie Wachtel's. Geo went along too. In the evening we finished the quilt.

Thurs 28 – Fair, 30 degrees, strong south winds. We worked around the place. In evening we were to Willard Probst's wedding dance at Daab Clubhouse.

March 1946

Fri 1 – Fair, 40 degrees, cloudy by noon, rain and colder towards evening. We cleaned the brooder house and Geo shucked corn.

Sat 2 – Fair, we cleaned up around the place. I baked bread and coffee cake.

Sun 3 – Fair. We moved things out of the other house today.

Mon 4 – Fair, stormy. I cleaned the upstairs in the other house today.

Tues 5 – Fair. I washed, then I went to a card party at Smithton with Marcella. We rented out our house today to Lester Smith.

Wed 6 – Fair. We were to Belleville with the eggs. Also stayed for a meeting in Belleville.

Thurs 7 – Fair. We and Metzgers were to the card party at the Grange.

Fri 8 – Rainy all day, getting colder, some sleet. We couldn't do much of anything except mix feed.

Sat 9 – White frost, hard frost, 20 degrees, fair. We worked around the house and cleaned the brooder house.

Sun 10 – Frost, fair, warmer. We were at church in morning & afternoon had a potluck supper at church hall. We had a lot of company in evening.

Mon 11 – Very pretty day. I washed and then helped Pop & the Smiths clean the yard.

Tues 12 – Fair. We were at Belleville in morning. In afternoon I was to Ceile Wachtel's quilting party. No frost today.

Wed 13 – Light rain to fair. We butchered 2 hogs today. One for Johnny & Katie and one for us. We put most of it into locker, 74 lbs.

Thurs 14 – Partly cloudy, warmer. We were at the George Lortz sale. We planted shade trees in the front yard. Henry Lang got them in our timber. Linden trees.

Fri 15 – Fair, very windy, warm. We cleaned the brooder house and worked about the place.

Sat 16 – Fair, very windy & showery. I started spading flower beds. We were at Orlin Skare's in the evening.

Sun 17 – Fair to cloudy and some rain, warm. Had my chicks out in the yard. We put on screen doors.

Mon 18 – Rainy all day. We were to my home bureau meeting at Mrs. Holcomb's.

Tues 19 – Very cloudy, colder, 45 degrees mostly all day. We were at Belleville. Ludger & Leo started to wire our house today.

Wed 20 – Fair, warm, very pretty day. The boys finished wiring the house and Mr. Dengler brought the pressure pump and connected the sink.

Thurs 21 – Fair, very pretty day. The Skares started to paint the rooms and build a closet in the other house. Henry Lang hauled his wheat.

Fri 22 – Fair. I washed the walls of the kitchen so that Orlin Skare could paint. Mr. Skare finished the closet today.

Sat 23 – Fair. We were at Millstadt. Then cleaned the brooder house and got firewood at Boobe's. Skares finished painting the rooms over there.

Sun 24 – We had my birthday party during the day and evening.

Mon 25 – Fair, very warm. I washed. In evening Johnny & Katie were here to put in my lower cabinet. We also celebrated my birthday.

Tues 26 – Fair, hot, 76 degrees, fair to cloudy. We took the eggs to Belleville. In the evening we went to W. Brandenburger's for her birthday, also Melvin's is on 27th.

Wed 27 – Fair, hot almost 80 degrees. Geo plowed. I cleaned the old brooder house to move the first chicks into it. Also set out potted plants.

Thurs 28 – Fair, very warm, 96 degrees. I cleaned the washhouse and Geo plowed for corn by the north chicken house.

Fri 29 – Fair, hot, 80 degrees, thundershowers by night. We moved our chicks into the old brooder house, 353 seven weeks old.

Sat 30 – Fair, warm. We cleaned the brooder house and worked about the yard.

Sun 31 – Very pretty day. We were at St. Louis at Uncle Henry's birthday celebration. Brandenburgers were here in the evening.

April 1946

Mon 1 – Fair, hot, 86 degrees. Geo plowed the backyard over there and I spaded and worked around outside.

Tues 2 – Fair, hot, 85 degrees. I washed and we got 315 chicks, a week and a half old. We set up the new electric brooder.

Wed 3 – Fair, not quite so hot. I washed off doors & windows in the other house and then I spaded in the flower beds.

Thurs 4 – We & Orlin Skare finished painting the inside house over there. In evening Ludger and Geo worked on our water system.

Fri 5 – Cool, 40 degrees but warmed up nicely. Pop & I were at Millstadt. Franklin and family are coming this evening.

Sat 6 – Franklin & his family are here and Bill & Anita also came for the afternoon. June Ann stayed overnight.

Sun 7 – Schillings and Kleins and Ludger were here for dinner. Boobe took Franklin to Millstadt bus station in afternoon.

Mon 8 – Gerry and I washed today and cleaned up the house. Mr. Smith paid the first rent $20.00 today.

Tues 9 – Geo & I took the eggs to Belleville and Gerry and the boys went to Millstadt with Marcella and stayed at Aunt Katie's.

Wed 10 – We baked cookies and then went to Schilling's a while. Geo plowed.

Thurs 11 – Very cloudy and cold, 40 degrees by morning. We all were at Marcella's for supper.

Fri 12 – We were at Herman's a while, then we stopped at Edna's. Baked rabbit cookies in the morning.

Sat 13 – Very pretty day, warmer. Franklin came today, also Bill & Anita. June stayed overnight. George Dintelmann crashed this evening.

Sun 14 – Sunday, very pretty day. Franklin, Gerry, and the boys went home again today. Bill & Anita took them to the station.

Mon 15 – Rained hard all morning. We went to Belleville in afternoon.

Tues 16 – The Smiths moved into our house today and Geo and I and Fred Wachtels went to Alton to Geo Dintelmann's funeral. Cool all day, but fair.

Wed 17 – Light frost, fair. I washed. Geo plowed.

Thurs 18 – Fair, very pretty day, warm. We cleaned the brooder house and I ironed. Geo plowed.

Fri 19 – Fair, very pretty day, hot. It's Good Friday today. Geo plowed. I worked in the yard. Went to church in evening.

Sat 20 – Fair, very pretty day. I mixed feed. Orlin or Orville Skares were here in the evening.

Sun 21 – Fair, very pretty Easter Sunday. We were at church, then went to Hesse's for dinner.

Mon 22 – Fair. I washed for Mrs. Smith, also worked in my garden. Geo plowed. Tommy plowed the alfalfa patch.

Tues 23 – Light rain mostly all day. We didn't do much. Leo & Alex killed 49 rats in two evenings with their dogs.

Wed 24 – Fair, warmer. I went to Belleville to see Minnie at the hospital. Afternoon I spaded in the flower beds. Geo planted the first corn.

Thurs 25 – Fair, cool. I washed, then I went to Clara's & helped her patch. Geo plowed.

Fri 26 – Fair, very cool all day. Geo plowed. I washed eggs and mixed feed, planted tomatoes and ironed.

Sat 27 – Fair, warmer. We cleaned the brooder house and mixed feed. Light rain in the night.

Sun 28 – Fair. Viola and Ralph took us along to Bill & Anita's. Rained in the night.

Mon 29 – Cloudy all day. I spaded and planted tomatoes. Geo plowed.

Tues 30 – Rain all day so I worked in the house. Geo mixed feed. Ludger put in our wash bowl.

May 1946

Wed 1 – Rained mostly all night and part of day. We were at Millstadt to get things to wire over to the shed for grinding.

Thurs 2 – Rain. Geo was grinding a lot of corn with his electric motor.

Fri 3 – Rain to fair. I washed. Dried very poorly, had to hang a lot of it on the porch.

Sat 4 – Rain mostly all day. I worked in the basement.

Sun 5 – Fair, very pretty day. We were at church at Freeburg. It was the Grange church Sunday. Then I was at guild meeting and Vogel School picnic in evening at Paderborn school play.

Mon 6 – Fair. I washed for Mrs. Smith and myself. John & Katie were here in the evening.

Tues 7 – Fair, very cool, stormy. I washed for Mrs. Westerheide and we put up our wire clothesline in the backyard.

Wed 8 – Fair, cool, very pretty day. We were to the annual county home bureau meeting at Christ Church hall in Belleville today. I was on the program, school days.

Thurs 9 – Fair to cloudy, rain by night. I set out some of my house plants. Geo disked in the corn land.

Fri 10 – Rain mostly all day. I was at Schilling's in the afternoon to help with the work as Clara hurt her leg with an ax. Geo mixed feed.

Sat 11 – Very cool. I did my Saturday work. Geo made firewood. I baked bread and coffee cake and an angel cake.

Sun 12 – Mothers Day, fair, very pretty day. Bill & Anita came and took us to Freeburg for dinner. Then we went to Hesse's and picked strawberries.

Mon 13 – Rainy all day. We took the strawberries to the locker. I'm writing this with the new fountain pen Bill & Anita gave me for Mothers Day.

Tues 14 – Very pretty day. I washed today. Geo worked around the place. Henry Lang was here a while.

Wed 15 – Cloudy, rain by 3 p.m. and rained slow most of the night. I worked in the lawn. Henry Lang mowed clover.

Thurs 16 – Rain. We worked around the house.

Fri 17 – Rained very hard all day, creeks were out.

Sat 18 – Clearing somewhat, can't do much of anything.

Sun 19 – Light shower early in morning. We went to church and afternoon we were at Schillings. Irwin and Mary called up in the evening.

Mon 20 – Light shower to fair. We were at the home bureau meeting at Mrs. Meta Groosman's.

Tues 21 – Fair, very pretty day. I washed. Geo worked on the shed roof.

Wed 22 – Very pretty day. I worked in the lawn and did some sewing. Geo worked on the shed roof.

Thurs 23 – Rainy all day. I sewed. Geo worked around the place. A hen hatched 14 chicks in the cow barn.

Fri 24 – Rainy all day, thundering. Geo shelled corn. I worked in the basement.

Sat 25 – Fair. I dressed chickens for Mrs. Westerheide and 2 for us for Sunday dinner.

Sun 26 – Very cloudy with light rain all day. Earl & Helen, Will & Mable, and Bill & Anita and June Ann were here.

Mon 27 – Fair. I washed for Mrs. Smith and then I chopped off weeds. Geo worked on his shed.

Tues 28 – Fair. I washed for Mrs. Westerheide. Geo worked on the shed roof.

Wed 29 – Fair. We were at Millstadt in the morning, then we worked around the place.

Thurs 30 – Fair. We went to the women's guild, had our supper and bazaar, and church in the evening.

Fri 31 – Showers now & then. Caught some chickens to sell. Also chopped weeds.

June 1946

Sat 1 – Chopped weeds again but it rained hard all afternoon.

Sun 2 – Very cloudy all day, cold 50 degrees. I was to the women's guild meeting and in the evening we were to Alma's birthday.

Mon 3 – Fair, cool. We cleaned the chicken house today, also picked dewberries.

Tues 4 – Fair, cool. Finished cleaning the chicken house and moved the hens, also picked dewberries.

Wed 5 – Fair, warmer, moved the young chickens. Canned dewberries and 4 pints of cherries.

Thurs 6 – Fair, warmer. Clara, Marcella, and I picked dewberries, each got about 2 gal. Then I washed yet.

Fri 7 – Fair, hot winds. Geo planted corn. I hoed in the garden and canned some beans. Got a letter from Mary & Irwin. They bought 2.8 acres.

Sat 8 – Fair, very hot, 93 degrees. I picked 2.5 gal. dewberries and took 6 quarts to locker. Geo planted corn on alfalfa patch.

Sun 9 – Fair, warm. We were at church. Then we had come and go company all afternoon.

Mon 10 – Very warm, 84 at 11 o'clock. I worked in the garden. Geo harrowed his corn. Romuald combined our winter oats.

Tues 11 – Fair, 90 degrees, windy. I picked 1.5 gal dewberries and worked in the garden. Geo laid-by corn and plowed to plant more corn.

Wed 12 – Fair, hot, windy. I washed. Geo & Henry Lang plowed for corn. A lot of dewberries were picked today. Stevie is 2 years old.

Thurs 13 – Fair, hot. We picked more dewberries, also apples.

Fri 14 – Fair, hot. Geo finished planting corn. I worked about the yard.

Sat 15 – Fair, hot. Franklin, Gerry, and the boys came this evening with Bill & Anita and June. Gerry & boys will stay all week.

Sun 16 – Fair, very hot. We had Uncle Henry & Bertha, Bill & Anita and June Ann, and Franklin's family for dinner & supper.

Mon 17 – Fair, hot, 95 degrees. We took Franklin to Belleville so he went to Dixon Springs with Mr. Tillmann.

Tues 18 – Fair, very hot, 98 degrees. We washed today and canned apple sauce and dewberries.

Wed 19 – Fair, hot. Got a windstorm by evening with a shower of rain and much cooler.

Thurs 20 – Cold, 64 degrees, very pretty day. We were at Marcella's a little while. Bill & Anita and John & Katie were here in evening.

Fri 21 – Fair, cool. Gerry & boys went along to Bill & Anita's last night.

Sat 22 – Fair, cool. We worked around the place.

Sun 23 – Fair, warmer. We were at church then we went to the picnic at Millstadt.

Mon 24 – Fair, hot. I washed for Mrs. Westerheide. Schillings finished combining on our place. Got about 500 bu in all.

Tues 25 – Partly cloudy, light shower. Schillings got 500 bu wheat from 25 acres.

Wed 26 – Very hot, 90 degrees. I washed for Mrs. Smith and worked in the garden.

Thurs 27 – Very hot. I helped Clara dress chickens. Then I canned beets and ironed.

Fri 28 – Very hot, up in the nineties. Geo mowed the road all the way past Knab's. Westerheides started combining wheat.

Sat 29 – Partly cloudy, warm. We worked around the place. I baked bread & coffee cake.

Sun 30 – Partly cloudy, thundered by afternoon. The Smiths and I were at Westerheide's.

July 1946

Mon 1 – Cooler, fair. Westerheides finished combining today. They got 300 bu in all from 30 acres.

Tues 2 – Fair, cooler. I sewed and mowed weeds.

Wed 3 – Fair. Shirley Smith's birthday. I mowed the lawn.

Thurs 4 – Fair, warmer. I washed the porch windows. Geo plowed by corn.

Fri 5 – Getting hot, very dry. I picked berries and washed for Mrs. Westerheide in the morning.

Sat 6 – 98 degrees, no rain. I scrubbed porch & kitchen floors and waxed them. We were to the wedding dance at the Grange.

Sun 7 – 100 degrees. Mr. & Mrs. Willard Probst were here. We paid our rock phosphate $113.22. Bill & Anita were here in the evening.

Mon 8 – 102 degrees, very dry. I canned blackberries. Geo worked in his corn.

Tues 9 – 100 degrees, very hard rain by 4 o'clock, creeks were out.

Wed 10 – Fair to a little shower late afternoon. I washed for Mrs. Smith. Mrs. Westerheide was here in the afternoon.

Thurs 11 – Cooler to fair. I helped cook for the threshers at Koerber's.

Fri 12 – Fair. I helped cook again at Koerber's. They finished threshing. Geo worked in his corn.

Sat 13 – Very cool this morning, much warmer by afternoon. I baked bread & coffee cake. Geo worked in the corn.

Sun 14 – Fair, very hot, 95. John & Katie were here.

Mon 15 – Very hot, fair. We were at Belleville to my home bureau meeting at May Carre's house. Also visited Minnie at the hospital.

Tues 16 – Very cloudy all day. I chopped weeds. Geo worked in the corn.

Wed 17 – Fair, very hot, 102. I washed. Had a thundershower.

Thurs 18 – Hot, 103. Henry Lang and the children were here.

Fri 19 – Very hot, 105, hottest day so far.

Sat 20 – Cooler, good rain all morning. We went to the Paderborn picnic in the evening.

Sun 21 – Fair, warm. We were at Edna's to fish dinner & supper. Bill & Anita & June Ann were there also. Brinkers came in the evening, paid ½ rent.

Mon 22 – Fair. Smiths moved out of the older house today. We worked around the place.

Tues 23 – Fair, hot. I was at Marcella's in the afternoon. Geo mowed weeds along the road.

Wed 24 – Fair, very hot, 100 degrees. We were at the fair at Belleville.

Thurs 25 – Fair, cooler by night. I helped Clara patch in afternoon. Geo mowed clover seed today for Henry Lang.

Fri 26 – Fair, cool, 61 degrees in morning but warmer later in the day. Geo mowed weeds in the pasture.

Sat 27 – Getting hot again. I baked coffee cake and dressed four chickens for Sunday dinner. Henry Lang combined 6 bu clover seed.

Sun 28 – Partly cloudy. Carlena & family, John & Katie, Edgar & family, Will Feder family, Pearl & Melvin, Bill & Anita & June, Henry & Bertha & Annie and the boys at home were here.

Mon 29 – Fair, hot. We worked around the place.

Tues 30 – Hot. We were at Belleville to get electric stuff for the other house towards evening. Ludger came and did the wiring. A hard rain came then.

Wed 31 – Very hot all day. I helped Clara in the afternoon. We fixed hog fence. Carlena & Elmer got 76 pullets from us this evening.

August 1946

Thurs 1 – 104 degrees. I cleaned the brooder house. Geo plowed. Very hot all day.

Fri 2 – Rain all morning. Geo & Boobe took 4 of our and 4 of Boobe's hogs to the yards. Weight 760 and one 135 @ $21.25. The 3 big ones brought $24.25.

Sat 3 – Very hot, in the nineties. We were at John & Katie's for supper as Edgar & Toddy were there, also Feders & Pearl & Melvin.

Sun 4 – Very hot, 100 degrees. We were at the picnic at Millstadt and then at Edna's to get prunes.

Mon 5 – Very hot, bad thunderstorms all afternoon, creeks were out. I canned peaches.

Tues 6 – Clara came and helped me peel & can peaches. Then afternoon I helped Clara peel peaches. Geo mixed feed.

Wed 7 – Fair, hot to cooler by night. I was at Schilling's in afternoon. In evening we and Gus & Alma went to see Mrs. Rapp.

Thurs 8 – Fair, hot. I canned 3 quarts of peaches. Then I helped Clara peel. Geo mixed feed.

Fri 9 – Partly cloudy to fair, 81 early in morning, very hot all day. I helped Marcella peel peaches. Geo got corn at Walter Brandenburger's.

Sat 10 – Fair, cool. I baked coffee cake & Clara's birthday cake. Bill & Anita and June Ann were here in the afternoon.

Sun 11 – Fair, very cool, 60 in morning, 75 by noon. We were at Clara's birthday party in the evening.

Mon 12 – Cloudy, cool, 61 degrees. I chopped and pulled weeds all day. Geo plowed.

Tues 13 – Very cloudy all day and cool. We fixed pasture fence and cleaned up around the shop. Light rain.

Wed 14 – Cool to warmer, heavy rain by night. Pop was to a road meeting. A big flood all over by morning.

Thurs 15 – Warmer, more hard rains, flood getting worse. Pop got Franklin at Millstadt. Rained 14 inches in 10 hours.

Fri 16 – More heavy rains. East St. Louis and Belleville having the worst floods in history. Water up to corn tassels in bottoms.

Sat 17 – Very hot, fair. Franklin went to St. Louis to get our tickets for our Calif. trip tomorrow. He drove thru deep water.

Sun 18 – Fair, cooler. Geo, Franklin, and I left for Texas. Henry took us to the station at St. Louis. Train left at 3:30 p.m.

Mon 19 – Fair, arrived at Texas by 3 o'clock afternoon. Mr. Brockette met us at Farwell Station, light rain by night.

Tues 20 – Cloudy, cool. Mr. Brockette took us out to see our farm and other nice places. At 8 p.m. we took the bus to Clovis, New Mexico.

Wed 21 – Cloudy, rainy. Franklin put us on the train at Clovis at 1:30 a.m. Then he took a train back to Kansas City at 2:30 a.m.

Thurs 22 – Fair. We were somewhere in Arizona.

Fri 23 – Fair. We arrived at Los Angeles by 7 a.m. and Irwin was there to meet us. Then we drove out to his home.

Sat 24 – Fair. We were enjoying a nice rest with Mary and the boys after our long trip. We all went to the beach in the afternoon.

Sun 25 – Fair, cool. We went out to work around Mary & Irwin's new home. We ate a lot of oranges off their trees.

Mon 26 – Fair. We were enjoying ourselves very much, playing with Stephen and Kenneth.

Tues 27 – Fair. We went out to Mary & Irv's house to do some work.

Wed 28 – Fair. Mary and the boys went to a card party and Geo and I went to a farm meeting with Irwin in the afternoon.

Thurs 29 – Fair. We went over to the house again to wash up the rooms and work around.

Fri 30 – Fair. We moved some things to the new home. Geo dug in the septic tank hole. This was at Irwin's home in Calif.

Sat 31 – Fair. We moved more things and filled up the front yard with ground.

September 1946

Sun 1 – Fair. Moving more things and getting ready for our trip to Atascadero.

Mon 2 – Fair. We left early for Atascadero. Arrived there by five p.m.

Tues 3 – Fair. We were enjoying a nice visit with Mary's folks.

Wed 4 – Fair. Irwin, Geo, and I left for our trip to Yosemite Park. Stayed overnight.

Thurs 5 – Fair. Left early for San Francisco and came over the skyline to go to Big Basin State Park. Stayed overnight.

Fri 6 – Fair. We left Big Basin to go back to Atascadero. Arrived there by 4:30 p.m.

Sat 7 – Fair. Spent a nice day with Mary's folks.

Sun 8 – Fair. We had another nice Sunday with Mary's folks.

Mon 9 – Fair. We left for home to Vista to live in Mary & Irwin's new home.

Tues 10 – Fair. We are working around to clean up things.

Wed 11 – Fair. Still working about the place.

Thurs 12 – Fair. We worked in the yard today. The men were here to wire the house.

Fri 13 – Fair. We washed today. Then we went to the beach. More wiring done.

Sat 14 – Fair. We worked about the place.

Sun 15 – Fair. We washed then we all went for a ride to old Mexico. Had a dinner for Irwin's birthday in the evening.

Mon 16 – Fair. Mary & I washed and waxed the floors and we left for home by 3:30 p.m. Irwin took us to Los Angeles.

Tues 17 – Cloudy, rainy. Enjoying our train ride back thru Calif. & Arizona & Texas.

Wed 18 – Cloudy, rainy. Arrived at Kansas City by 9:30 p.m. Got on the Wabash by 11:30 p.m.

Thurs 19 – Fair. Arrived at St. Louis by 8:15 a.m. Took the bus to Belleville, then Hecker bus to Brandenburger Road.

Fri 20 – Rain in morning. Afternoon I started cleaning the yard. Were at Marcella's and Boobe's in the evening.

Sat 21 – Fair. We were at Millstadt today. Also at Smithton to the bank.

Sun 22 – Fair. Bill, Anita, and June Ann were here. Also Frank Kleins.

Mon 23 – Rain, heavy thru the night, then fair. I potted my flowers and then we picked apples.

Tues 24 – Fair. I washed today and picked apples. Got our paint today for the other house.

Wed 25 – Canned apple sauce and worked around the house.

Thurs 26 – Fair. We cleaned the chicken house and picked pears.

Fri 27 – Fair. We went to the Progressive Grange for my home bureau meeting. Beulah & Edwin were here in evening.

Sat 28 – fair, hot, cloudy by night. I baked coffee cake and ironed and carried in wood for the winter.

Sun 29 – Fair, very cool. We were at church in morning. Again in afternoon to William Schneider's wedding. Will & Mable and Bill & Anita came.

Mon 30 – Fair, cold 43 degrees. I picked apples. Earl & Helen were here.

October 1946

Tues 1 – Fair, very cool. Finished picking apples. Then we went to Smithton & Millstadt. Bill, Anita, & June came in afternoon.

Wed 2 – Fair, light frost. We started to paint the other house.

Thurs 3 – Fair, light frost. We painted all day.

Fri 4 – Fair, warmer. We painted all day.

Sat 5 – Fair, hot. We painted mostly all day. In the evening we visited with Grandma Lang. She is sick.

Sun 6 – Fair, hot. Gus & Alma took us along to visit with Mrs. Dora Mueth at New Athens. Were at church in evening.

Mon 7 – Fair, very hot. Schillings started to sow wheat on our land. Louis & Hattie were here for dinner. We painted after they left.

Tues 8 – Fair, hot. We painted in the morning. In the afternoon I went to the autumn festival at Millstadt Church with Emma Barthel.

Wed 9 – Fair, hot. We painted all day, finished first coat. Clara was here in the afternoon.

Thurs 10 – Fair to cloudy, dust storm by afternoon, shower by night. I was at Turkey Hill Grange for lesson, then at women's guild meeting in evening at Floraville.

Fri 11 – Cloudy, much cooler. Franklin, Gerry, and the boys came at 5:30 evening, stayed until Sunday noon.

Sat 12 – Fair, heavy frost, 32 degrees. We & Franklin and family had a nice day together. Bill, Anita, June, and Johnny & Katie were here too.

Sun 13 – Fair, 36 degrees. Franklin & Gerry and Geo & Richard left at 12:30 noon. In the evening we were at Mrs. F. Klein's birthday party.

Mon 14 – Fair. We fixed the door at the other house. Leo painted the gables and dormer windows. We also blood tested our chickens.

Tues 15 – Fair. We were to see sister Minnie at the hospital in the morning. Afternoon we painted.

Wed 16 – Fair. We painted all day.

Thurs 17 – Rainy all day, hard rain by night. Walter Ettling, Ruth Kempf, Adele Hoffman, Emma Barthel, and I were at meeting at East St. Louis.

Fri 18 – Cloudy, warm. Grandma Lang died today.

Sat 19 – Fair, much cooler. We decorated the church today for the harvest fest tomorrow.

Sun 20 – Fair, very cool. We were at church. Henry & Bertha and Uncle Wills & Earl & Helen and Bill, Anita, & June Ann were here.

Mon 21 – Fair. I washed in morning. Bill & Marie Schlueter were here. We went to Grandma Lang's funeral today.

Tues 22 – Fair. We painted all day except in the morning. I ironed.

Wed 23 – We painted mostly all day. Were at Brandenburger's in the evening.

Thurs 24 – Cloudy & very stormy, hard rain by night. We shucked and shelled corn and mixed feed.

Fri 25 – Fair, cooler, very pretty day. We cleaned off the porches over there and painted some. Marie painted 2 doors and front porch floor.

Sat 26 – Fair, very pretty day. I painted. Geo shucked corn.

Sun 27 – Fair, very warm. We were at Ralph & Viola's today. In evening Boobe Kleins & grandma Klein, Gus Metzgers and Brinkers were here.

Mon 28 – Fair, very warm. I baked coffee cake and bread and painted.

Tues 29 – Fair, warm, 82 degrees. We took baked stuff to Freeburg for the Institute. Then I painted and in the evening we went to Waterloo. Tobbie Schuchardt died.

Wed 30 – Fair, hot, 84 degrees. We were at the Farmers Institute at Freeburg. Afternoon and evening, I got 4 blue ribbons on my baked stuff.

Thurs 31 – Rain all day, a little cooler. We couldn't do much of anything.

November 1946

Fri 1 – Warm, rain all day.

Sat 2 – Warm, rain all day.

Sun 3 – Warm to a little cooler, light rain at times. We were at church. Then Henry & Edna and Bill, Anita, and June came. Were at Gus's birthday in evening.

Mon 4 – Cloudy all day, cooler. We chopped out old peach trees.

Tues 5 – Cloudy. I helped Schillings paint at the Karban place.

Wed 6 – Cloudy to rain by afternoon and all night. We were at Belleville to the Farm Bureau dinner.

Thurs 7 – Fair, colder. I was at Schilling's to help paint at Karban's place.

Fri 8 – Cold and fair, no frost tho. I painted on the porch ceiling on the house over there.

Sat 9 – Rain mostly all day and night. I finished painting the porch ceiling over on the other house.

Sun 10 – Cloudy and cold all day. We were at Carlena's for dinner for Christie's birthday. Paul and Cecilia Wachtel came in evening.

Mon 11 – Very cloudy and cold. I got my hair set at Leona's. Then I baked 2 angel cakes for Romuald's wedding.

Tues 12 – Fair, very pretty day for the Schilling – Wachtel wedding. We went along to the dance in the evening with Marcella and Boobe.

Wed 13 – Fair, very pretty day. We painted on the porches again. Geo painted the one ceiling.

Thurs 14 – Fair, warmer, light frost. I painted the storm windows. Geo painted porch ceiling. I also took off the screens here.

Fri 15 – Cloudy all day, rain by night. We went to the potluck at the Grange. Rained very hard as we drove home at 10:30.

Sat 16 – Fair, cooler. We put up the storm windows. Got one load of road rock for the yard.

Sun 17 – Fair, cold, 28. We were at church. I gave my report. To church again in evening, then to Boobe's birthday. Bill, Anita & June were here.

Mon 18 – Fair, cold, 26 degrees. We went to Belleville then to Groth's for home bureau meeting.

Tues 19 – 30 degrees, fair. I painted porch wall. Geo painted the porch roof.

Wed 20 – Fair, nice & warm. I painted the porch wall over at the other house. Geo shucked corn and made firewood.

Thurs 21 – Partly cloudy, warm, but cooler late in evening. Marie & I painted front porch floor. Then Marie painted the back doors.

Fri 22 – Fair, 30 degrees. I painted the screens for the other house. Geo and Mr. Brinker set up the mailbox. Geo also made firewood.

Sat 23 – Fair to cloudy, very stormy all day, little frost. We painted the outhouse and made firewood.

Sun 24 – Very stormy, south winds, no frost, cloudy. We stayed home all day, but want to go to Frank Klein's birthday tonight.

Mon 25 – Cold rain all day. I cleaned the bedroom in the evening. We had supper with Marie & Lester, Lester's birthday.

Tues 26 – Fair, cold but no frost. Geo mixed feed and I cleaned in the house.

Wed 27 – Fair, very pretty day. I washed and then cleaned the bedroom and waxed the floor.

Thurs 28 – Fair, light frost, very pretty day, about 60 at noon. We and Bill, Anita & June Ann were at Hesse's for Thanksgiving dinner.

Fri 29 – Fair, warm, no frost, very pretty day. I washed & ironed my drapes. Geo husked corn.

Sat 30 – Fair, very pretty day altho turning colder by night. I cleaned the bathroom. Geo shucked corn.

December 1946

Sun 1 – Cloudy, windy, and cold. We were at June Ann's birthday party. Wachtels (Fred) and Annie were here in the evening.

Mon 2 – Fair, cold, 18 degrees. I worked in the house. John & Etta came by afternoon, stayed overnight.

Tues 3 – John & Etta left at noon. Then Marie, Larry, & Mary Ann, and I went to Schilling's. It was so nice and warm.

Wed 4 – Fair, warmer, 27 early, then about 50 by noon. We were at Belleville today.

Thurs 5 – Fair, warm, no frost. I worked in the house. Ben Boveings were here in the evening.

Fri 6 – Fair, warm. I scrubbed the living room floor in the evening. We were at Marie Brinker's birthday party.

Sat 7 – I varnished the living room floor and worked out in the yard a while.

Sun 8 – Fair, warm. Herman & Frank were here for dinner. Then Mary & Lillian came in the afternoon.

Mon 9 – Fair to cloudy & showers, rain by night. We were at Waterloo to get a muffler for the coupe.

Tues 10 – Very cloudy, a little cooler. I cleaned upstairs. Then I washed. Geo cleaned along the roadside.

Wed 11 – Cloudy, cooler. I worked about the house. Geo mixed feed.

Thurs 12 – Cloudy, warm. We were to the oil meeting today at Belleville. Rain to much colder as we were on our way home.

Fri 13 – No entry.

Sat 14 – No entry.

Sun 15 – Cloudy, cold, damp weather. We were at church and afternoon I made the Christmas tree and got things ready for the meeting.

Mon 16 – Cloudy, warm, 60 degrees. We had the Xmas potluck dinner of the home bureau here today.

Tues 17 – Clear, cold, 24 degrees. I cleaned up in the house. Geo worked along the road. We got a Xmas box from Mary & Irwin.

Wed 18 – Fair. Geo worked along the road. I shucked corn by the house here.

Thurs 19 – Fair. We worked around the place.

Fri 20 – Fair. We worked around the place. We were at Oscar Koerber's birthday in the evening.

Sat 21 – Fair, cooler. I cleaned the kitchen & porch. Geo shucked corn. Boobe took us along to the Grange income tax meeting.

Sun 22 – Fair, very pretty and warm day. We went to Earl & Helen's for dinner. Bill & Anita got us at Millstadt.

Mon 23 – Fair, warm. We shucked corn and worked around the place.

Tues 24 – Fair, warm. We were at Millstadt. Got some meat and fruit from the locker. Were at church in evening.

Wed 25 – Fair, very pretty day, warm. Bill & Anita came and took us along to Vera & Siegel Hesse's for Xmas dinner.

Thurs 26 – Fair, very pretty and warm day. We cleaned the chicken house, also shucked some corn. Were at Fred Wachtel's in evening.

Fri 27 – Fair, very warm, strong southwest winds. We took the coupe to Smithton to have it fixed. Were at Schilling's in evening.

Sat 28 – Cooler, very cloudy, rain by nite. I washed, then shucked corn. Geo made firewood and shelled corn.

Sun 29 – Snow flurries, much colder, 22 at 7:00 a.m., 17 at 11:00 a.m., 14 above by nite. Bill & Anita and June Ann came and had supper with us.

Mon 30 – 14 above, light snow to fair, warmed up to 22. I have a bad cold so I didn't do much. Geo made firewood.

Tues 31 – Cloudy, 13 degrees, warmed up to 20. I pasted pictures in my scrapbook. Geo made firewood.

January 1947

Wed 1 – Cloudy, cold, 16 at 8:00 a.m., 22 by noon, sleet falling mostly all day. Geo & I walked to Klein's in the afternoon. Schillings were there too. Received $132.00 from Texas for cotton insurance.

Thurs 2 – 13 above, cloudy, snowing a little. I helped Clara patch. It was slick ice by night.

Fri 3 – 13 above. Edna called up that Henry would come and get our hog and butcher it at their place so I went along & stayed overnight.

Sat 4 – Fair, cold, 2 above. Henry took me home, went thru Millstadt & left 17 lbs pork sausage mix at the locker. Roads icy.

Sun 5 – 13 above, fair, got up to 30. Bill & Anita brought Franklin, Gerry and the boys. Franklin went along back. Gerry & the boys stayed.

Mon 6 – 13 above, very icy roads. We couldn't do much of anything. The boys helped gather eggs. W. Merhman got a 339 lb hog @ $19.60 per 100 weight, $66.68.

Tues 7 – 20 above, fair, warmed up by noon to 35. We took the boys out for a walk to the mailbox.

Wed 8 – 25 degrees, fair all day. I washed. Then I smoked the pork sausage.

Thurs 9 – 35 degrees, warmed up to 45. I fried in 4 gals pork sausage and made brine for the ham & bacon.

Fri 10 – 35 degrees, fair, warmer. I patched. Gerry & Georgie walked to Marcella's. In evening we cut quilt patches.

Sat 11 – 35 degrees, partly cloudy. Gerry washed out a few things. I did my Saturday work and patched.

Sun 12 – No frost, rainy all day. Helen and Earl came to get a 305 lb hog @ $20.50 per 100 weight. Beulah and Edwin were here for supper.

Mon 13 – No frost, very deep mud. I fried in bacon in morning. Afternoon we went to Belleville with Schillings to make out income report.

Tues 14 – 30 degrees, fair. We cleaned one hen house and brought in some wood.

Wed 15 – Fair. We washed. Then I worked along the road to Klein's while Gerry did the ironing.

Thurs 16 – Fair, hard frost, 26 degrees. Geo & I worked along the road, cut off brush.

Fri 17 – Fair. Geo & I went to Millstadt to get cinders for our road. In evening Geo & Gerry met Franklin at the Brandenburger Road.

Sat 18 – Cloudy, frost in morning. Franklin & Gerry walked over the farm. Beulah, Edwin & Robin came and had supper with us.

Sun 19 – Very cloudy, warm, rained all night. Bill, Anita, and June Ann came and took Gerry and the boys and Franklin and me along to Hesse's for dinner. Gerry, Franklin & boys went along to Bill's. Walter Merhman got a 500 lb hog @ $20.00 per 100 weight, $100.00.

Mon 20 – 40 degrees, rainy. Geo, Patsy, and I went to the home bureau meeting at Henry Stahlman's house. It snowed then cleared up, got much colder.

Tues 21 – Fair, much colder, eleven above. I washed. Was too cold to do much.

Wed 22 – Fair, some warmer, 20 above. Marcella took sick last night so Boobe came and got me. Received from Waterloo milk company $4.00 for interest.

Thurs 23 – Fair, warmer. I was at Klein's in the afternoon. Marcella was much better.

Fri 24 – Fair, warm. I raked in the yard.

Sat 25 – Fair, warm, beautiful day. I baked coffee cake and cleaned. Geo husked corn.

Sun 26 – Fair, very pretty day, warm. We were at church. I was installed to a member of the consistory & citizenship. We paid our 1946 and 1947 church dues @ 10 dollars for each year, $20 in all.

Mon 27 – Partly cloudy, 45 degrees. I worked on the road to close up ruts. Geo shucked corn and mixed feed.

Tues 28 – Fair, still warm. We took our first hatching eggs to Belleville and ordered our chicks for March 7th.

Wed 29 – Very cloudy, rainy. I helped Clara patch & bake cookies. In the night it rained & thundered, creeks were out. 69 degrees.

Thurs 30 – Partly cloudy, colder, strong northwest winds. Geo & Boobe went to a meeting at the brick school in the evening.

Fri 31 – Fair, 20 degrees, warmed up to 38. We got our refrigerator today. Geo husked some corn. I patched.

February 1947

Sat 1 – Fair, cold, strong west winds, 30 degrees at 7:00 a.m., 24 by 10:00 a.m. We didn't do much work.

Sun 2 – Cold, 17 degrees. Bill & Anita brought Franklin, Gerry and the boys out. Aunt Katies and Howard Alberts were here also.

Mon 3 – Fair, getting warmer. We took Franklin to Belleville to bus station. He had to go back by train. We bought a battery.

Tues 4 – Fair, cold, 10 above, strong NW winds. We baked cookies and sewed quilt blocks.

Wed 5 – Fair, cold, 7 above, strong NW winds all day. Gerry & I washed. Pop mixed feed.

Thurs 6 – Cloudy, 27 degrees, snow flurries in afternoon and getting colder, NW winds. Patsy and I were to the home bureau meeting at Freeburg.

Fri 7 – Fair, colder, 7 above, strong winds all day. I stayed with Marcella's children while they went to town.

Sat 8 – 8 above, still strong winds, fair.

Sun 9 – Fair, cold, 7 above. Brinkers were here for dinner. Willie Krehers and Bill & Anita & June Ann came in evening.

Mon 10 – Fair, 14 above. We sewed quilt blocks.

Tues 11 – 17 above, fair. We took the eggs to Belleville.

Wed 12 – 20 degrees. I was to a quilting at Clara's.

Thurs 13 – Nice & warm, 50 at noon. Gerry & boys & I were at Clara's to quilt.

Fri 14 – Fair, very pretty day. We washed. Then I went to help Clara finish her quilt. Franklin came in evening.

Sat 15 – Fair, very pretty day, warm. Franklin & Gerry & Georgie were at Belleville. Pop & I were to the Ralph Keim funeral in the afternoon.

Sun 16 – Very cloudy to fair. Bill, Anita, and Gerry and the boys and Geo & I were at Seibert's for dinner. Franklin left for Urbana at 11:30 that morning.

Mon 17 – Fair, very pretty & warm day, no frost. Gerry, the boys, and I went to my home bureau meeting at Alex Brandenburger's. Walter Merhman got a hog, 440 lbs @ 22 cents a lb, $96.80.

Tues 18 – Fair to cloudy and snow by nite. I was at the Kreher wedding all day. Sister Minnie died last night so we and Clara went to Millstadt with Boobe. (*Minnie Sponemann was the third oldest of Katie's ten siblings. She had been widowed since 1940. They had no children.*)

Wed 19 – Fair, 20 degrees. I was sick with earache all day and could not go to Minnie's funeral.

Thurs 20 – Fair, 17 degrees. Geo and Gerry went to Minnie's funeral. Boys and I stayed in the house.

Fri 21 – 20 degrees. Geo took me to the doctor for my cold and earache.

Sat 22 – Fair, cold, 17 degrees. We baked cookies. Mrs. Brinker brought a birthday cake over for Georgie's birthday.

Sun 23 – Cold, 10 above. Franklin took Gerry and the boys along home today.

Mon 24 – Cloudy, snow flurries, 20 above, stormy all day. I worked with cleaning up closets. Geo made firewood.

Tues 25 – Fair, 22 degrees, stormy. Geo and I went to the doctor for my ear. John & Katie were here in morning.

Wed 26 – Fair, 23 degrees. I sewed on Mary's pad. Geo made firewood. Geo & Marie took the eggs to Belleville.

Thurs 27 – Fair, warmer, 22 degrees. I washed. Marie hung it out for me. I also ironed in the evening.

Fri 28 – Colder, snow flurries. I patched and then sewed on Mary's pad again.

March 1947

Sat 1 – Cold, 18 above, snow all day, 5 inches by night, it drifted pretty bad.

Sun 2 – Cold, snow flurries, windy, 15 above. We stayed home all day.

Mon 3 – Fair, cold, 10 above. I went to Belleville with Schillings to fill out income report.

Tues 4 – 24 above, warmed up to 45, snow melted quite a bit. We took the eggs to Smithton, then we cleaned out the brooder house.

Wed 5 – 33 degrees. We carried in wood & coal and set up the brooder. By afternoon it snowed heavy and they brought our chicks, 357.

Thurs 6 – 30 degrees, clearing. We couldn't do much of anything except taking care of the chicks.

Fri 7 – Fair, 32 degrees. Geo and I both have a cold. Didn't do any work.

Sat 8 – 28 degrees, fair, getting warmer. We still have a cold and can't do much of anything.

Sun 9 – Fair, 24 degrees, warmed up to 45. They took Grandpa Brinker to the hospital today.

Mon 10 – 29 degrees, fair, thawed a lot today. We made firewood. Henry Lang sowed clover here today.

Tues 11 – Fair. We took the eggs to Belleville. Then I carried in wood and coal.

Wed 12 – Fair, warm. Had the bed things out to air. Then Marie helped me turn the rug in bedroom. Ed Feders were here.

Thurs 13 – Rainy all day, 45 degrees. I worked about the house.

Fri 14 – Cloudy, cold. Couldn't do much of anything.

Sat 15 – Fair, cold. I worked about the house. Geo shucked corn.

Sun 16 – Fair, frost. We were all at home at Herman's today. In the evening Bill & Anita were here.

Mon 17 – Fair, light snow during the night. Patsy and I were to the home bureau meeting at Mrs. Barthel's.

Tues 18 – Fair, warmer. We took the eggs to Belleville. No frost today.

Wed 19 – Fair, nice and warm. Geo hauled 2 loads of cinders and I worked about the yard.

Thurs 20 – Fair. Geo took me to Smithton. There I took the bus to Belleville. Went to Dr. Altrick for my ear. Then took the frozen food lesson at Ill. Power Co. Then got a cold wave at Leona's.

Fri 21 – Fair, cold, very stormy. Couldn't do more than just the feeding and house work.

Sat 22 – Fair, warm. We were at Millstadt to get cinders. Then I raked some yard and cleaned the porch. Willard Probst hauled more rock on road.

Sun 23 – Fair to cloudy, showers at times. We were at Waterloo church for Christian's confirmation. (*Christian Gummersheimer is Katie's nephew.*) In evening the crowd came to celebrate my birthday.

Mon 24 – Foggy, then thunder, hail, rain, and snowstorm, getting much colder, very stormy.

Tues 25 – Rain, very stormy, northwest winds, 33 degrees, snow flurries. George's Brother Henry Reiss was here all day for my birthday. I got a lot of cards today. Irwin & Mary called up in the evening. I paid Henry Reiss $24.00 for interest today on $600.00 note.

Wed 26 – 25 degrees, fair to cloudy. We took the eggs to Belleville. In the evening we went to W. Brandenburger's for her birthday, also Melvin's is on 27th.

Thurs 27 – Snowing, about 10 inches deep already, clearing by noon, 33 degrees in morning, warmed up some by noon.

Fri 28 – Fair, 33 degrees, got to 56 by noon. I washed & ironed some. Geo shucked corn and made firewood.

Sat 29 – Fair, 44 degrees in morning, 60 during noon. I ironed and did my Saturday work. Geo shucked corn. Franklin came at six in evening.

Sun 30 – Fair, 26 degrees in morning. Franklin, Geo and I went to church at Millstadt and then out to Edna's for dinner. In eve we went to Mrs. Orville Koerber's birthday.

Mon 31 – Cloudy, 38 degrees, to 50 by noon, thundershowers late afternoon. We were at Belleville in the morning. Got a load of feed.

April 1947

Tues 1 – Cloudy, light thundershowers. I was at Clara's in the afternoon. In the morning we husked corn.

Wed 2 – Fair to cloudy, getting colder, 40 in morning. We husked corn and Geo went grinding at Schilling's.

Thurs 3 – Cloudy, 50 degrees, some showers. We shucked corn. Then I raked the lawn. In evening we were at Marcella & Boobe's.

Fri 4 – 51 degrees, showery to fair. We were at church in the evening. I was on the program.

Sat 5 – 70 degrees in morning, thunder, rain all day, very stormy, creeks were out in low places.

Sun 6 – 51 degrees, fair. Today was Easter. We were at church and afternoon we were at Rapp's. Frank, Leo, & Alex came in evening.

Mon 7 – Fair, very pretty day, 38 degrees in morning, warmed up to 55 by noon. We pruned trees & loaded 8 hogs for tomorrow.

Tues 8 – 42 degrees, started to rain by 9 o'clock. Geo & Oscar Koerber took a load of hogs to the yards. I shucked corn and did the feeding. We sold our last sow, weighed 595 lbs @ $22.50 = $133.87. One hog, 220 lbs @ $25.75 = $56.65. Six hogs 1395 lbs @ $25.75 = $359.21.

Wed 9 – Fair to cloudy, showers by night. We & Metzgers were to the card party at Paderborn. We shucked some corn today.

Thurs 10 – Fair to cloudy, 56 in morning, 75 by noon, thundershowers & hail by 4 o'clock. I sowed my first lettuce today.

Fri 11 – Cloudy to fair. We worked on the new shed and we cleaned the brooder house.

Sat 12 – Fair, 40 degrees. I baked bread & coffee cake and prepared for the company we are getting tomorrow.

Sun 13 – Fair, 45 degrees. Henry and Ed Cook, Uncle Will, Bill & Anita & June Ann, Viola & Ralph & family, Katie Petry, Herman & Frank, Lena & Ed were here.

Mon 14 – Fair, warmed up nicely, very pretty day. Had my chicks out for the first time. Set out a lot of my potted plants.

Tues 15 – Cloudy, 50 in morning, light rain, hard shower in evening. I got some flowers at Marcella's. We butchered a small hog.

Wed 16 – Light drizzle in morning, colder, 38. I patched. Geo made firewood.

Thurs 17 – Fair, cold, 32, white frost, ice on water pails. We went to Belleville to get feed. Afternoon I worked about the yard.

Fri 18 – 49 degrees, fair, warmed up nicely. We got four loads of rock on the Schaeffer place. I also transplanted the clematis.

Sat 19 – 57 degrees, thundershowers till 10 a.m., then clearing. We went to Millstadt to get cinders. I spaded some yet in the garden.

Sun 20 – Cloudy, rainy & cold all day. We were at church and afternoon we had company. In evening the crowd came to celebrate Pop's birthday.

Mon 21 – Cloudy to fair, 40 degrees. Patsy & I went to HB meeting at Mrs. Herman's. I gave lesson on frozen meat & Margie Skare on fruit & vegetables.

Tues 22 – Cloudy to fair, 45 degrees. Bill & Anita & June Ann, Johnny & Katie were here in evening for Pop's birthday.

Wed 23 – Fair. We got our concrete for feed house floor today. Afternoon Katie and Mary & Lillian and I went to Mrs. Keim's funeral.

Thurs 24 – Rain all day & night, creeks were out. We had been at Belleville in morning to get feed.

Fri 25 – 42 degrees, cloudy to fair, still awful wet. We put water in rat holes and worked around the place.

Sat 26 – Fair, 45 degrees. I washed and afternoon Patsy and I went to the bridal shower for Margie Groth. Geo worked on brooder house.

Sun 27 – Fair, very pretty day. We had company all day long but we did clean the brooder house in the morning.

Mon 28 – Fair to cloudy. I worked around outside all day. Mr. Weible got a bred gilt today, 190 lbs @ 25 cents a lb = $48.25.

Tues 29 – Thundershowers early in morning. In evening Schillings, Kleins and we went too visit Boveings.

Wed 30 – Fair, very pretty day, very warm. I cleaned and scrubbed all of the upstairs. In evening were to the consistory meeting. We planned to have church steeple repaired & painted.

May 1947

Thurs 1 – Showers all day long. I cleaned up the old brooder house between showers. Geo tore down the brooder house in pasture.

Fri 2 – 55 degrees, very stormy, cloudy with showers. Geo is mixing feed. I cleaned in the house. We butchered a 100 lb hog.

Sat 3 – Fair, cool. We were at Millstadt, took 2 hams to locker. Then I baked coffee cake and did my Saturday work. Geo husked corn.

Sun 4 – Fair, very pretty & warm day. Hesses were here for dinner. Bill & Anita came in evening. Mrs. F. Klein and Eileen marked my quilt.

Mon 5 – Fair, 50 early in morning, much warmer during noon. I spaded the flower bed. Geo husked corn.

Tues 6 – Fair, warm. We were at Belleville to visit Katie at the hospital. Afternoon I worked in the garden. Geo husked corn.

Wed 7 – Fair, cooler, 45 degrees, cold north wind. Canned pineapple, 16 quarts from 13 pineapples, 35 cents each. Geo husked corn.

Thurs 8 – Fair, very cool all day. I worked in the garden till noon. Then I helped Clara patch.

Fri 9 – Fair, white frost. We were at Edna's. Afternoon at the Freeburg High School play. In evening with Metzgers.

Sat 10 – Fair. I worked in garden, planted beans. Emma Barthel, Elisa Koerber, Ann Franke and Alma Metzger were here in evening. We had a meeting.

Sun 11 – Fair, cool. We and Gus Metzgers were at Bill and Anita's for dinner. It was Mothers Day.

Mon 12 – Fair to cloudy, stormy and a good rain by afternoon. We were to see about a horse at Leingang's. Also got plants at Millstadt.

Tues 13 – Good rain last night, fair today. Leingang brought the horse today, 85 dollars, collar 3 dollars.

Wed 14 – Fair, very hot today. I washed and then worked in the garden. Geo disked with the new horse.

Thurs 15 – Fair to cloudy, shower by night, very hot all day. Johnny & Jakie came to put up the frame for the feed house. I planted cucumbers.

Fri 16 – Rain. Can't do much of anything. Sold 26 spring chickens today at just 12 weeks old. Averaged 3 lbs each @ 34 cents a lb.

Sat 17 – Fair to heavy thundershowers by afternoon. Geo and I were at Columbia in morning to get tin roofing for feed house.

Sun 18 – Fair, very pretty day. We were at church. Afternoon Henry & Bertha came. In evening Bill & Anita and June Ann & Henry Langs were here.

Mon 19 – Fair. Today we had Mrs. Glauber's baby shower at Mrs. Seibert's. Marcella, Marie, and Bess Glauber went along too.

Tues 20 – Cloudy. Geo disked Brinker's garden. Afternoon it rained, rained very hard by evening.

Wed 21 – Fair. We worked on the feed house. Toward evening O. Koerber and Geo hauled 9 of our hogs to the yards. Boobe & Marcella were here in evening.

Thurs 22 – Fair. We cleaned the hen house and worked on the feed house.

Fri 23 – Cloudy, hot, rain by late afternoon. We worked on feed house and husked corn. Sold 35 spring chickens @ .34 a lb.

Sat 24 – Cloudy, hard rain by night. We were in Belleville in morning. Helped clean church hall afternoon then I mowed my lawn.

Sun 25 – Fair, very cool. We were at church. Afternoon we picked our strawberries, about 3 qts.

Mon 26 – Fair. We cleaned the upstairs part of the granary and then we finished husking corn here by the house.

Tues 27 – Fair to cloudy, light drizzle. We cleaned the upstairs of the granary and were at Red Bud today.

Wed 28 – We finished cleaning the granary and chopped old trees and worked about the yard.

Thurs 29 – We worked about the yard, cleaning up for Irwin & Stevie are coming June 1st.

Fri 30 – Fair. I worked in the garden. Also helped Geo with the new shed.

Sat 31 – Fair. We were at Millstadt today and then I mowed the lawn.

June 1947

Sun 1 – Very cloudy and rainy, very stormy in morning. Irwin and Stevie came today. Henry brought them out here.

Mon 2 – No entry.

Tues 3 – No entry.

Wed 4 – No entry.

Thurs 5 – No entry.

Fri 6 – No entry.

Sat 7 – Partly cloudy. Henry Lang plowed our corn land today. Rained and stormed by night. Geo planted his first corn today.

Sun 8 – Fair, very warm. We had 47 people here today. They all wanted to visit Irwin. June stayed overnight.

Mon 9 – Fair. Henry Lang came to finish plowing. Geo started to disk. Bill, Anita came to spend the afternoon with us and Irwin.

Tues 10 – Fair. We, Irwin, Stevie, and June were at Millstadt. Geo planted corn in the big field here.

Wed 11 – Geo planted more corn. I washed some clothes. Irwin fixed the truck cab roof. Bill & Anita got June Ann this evening.

Thurs 12 – Fair. Stevie's birthday today. Marie and the children were here for dinner. We took Irwin & Stevie to the station this evening.

Fri 13 – Cloudy and very cold all day, strong NW winds. I worked in the garden. Geo finished planting corn by the house here.

Sat 14 – Fair, cold, 54 in morning, strong winds all day. I worked in the garden.

Sun 15 – Fair. We were at Waterloo at sister Mary's birthday. Also went to Carlena & Elmer's. Elmer lost 2 fingers on the tractor.

Mon 16 – Fair, cloudy. I worked in the garden. Geo planted corn. I also cooked strawberry preserves.

Tues 17 – Fair to cloudy. I pulled weeds till noon. Then I helped Clara patch. Geo worked in the corn.

Wed 18 – Cloudy, showery. I worked in the garden. Geo worked in his corn.

Thurs 19 – Cloudy and very cool. We were to the Bertha Probst funeral.

Fri 20 – Cloudy, cool, showers. We were to the John Englert funeral. Then Clara helped me butcher chickens for locker.

Sat 21 – Cloudy to fair and also a heavy shower. We took our chickens to the locker. Elmer & Carlena were here.

Sun 22 – Cloudy, showery. We shelled corn from Edwin. John, Katie and Mrs. Deisel were here in evening.

Mon 23 – Cloudy, cool. I picked dewberries and also washed. But it rained hard by noon.

Tues 24 – Cloudy to fair and warmer. Kleins, Schillings, and I picked dewberries. Then Geo & I took 12 qts to the locker.

Wed 25 – Raining. Marie and I picked some dewberries in morning. Early peaches are ripening now. We got our AAA check today, $138.00 and took it to the bank.

Thurs 26 – Fair, 81 degrees, heavy fog. We are both hoeing weeds also picked some dewberries.

Fri 27 – Rained hard till noon. I picked some berries. Geo worked around the place.

Sat 28 – A lot of berries were picked today. I picked and seeded my cherries, got 3 pints.

Sun 29 – Cloudy to fair and very warm. Viola & family were here. They also picked berries. We took 9 hogs to the yards in evening.

Mon 30 – Very hot, 95 by noon. Schillings started to combine in the 20-acre field. Brought us 45 bu. Then by evening it rained very hard and stormed.

July 1947

Tues 1 – Clearing. We had about 2.5 in. rain last night and the highest water in the bottoms than ever.

Wed 2 – Fair, cool. I picked & canned beans. Schillings combined some wheat. Clara & Frank and I picked the apricots.

Thurs 3 – Clear, cool to warmer, 69 in morning. Viola & Ralph got the apricots today. I canned beans.

Fri 4 – Bill, Anita, June & I went to Urbana today to spend the weekend with Franklin, Gerry, and the boys.

Sat 5 – We were at Urbana. It rained there. Also some here.

Sun 6 – Rainy. We were at Urbana. Came home at 5:30 p.m. Bill & Anita took some beans & pickles along home.

Mon 7 – Fair. Henry Lang combined wheat. Geo & I took a load to Belleville, 14 bu got 56 test. Price $2.04 a bu.

Tues 8 – Fair, cool. I picked up apricots & apples, took some to Clara. Then I chopped weeds in my backyard.

Wed 9 – Fair, cool. Clara & I picked our apricots. I also helped her with some work. Then I picked peaches at home & took them to Boobe.

Thurs 10 – Fair, cool all day. I picked beans, so Marie & I canned 14 quarts in her cooker. Schillings finished combining wheat here, 806 bu.

Fri 11 – Fair, warmer. Geo plowed by (*cultivated*) his first corn. I picked peaches and also the first blackberries.

Sat 12 – We took a bu. of peaches to Rapp's. Then Geo worked in his corn and I did my Saturday work. Will & Lena Feder came in evening.

Sun 13 – Henry & Bertha came and got us to go to Lizzie Beuchley's at Belleville for dinner. It was Helen's birthday on the 14th.

Mon 14 – Fair, warm to hot. I cut the pickles and canned 10 quarts. Also made some sauerkraut.

Tues 15 – Fair. Geo plowed corn. I cut weeds and picked beans and blackberries. John & Katie were here in the evening.

Wed 16 – Fair, very hot, 96 at noon, hot all night. We canned 7 quarts beans. Geo plowed by corn.

Thurs 17 – Fair, hot, 95 degrees during noon, 78 early in morning. I canned 10 quarts of applesauce, also 3 quarts beans.

Fri 18 – Partly cloudy to fair, hot in morning, cooled off towards evening. Geo plowed corn and I chopped weeds and washed.

Sat 19 – Very cool, 62 in morning, fair, north winds. I mowed the lawn and cut weeds. Geo plowed by corn.

Sun 20 – Partly cloudy, cool, good shower by night.

Mon 21 – Fair, very cool, 50 degrees, cool all day. We were to my home bureau meeting at Wiskamp's. Clara Probst went along with us.

Tues 22 – Fair, cool, 50 degrees. I cut weeds and canned pickles. Geo worked in his corn.

Wed 23 – Fair, cool, 52 degrees. I cut weeds and picked blackberries. Geo worked in his corn.

Thurs 24 – Fair, cool, 60 degrees. We went to Belleville. Got 1000 lbs tankage at Streck's. Also went to the fair for about 2 hours. *(Streck's was a slaughterhouse so "tankage" is meat/bone meal sold as food for chickens and/or pigs.)*

Fri 25 – Fair to cloudy, 70 degrees, light drizzle. Mrs. Westerheide was here all morning. In the evening Boobe & Marcella and Mary Klein were here.

Sat 26 – 70 degrees, partly cloudy, got up to 95 by afternoon. I did my Saturday work.

Sun 27 – Fair, hot, 96. We were at church and afternoon we went to picnic at Smithton. In evening we went to consistory meeting.

Mon 28 – Fair, hot, 98. Geo worked in the corn and I cleaned in the basement.

Tues 29 – Fair, hot, 98. I picked blackberries and then worked in the basement. Geo worked in the corn.

Wed 30 – Fair, hot, 101 degrees. I was to a quilting at Clara's in the afternoon. In evening I picked blackberries.

Thurs 31 – Fair, hot, 99 degrees. We were to the funeral of Aunt Dora Feder at Belleville.

August 1947

Fri 1 – Fair, hot, 100 degrees. I worked in basement. Charles Helfrichs were here in afternoon. Were at Grange meeting in evening.

Sat 2 – Fair, hot, 102 in shade. I washed and worked in the basement. Mr. Westerheide was here in afternoon. John & Katie in evening.

Sun 3 – Fair, very hot, 103 in the shade. We were at Herman's and Frankie's in morning and towards eve, Bill, Anita & June came.

Mon 4 – Fair, very hot, 103 to 104. I cleaned in the basement. It was too hot to do much.

Tues 5 – Fair, hot, 103 degrees. We visited at Metzger's in evening.

Wed 6 – Fair, hot, 102 degrees. I cleaned in the basement. Clara Schilling got gored by a bull in morning. We went to see here in evening.

Thurs 7 – Fair, hot to cooler by night. I was at Schilling's in afternoon. In evening we and Gus & Alma went to see Mrs. Rapp.

Fri 8 – Fair, a little cooler, 92 at noon. I baked bread & coffee cake. Pop chopped weeds. Ludger cut the red clover for seed.

Sat 9 – Fair, hot. Franklin, Gerry, and the boys came. Gerry and the boys will stay 2 weeks while Franklin goes to Mo.

Sun 10 – Fair, hot. Uncle Henry came and got us at Millstadt to go to Lucille Dietz's for dinner.

Mon 11 – Fair, hot, always around 95 to 100 degrees, no rain yet. I went to Schillings to help wash and patch.

Tues 12 – Fair, hot. Gerry & boys and Geo & I all went to Sander's to see the twin girls.

Wed 13 – Fair, hot. We all went to Clara Schilling's birthday in the afternoon.

Thurs 14 – Fair, hot. Georgie had fever all day, but is better now.

Fri 15 – Fair, hot. We had a little shower last night. Georgie is fine again.

Sat 16 – Fair, hot. We all went to Edwin & Beulah's for dinner and supper.

Sun 17 – Fair, hot. Bill, Anita, and June Ann came for dinner. Gerry & boys went home with them.

Mon 18 – Fair, hot. Geo & I went to the home bureau meeting at Hesse's.

Tues 19 – Fair, hot. We were at Millstadt. Otherwise we didn't work much except peel apples for applesauce.

Wed 20 – Fair, hot. Yesterday Louis Guidetti and Jimmie Bode from California were here for supper, also Gerry & boys and Bill, Anita & June. *(Louis Guidetti was a Marine Corps officer based in San Diego who befriended Katie and George on their train trip last year to California. They exchanged letters for months and then he visited the Reiss farm this day.)*

Thurs 21 – Fair, hot, 102 degrees. I was at Schilling's all day.

Fri 22 – Fair, hot. I canned applesauce and made tomato preserves.

Sat 23 – Fair, hot. I picked some apples. We were to Mrs. F. Gasser's funeral. And in evening we were to visit Westerheides.

Sun 24 – Fair, very hot, around 100. We were at Bill & Anita's to see Franklin, Gerry & boys. They left for Urbana this evening.

Mon 25 – Very hot, thundering all around by evening. We got our hardest rain in history, 5.5 to 6 inches in two hours.

Tues 26 – Partly cloudy, hard rain by noon, hot. We paid our taxes today for 1946, $270.00.

Wed 27 – Fair, hot. I'm preparing to go to Urbana today.

Thurs 28 – Fair, hot, 93. Boobe Kleins, Mary Klein, and I went to Urbana today to see the Sportsfest. Orville, Marie, and Wilbur Franks also went.

Fri 29 – Cloudy to a shower by night at Urbana. Fair at home here tho. We celebrated Mary Lou Klein's first birthday at Franklin's & Gerry's today.

Sat 30 – Fair, hot, 95. We came back from Urbana at noon today. Then I canned some peaches yet.

Sun 31 – Hot, thundershowers till noon. We were at the Millstadt Homecoming picnic.

September 1947

Mon 1 – Cooler, fair.

Tues 2 – Fair, hot. I worked with my peaches. Geo rested as it was Labor Day (*yesterday*).

Wed 3 – Fair, hot. We were at Belleville. I bought my gray coat and shirts for Geo.

Thurs 4 – Fair, hot. I worked with the peaches and cut weeds.

Fri 5 – Hot. I canned peaches and worked about the place. In the evening we were to the road meeting by the Bince Bridge.

Sat 6 – We chopped brush and trees off at the orchard in the 20 acres and then I baked bread and cake for Sunday.

Sun 7 – Fair, hot. Johnny Rapps and Herman and Frank were here. In evening Bill, Anita and June and Gus Metzgers were here.

Mon 8 – Fair, hot. Geo and I started to chop down trees along the wheat field on the other place.

Tues 9 – Fair, hot, 95. We chopped more trees and made firewood of them.

Wed 10 – Fair, hot, 100 degrees. We chopped more trees. Afternoon I worked with the peaches.

Thurs 11 – Fair to cloudy, good rain towards evening. We went to the guild meeting. I gave the program.

Fri 12 – Fair, cool, and nice. Oscar Koerber took 2 hogs to Streck's for us. They weighed 490 lbs, got $29.60 for them, our best price.

Sat 13 – We worked with the wood again, made some fence posts and I baked 2 cakes for the Grange chicken supper.

Sun 14 – Fair, cool to hot and a shower in the night. We were at the Grange picnic & chicken supper.

Mon 15 – Very cool, 56 degrees. Cool all day. We chopped more trees all day and made firewood.

Tues 16 – Cool. We worked in the woods again.

Wed 17 – Fair, cool. We worked in the woods on the Schaefer place.

Thurs 18 – Fair, warm. Patsy came and we went to Daab's Clubhouse for our district meeting & potluck dinner.

Fri 19 – Fair, pretty hot, 90 degrees. We worked in the woods till noon and then I washed and Geo mixed feed.

Sat 20 – Fair, hot, 86. We worked in the woods again. Afternoon we got word that Etta died, funeral will be Monday Sept 22.

Sun 21 – Rain mostly all day and much cooler. Johnny and Katie came in the evening to get cling peaches.

Mon 22 – Fair, cold, 54 degrees. Geo went to Sikeston with Ralph Bald and Katie Petry. I worked around the house.

Tues 23 – Cold, 38 degrees. We worked on the Schaeffer place clearing away trees. Clara & I picked up apples yesterday for cider & apple butter.

Wed 24 – Cold, 42 degrees. We worked with clearing trees and brush. This evening we want to peel apples at Schilling's.

Thurs 25 – Fair, cool. I helped Clara cook apple butter. Geo mixed feed.

Fri 26 – Fair, cooler. We worked on the Schaefer place making firewood and cleaning up brush.

Sat 27 – Fair. We worked in the timber in the morning. Afternoon Helen & Earl were here to take measurements for our hot water system.

Sun 28 – Fair to cloudy. Lizzie Buechle, Helen & Orville, and Janet Jung were here for dinner, also John & Katie, Will & Mable, Bill & Anita, and June Ann.

Mon 29 – Fair, cold, 42 degrees. We worked in the timber again and took a lot of firewood home.

Tues 30 – Fair, cold 44 degrees. We worked in the timber. In evening we and Westerheides went to booster night at Grange. We got our silver star pins.

October 1947

Wed 1 – Fair, cold, 50 degrees. We worked in the timber again. Afternoon we were at Millstadt.

Thurs 2 – Fair, warmer. We worked with the firewood again. Afternoon we took apples to Schilling's. They took them to St. Louis.

Fri 3 – Fair, hot winds. I picket up a gal of hickory nuts. We made firewood again.

Sat 4 – Rained hard for about 2 hours, then cleared up. Pop got Franklin & family at Millstadt this morning.

Sun 5 – Fair, cool. Bill & Anita came for dinner. We had picture show in evening.

Mon 6 – Fair. Franklin, Gerry, and the boys and we are enjoying a week together.

Tues 7 – Fair, cool. We all picked apples. Franklin & the boys gathered nuts. Pop & I were to the Tom Brenneman Show at Smithton.

Wed 8 – Fair. Franklin & Gerry picked apples & pears today and gathered nuts.

Thurs 9 – Fair. We expressed boxes of apples & nuts to Urbana also one to Irwin. George & Richard are having a grand time.

Fri 10 – Fair. Franklin & Gerry got 2 sacks full of walnuts in the long bottom.

Sat 11 – Fair, warm. Franklin, Gerry, and the boys left this evening to go home tomorrow. Will stay at Bill & Anita's tonight.

Sun 12 – Fair. Henry & Bertha and Elmer & Carlena & family were here. We were at church in evening, then to Lena Klein's birthday party.

Mon 13 – Fair, warm. Schillings finished sowing wheat on the Schaefer place. Geo pruned the blackberries. I cleaned the lane.

Tues 14 – Fair, warm. We worked on cleaning the lane. After noon we and Alma went to Millstadt to church festival.

Wed 15 – Fair, warm. We picked some apples and worked about the place. I also canned apples.

Thurs 16 – Fair, very warm, 80 degrees. Geo is repairing the washhouse roof. I worked in the lane and sorted apples.

Fri 17 – Very warm, 82 degrees, thunder and rain by evening. Marie and Mary Ann had dinner with us. Geo finished the roof on the washhouse. Got $18 rent from Mr. Roy F. Howerton.

Sat 18 – Fair, warm. We took the Brinker boys to the barber at Millstadt in the morning and afternoon Mrs. Westerheide was here.

Sun 19 – Fair, cooler. Brinkers moved out today and Howertons moved in today.

Mon 20 – Fair, warm. Patsy & I were to the home bureau meeting at Mrs. Germann's. I washed in morning.

Tues 21 – Fair, warm. We are tearing down the old chicken shed to use lumber to build our auto shed here.

Wed 22 – Fair, warm, 78 degrees. We worked on our shed. Went quilting at Floraville in evening.

Thurs 23 – Fair, warm, 84 degrees. We worked on shed. Mrs. Westerheide was here in afternoon.

Fri 24 – Cloudy, warm. We worked on the shed and I potted more flowers and gathered pecans. Shower by night.

Sat 25 – Rained mostly all day. We worked on shed between showers.

Sun 26 – Rained all day. We were home all day.

Mon 27 – Fair, cooler. We picked up apples and had cider made at Armbruster's, 15 gals at 4 cents a gal. We had about 4 bushels apples.

Tues 28 – Rainy all day. We went to Smithton to get feed crushed. Visited with Mrs. Peter Wachtel a little while.

Wed 29 – Cloudy, rain in morning. Worked on our shed in afternoon. Westerheide's and I were to Patsy's birthday party last night.

Thurs 30 – Fair, warmer. In morning we cleaned chicken house. Afternoon we were at Belleville. Rain by night.

Fri 31 – Rainy all day and all night. Got our chickens blood tested today. No reactors at all. Also sold 3 pigs to a man from East St. Louis.

November 1947

Sat 1 – Rainy all day, 50 degrees, couldn't do more than feeding and my house work.

Sun 2 – Cloudy all day. We were at home with Herman & Frankie, got a half bu potatoes. In evening we were at Gus Metzger's birthday party.

Mon 3 – Cloudy. We cleaned the brooder house. Got a letter from Irwin today saying that Mary Kay was born on Nov 1st.

Tues 4 – Showery most of the day. In evening we were at the Paderborn card party. I dressed 3 young hens to take to the locker tomorrow, Nov 5.

Wed 5 – Fair, colder. We were to the farm bureau dinner today. In evening Boobe came and paid us 24 cents a lb for 22 lbs of lard.

Thurs 6 – Fair to cloudy, rain by night, very stormy all day, lightninged & thundered in evening. Geo got the roof finished on the shed here.

Fri 7 – Fair, colder, very stormy, NW winds. We brought in firewood.

Sat 8 – Fair, cold, 32 in morning. Geo husked corn. I did my baking and Saturday work.

Sun 9 – Cold hard freeze, 26 early in morning. Earl & Helen, Will & Mable, Bill & Anita & June were here. We were at church in morning & evening.

Mon 10 – Rain and warmer. I set up my quilt today, that blue and white one for Gerry.

Tues 11 – Fair, cold, hard freeze. Had quilting afternoon and evening.

Wed 12 – Fair, cold. We worked on the shed. In evening we went to Mary Klein's birthday party at Koerber's. Marcella & Boobe took us along.

Thurs 13 – Cloudy, cold, 27 degrees. We worked on the shed all day.

Fri 14 – Cloudy, rain by afternoon. We took one hog to Belleville today. The highway men were in the bottom and said they would start Monday.

Sat 15 – Cloudy, cold all day. We picked the last pears and took some to Klein's. I'm still quilting but it's almost done.

Sun 16 – Fair, 36 degrees, windy. We were at Boobe's birthday in the evening.

Mon 17 – Fair, very pretty day. We were to my home bureau meeting at Meta Grossman's. Clara & Marcella came in evening to finish quilt.

Tues 18 – First snow, about an inch but was gone by night, turned to light rain, 33 degrees. We made firewood.

Wed 19 – Cloudy to fair, later a shower. I washed then I helped Clara cook pear butter. After that I helped shuck corn.

Thurs 20 – Fair, warmer. We were at Millstadt today. Got my hair fixed at Lillian's beauty shop. Shucked corn in morning.

Fri 21 – Cloudy & warmer, 54, rain by night. We shucked corn today and shelled & ground it. Mrs. Westerheide was here.

Sat 22 – Cloudy to fair, cold but not freezing. Helen & Orville Jung and Lizzie Buechley were here in evening. Tomorrow night we will go to Frank Klein's birthday.

Sun 23 – Cloudy, sleet showers & rain by night. Earl put in our feed house light. Preacher was here for dinner. Bill, Anita, June & Bill's partner came afternoon.

Mon 24 – Cloudy, very strong NW winds, getting much colder, snow flurries in morning. Mrs. Westerheide was here most of the day.

Tues 25 – Fair, cold. John Reiss from Sikeston came in morning, also Uncle Henry. He took me & Geo to Turkey Hill Grange where I had to take a lesson.

Wed 26 – Cloudy, snow by night, 25 degrees, ground frozen hard. Mrs. Westerheide came and her & I went to New Athens, took our radio along to get it fixed.

Thurs 27 – Fair. Franklin came in the morning. Bill and one of his fellows he works with came out hunting. Anita came in the morning with their car.

Fri 28 – Fair. Geo & I took Franklin to Belleville to the bus station. First we stopped at bank at Smithton to make a loan for our Texas well.

Sat 29 – Very cloudy & cold all day, ground was frozen in morning. We husked corn and shelled it. Then I did my Saturday work.

Sun 30 – Fair, cold, 15 above in morning. We were at Bill & Anita's for June's birthday dinner.

December 1947

Mon 1 – Fair, very pretty day. I washed and ironed. Geo spread fertilizer by the apple trees.

Tues 2 – Fair, pretty day, warm. I planted tulip bulbs and worked about the yard.

Wed 3 – Partly cloudy, warm, 60 degrees. Ed Feders were here and fixed my mantel clock. I raked in the yard.

Thurs 4 – Warm, 60 degrees, rainy to fair by night. We butchered today. Our renters got half the hog. O. Koerber brought us a load of coal, 69 bu.

Fri 5 – Fair, colder, 33 in morning. We mailed Gerry some cedar twigs. We were at Millstadt. Took 1 ham & 1 shoulder to the locker.

Sat 6 – Fair to a light rain. I worked in the house. Geo shucked corn and mixed feed.

Sun 7 – Fair, warm 55 degrees, but colder by night. Were at church first then to the Brietshaft wedding at church. Then at J. Rapp's. In evening we were to Romuald's birthday.

Mon 8 – Fair, very pretty day, cold tho, 25 in morning. Mrs. Westerheide came and took me along to New Athens. Evening Boobe & Schillings & we were at Grange for income tax.

Tues 9 – Fair, cold, 22 degrees. We worked around the place. Hauled in a lot of wood.

Wed 10 – Very cloudy, 31 degrees at noon, 27 in morning, about an inch of sleet fell during the night. Geo & Roy cut a bee tree today.

Thurs 11 – Cloudy and cold all day, 26 degrees. In evening we were at women's guild meeting and Xmas party.

Fri 12 – Cloudy, cold, 27 degrees. I baked cookies all day. Geo husked corn.

Sat 13 – Fair, very pretty day, warm. I washed and did my Saturday work. Geo mixed feed and made firewood.

Sun 14 – Fair, warmer, very pretty day. We were at church and afternoon Edna & children were here. And in evening Schillings were all here.

Mon 15 – Fair, turning to heavy snow by afternoon. Marcella drove and we all went to Patsy's home bureau meeting and Xmas party.

Tues 16 – Fair, warmer, 17 degrees early in the morning. I helped Clara bake Xmas cookies.

Wed 17 – 27 degrees, fair and warmer thru the day. We were at the oil meeting at Belleville.

Thurs 18 – Fair, warm, 55 by noon. We worked about the place.

Fri 19 – Fair, very pretty day, 34 in morning, 56 by noon. We were at Smithton to get grinding done.

Sat 20 – Fair, warm, 60 by noon. We worked about the place.

Sun 21 – Cloudy to fair. We were at church then Bill, Anita & June came and had dinner with us. In eve we were at O. Koerber's birthday.

Mon 22 – Cloudy to fair, 27 in morning, but warmer by evening. I baked cookies and washed windows. Geo made firewood.

Tues 23 – Fair, 28 degrees. We went to Bill & Anita's towards evening to see June Ann's program at her school.

Wed 24 – Fair, 26 degrees. We came home at 9 a.m. from Bill & Anita's. Then in evening we went to church. Betty & Verna were along.

Thurs 25 – Cloudy & cold, 23 to fair & warmer, 32 by evening. Bill & Anita & June Ann had dinner with us. Then we all went to Hesse's for supper.

Fri 26 – Fair, a beautiful day, 32 degrees. I worked on the income report. Geo & Roy made firewood.

Sat 27 – Fair, very pretty day. We cleaned the chicken house and then got some wood again.

Sun 28 – Fair, very pretty day, warm. Mary & Lillian were here for dinner. In evening we were at Metzger's.

Mon 29 – Fair, warm, 59 degrees. We were at Belleville to see Emmett about the income tax.

Tues 30 – Fair, warm, 64 degrees. I washed and then we put roofing on north outside wall of the feed house. Went to Westerheide's in evening.

Wed 31 – Getting cold and rained all day long. We sold some old iron today to Wilde. I ironed & patched. Geo did the feeding.

January 1948

Thurs 1 – 34 degrees, thunder & lightning, heavy rain, turned to snow by 10 o'clock.

Fri 2 – 24 degrees, fair. I baked cookies. Geo mixed feed. It was too icy to work outside.

Sat 3 – Fair, 26 degrees. I walked to Schillings and went to Belleville to file our income tax report. There is still some snow on ground.

Sun 4 – Fair, stormy, 32 degrees. I was at the guild meeting in afternoon and in the evening we were at Robert Probst birthday.

Mon 5 – Fair, 28 degrees. We were at Millstadt. Took chickens in to sell. We were to the consistory meeting in the evening.

Tues 6 – Fair, 28 degrees, warmed up to 50. I helped Marcella take off wallpaper.

Wed 7 – Fair, 30 degrees, warmed up to 55. Geo husked corn and worked on the hog fence. I patched.

Thurs 8 – Fair, warm, 60 degrees by noon. Mrs. Westerheide was here mostly all day. I darned stockings.

Fri 9 – Fair, colder, no frost in morning, 33 by 10 p.m. We butchered at Henry Lang's today and took 2 hams, 2 shoulders, and 2 backbones for pork chops to locker.

Sat 10 – Fair, colder, 29 degrees, warmed up to 40 by noon. I rendered the lard today, made 6 gallons. Geo was at the telephone meeting.

Sun 11 – Cloudy, cold. Frank & Herman, Bill & Anita & June Ann, and Helen & Earl were here for dinner. By 2:30 we went to church meeting. John & Katie were here in evening.

Mon 12 – Fair, no frost, warm. We took Earl's hog to Millstadt and loaded Bill's hog for the next day. Got much colder by evening.

Tues 13 – Fair, 18 above, strong NW winds. We were at Millstadt by 8:30 with Bill's hog, and then we stayed and helped Mr. Marker with the butchering.

Wed 14 – One inch snow, cold, 7 above, didn't get over 20 all day. I rendered the lard for Bill & Anita.

Thurs 15 – 2 degrees, fair, warmed up to 45. Fried in sausage and put bacon in brine, and washed some clothes by hand.

Fri 16 – Cloudy, very cold, 10 above. We couldn't do much of anything.

Sat 17 – Cold, 7 above. Bill & Anita were here to get their meat at Knab's.

Sun 18 – Cold, 5 above, warmed up to 20. Henry & Bertha were here for dinner. In evening we were at Schillings.

Mon 19 – 25 degrees, fair. We were to my home bureau meeting at Holcomb's.

Tues 20 – Fair, warmer, 22 degrees. We were to the Grange's 27 year birthday party, program & dance.

Wed 21 – 28 degrees, fair. I washed and baked a cake to go to a quilting at Floraville. In evening we & Schillings were at a quilting at Boveing's.

Thurs 22 – 15 above, snowing all day. I ironed and sewed. Geo did the feeding. It never got above 15 all day, by eight in evening it was down to 7 above, clearing.

Fri 23 – 10 above, fair to colder, never got above 15 all day. Geo mixed feed and I sowed a slip and some aprons.

Sat 24 – 2 below zero, fair, warmed up to 25 for a short time. Geo made some firewood. I fried in bacon and sewed carpet strips.

Sun 25 – 12 above, fair to cloudy. I walked to Klein's and then drove to church with Metzgers. We had installation at church today. Were at Klein's in evening.

Mon 26 – 15 above, warmed up to 20, started snowing by eleven and snowed all day. Geo & I drove to Belleville to sign our AAA papers.

Tues 27 – 10 above, fair. I sewed and patched. We signed up to pay $50 to the new hospital as soon as they start building.

Wed 28 – 5 below zero, our coldest day so far, ground still covered with snow. I darned stockings and sewed quilt blocks together.

Thurs 29 – Zero, never got above 15 all day. I sewed on my quilt.

Fri 30 – 20 degrees, cloudy. Geo went to Smithton to have feed ground. I helped Clara bake cookies.

Sat 31 – 14 degrees, snowing most of the day, about 7 inches deep. I sewed and prepared eats for Sunday dinner.

February 1948

Sun 1 – 12 degrees, fair, warmed up to 40. John & Katie, Edna & Henry, Lavern, Harold, Vera, & Myrtle Lang, Pearl & Melvin, and John Rapps were here in the evening.

Mon 2 – Fair, 22 degrees, thawed a lot today. I sewed. Geo mixed feed and made firewood.

Tues 3 – 18 degrees, snowed turned to sleet and rain towards evening. I worked on my quilt. Geo made firewood.

Wed 4 – 20 degrees, cloudy & foggy. I went to Belleville with Schillings. Then I stayed and helped Clara patch. Geo made firewood.

Thurs 5 – 24 degrees, cloudy, snowed all afternoon. I worked on my quilt. Geo mixed feed.

Fri 6 – 8 above, fair, warmed up to 32. We went to Smithton to get feed crushed. Also paid off one hundred dollars at the bank.

Sat 7 – 22 degrees in morning, cloudy. I set up my quilt and quilted all evening.

Sun 8 – 7 above, fair to cloudy. Clara, Rudy, Alex, and Frank Schilling were here. We marked my quilt. Bill, Anita & June came towards evening.

Mon 9 – 7 above, fair. I quilted and baked a cake and cleaned up for my quilting tomorrow.

Tues 10 – 10 above, fair, thawing by noon. 8 couples came in the evening for my quilting.

Wed 11 – 35 and rainy all day. I was at the church quilting. Had consistory meeting after church.

Thurs 12 – 23, cloudy, turning to rain and slick ice by night. Clara and Anna Wachtel were here to help me quilt.

Fri 13 – 25 degrees, cloudy, rain turning to slick ice and snow by night. I quilted all day.

Sat 14 – 22 degrees, fair. I quilted. Geo did the feeding.

Sun 15 – 24 degrees, warmed up to 45 degrees by noon. I finished my quilt. Geo listened to the radio.

Mon 16 – 40 degrees, fair. Patsy and I were to the home bureau meeting at Mrs. Kayon's.

Tues 17 – Fair, very warm, 65 by noon. I moved my flowers out of the basement to the sun porch.

Wed 18 – Fair to partly cloudy, 55. I washed and then I went quilting at the church hall. Stayed for church in evening.

Thurs 19 – 48 degrees, fair, turning colder, windy all day. I went to St. Paul's Church at Belleville with Ida Gasser.

Fri 20 – 18 degrees, fair. Patsy and I were at Belleville to take the home bureau lesson. In evening we went to Turkey Hill Grange play.

Sat 21 – 22 in morning, 29 by noon, snowing heavy. Couldn't do much work.

Sun 22 – Fair, cold 16 above. We were at church. Afternoon Will & Mable and their friends were here. In evening we were at Marcella's birthday.

Mon 23 – Fair, 39 degrees. Geo got some feed ground at Smithton. I quilted on Georgie's quilt.

Tues 24 – 38 degrees, cloudy, some rain. I quilted. Geo and Roy made posts.

Wed 25 – Very warm, around 55. We walked to church in evening. Had a Grange meeting after church.

Thurs 26 – Warm around 60 by noon, rainy all day.

Fri 27 – Rained all morning, had a bad storm by 2 o'clock which took the roof off our granary. Roy & Geo butchered for Roy.

Sat 28 – Fair, turning colder. I quilted and did my Saturday work. Geo shucked corn.

Sun 29 – 30 degrees, fair. Ralph and Viola & family and Bill, Anita and June Ann were here for dinner.

March 1948

Mon 1 – Rained mostly all day. I finished Georgie's quilt. Geo mixed feed.

Tues 2 – 40 degrees, cloudy all day. Mrs. Westerheide came and took me along to her sister's and we also visited Alvina Rapp at hospital.

Wed 3 – 29 degrees, snowing and getting colder. Alma & Gus took me along to the quilting at Floraville. We stayed for church in evening.

Thurs 4 – 25 degrees, fair. We were at Belleville. Got tankage and tin roofing at Millstadt. Afternoon & evening Alma & I were quilting at Tillie Lindaur's.

Fri 5 – Fair, 28 degrees, cold east wind. I worked about the house. Geo husked corn. I paid my guild dues today for 1948.

Sat 6 – Rained till noon, then cloudy & colder by night. I worked in the house. Geo shucked corn. We were to the guild meeting.

Sun 7 – Fair, colder, 28 degrees. We were at church, then went to Hoffman's a while.

Mon 8 – Fair to cloudy, 22. I went to Belleville with Schillings. In evening Mr. Helms & Mr. Eckert organized the Floraville Grange.

Tues 9 – Fair, 27 degrees. Geo & I put part of the granary roof back on, and we also took 30 doz eggs to Conner's for hatching.

Wed 10 – 24 degrees, snowing all day, 20 by noon, 17 by evening, still snowing. Johnny put up my drop ceiling & cabinet. Miss Brinkley was here, asked me to be 4H leader.

Thurs 11 – Clear, cold, 7 above, snow is about 8 inch deep with 3 foot drifts in our yard, warmed up to 20 by noon but dropped to 14 by night.

Fri 12 – Clear, zero, warmed up to 32 by noon. Ludger put a light above my sink today.

Sat 13 – Clear, 24 degrees, a lot of snow melted today. We went voting at the school.

Sun 14 – 32 degrees, fair. Herman and Frank and Bill, Anita, and June Ann were here for dinner.

Mon 15 – Very cloudy all day, windy. Patsy, Ardell, and I were to the home bureau meeting at Mrs. Jones.

Tues 16 – Fair, warm. I raked the yard and helped Geo put some tin roofing on the granary. The charter of the Grange was closed tonight, 53 members.

Wed 17 – Fair, warm, 68 degrees. I worked about the yard. Were at church in the evening.

Thurs 18 – Cloudy, showers by night, warmer, about 70. We got a new battery for the truck today. I also helped quilt at the church hall.

Fri 19 – Storm and hard rain all morning. We and Mrs. Kniern went to the 4H organization meeting at Belleville. 74 degrees.

Sat 20 – Very warm, cloudy to fair, 80 degrees. We were at Leroy Muskopf's in evening to have a Grange bylaws meeting.

Sun 21 – Cloudy, warm. We were at church. Afternoon it rained. Were to the 4H play in evening.

Mon 22 – Cloudy all day, rain by night, 47 degrees. I cleaned the bedrooms. Geo worked in the sewer.

Tues 23 – Very cloudy, showers, warmer. I cleaned in the house. We were at Orville Koerber's in evening.

Wed 24 – Fair to cloudy. We worked about the place. Were at church in evening.

Thurs 25 – Fair, warm. We were at Millstadt. Then quilted at church and Grange meeting in evening.

Fri 26 – Cloudy, rain & hail by afternoon and colder, stormy. Were at church in evening.

Sat 27 – Cloudy, very cold, 34 degrees, light snow and drizzle. Bill & Anita brought Franklin & Gerry and the boys out to our place.

Sun 28 – Hard frost, 25 degrees, fair. Bill, Anita, June, Franklin and Gerry and boys and Pop went to church. We had the birthday club in evening.

Mon 29 – Fair, very windy, 40 degrees. We, Gerry and the boys cleaned out the brooder house and set up the brooder.

Tues 30 – Cloudy, windy, looked like rain, 49 degrees. We want to move some shrubs today.

Wed 31 – Rained mostly all day. Alma and I helped clean the church hall. Then Gerry and I sewed on my dress.

April 1948

Thurs 1 – Fair. Gerry and boys and I walked to Schilling's for a short while. Boobe, Marcella and children had supper with us in evening.

Fri 2 – We organized a girls' 4H Club at Floraville this evening. Also took in women's guild meeting. We washed and ironed today.

Sat 3 – Fair, warmer. Franklin came today. Emil & Clara Haredrich and daughter were here for supper.

Sun 4 – Fair, very pretty day. Bill, Anita, & June Ann had dinner with us and then they took Franklin and Gerry and the boys to St. Louis train.

Mon 5 – Fair, very warm, shower by night. We took some old chickens and roosters to Millstadt, hens 30 cents, roosters 14 cents a lb. Rain by nite.

Tues 6 – 54 degrees, very cloudy and foggy, then fair. I was to a church doings at Millstadt. In evening we had our Tom Brenneman Show.

Wed 7 – Fair to cloudy, 75 degrees, lightninged by night. We went to card party at Paderborn. Worked in the garden, planted some potatoes.

Thurs 8 – Fair, getting much cooler, 54 by evening. Went to our Grange meeting.

Fri 9 – 41 degrees, windy all day. I did more gardening. Mrs. Westerheide was here in afternoon.

Sat 10 – Cloudy, light rain to fair. I worked in garden all day. 47 degrees in morning, windy all day.

Sun 11 – Cloudy, much warmer, around 70, hard shower by afternoon. We were at church. Rain all night.

Mon 12 – 47 degrees, rain all day, thundershowers by night. We had a 4H meeting at the church hall.

Tues 13 – 43 degrees, drizzle all day. Clara came in afternoon. Went to Frank Klein's quilting in evening.

Wed 14 – Partly cloudy to fair, very pretty day. I raked in the chicken yard. Geo shucked corn.

Thurs 15 – Fair, 48 degrees. I washed and then raked in the chicken yard. Geo shucked corn. Warmed up by noon. I planted cannas.

Fri 16 – Fair, 52 degrees. Oscar Koerber & Geo took 2 sows and 2 straight hogs to Streck's.

Sat 17 – 57 degrees, fair, very pretty day. I transplanted shrubs and flowers and raked the back yard. Geo disked the corn land.

Sun 18 – Fair, cool, beautiful day. We and Metzers were at Clara Probst home this afternoon.

Mon 19 – Fair, very windy and very warm. Patsy and I were at the home bureau meeting at Anna Stuts'. We gave the lesson.

Tues 20 – Fair to cloudy, cooler by night. Fred Wachtels came and took us along to Dintelmann's to see the new baby.

Wed 21 – Fair, 49 degrees. We were at Smithton. Then went to Millstadt, got meat from the locker and had the car fixed.

Thurs 22 – Fair, warmer. We went to the Grange meeting, celebrated Geo's birthday.

Fri 23 – Fair, very warm, around 80. We took 2 hogs to Belleville and then went to the 4H leaders' meeting. Mrs. Keinrim came home with us.

Sat 24 – Fair, 65 degrees in morning, 85 by 3:00 p.m., windy. Geo disked corn rows and I canned some pineapple and did Saturday work.

Sun 25 – Fair, windy, about 85 degrees. John from Sikeston, Henry & Bertha, Bill & Anita & June and Hesses were here for dinner. Birthday club came in evening.

Mon 26 – Had a good rain this morning. Canned more pineapples. Geo disked corn land.

Tues 27 – Fair, very pretty day, cool. I went to Maeystown church meeting with Mrs. Barthel and 4 other ladies.

Wed 28 – Fair, warmer. We worked around outside.

Thurs 29 – Fair, warm. We worked about the farm.

Fri 30 – Fair. We took 2 hogs to Belleville, got $21.10.

May 1948

Sat 1 – Fair, getting colder. I did my Saturday work. Geo worked in the field.

Sun 2 – Very cloudy, cold. We went to Alton with Bill and Anita.

Mon 3 – Fair. I washed and then worked in the garden.

Tues 4 – Fair. Geo disked and I worked about the house, also helped Clara patch.

Wed 5 – Fair to cloudy, getting colder. We worked about the place. I was to the women's guild meeting at Smithton.

Thus 6 – Cold, rainy all day. I set up Mrs. Westerheide's quilt.

Fri 7 – Fair, cool. We took 2 hogs to Belleville and did some shopping. Got $20.85.

Sat 8 – Fair, very warm, 75. I worked in my yard and garden. Geo shucked corn and disked some.

Sun 9 – We were at church, then Boobe & Marcella took us along to Brinker's. Were at church in evening.

Mon 10 – Fair to cloudy. Were at 4H meeting. And I quilted on Mrs. Westerheide's quilt.

Tues 11 – Rained mostly all night, cloudy all day. I picked my first strawberries. John & Katie were here in evening.

Wed 12 – Rainy, cold all day. Clara helped me quilt. Orlin was here to fix granary roof. I got a box of oranges & limes from Irwin.

Thurs 13 – Cloudy, cool. We were at the Grange meeting in evening.

Fri 14 – Fair. We took 2 hogs to Belleville.

Sat 15 – Rainy all day. We were at Frank Klein's cooking party in evening.

Sun 16 – Fair, very pretty day. We and Metzgers were at John & Katie's for dinner & supper. Willie, Anita, and June were here in evening.

Mon 17 – Fair, very pretty day. Patsy and I were to home bureau meeting at Angel's. I set out my last geraniums.

Tues 18 – Fair, 59 degrees. Transplanted more flowers. Got $21.35 for the last 2 hogs.

Wed 19 – Fair, beautiful day, 59 in morning, warmed up to 75. Henry Lang cut some clover. Geo disked corn land. I cleaned garden.

Thurs 20 – Fair, 59 in morning. I worked in the garden. Geo disked corn land.

Fri 21 – Fair, cool to hot by noon. We took 2 hogs to Belleville. They weighed 465 lbs. Afternoon Geo planted his first corn for this year.

Sat 22 – Fair, 60 degrees early. I mowed lawn and did my Saturday work. Geo planted corn.

Sun 23 – Fair. Geo is planting corn. I worked in the garden.

Mon 24 – Fair, cool. I worked around the yard. Also helped Marcella pick strawberries.

Tues 25 – Fair, very cool all day, 49 degrees. In morning we took 10 qts strawberries to the locker.

Wed 26 – Fair, warmer. Geo finished planting corn. We cleaned the brooder house.

Thurs 27 – No entry.

Fri 28 – Fair. We worked about the place. Were at Belleville with 2 hogs.

Sat 29 – Fair, very warm. I patched all day.

Sun 30 – Fair. Were at church, then went to John & Katie's for dinner. Then to Mrs. Seib's about strawberries. Alma's birthday in evening.

Mon 31 – Fair, hot. I sewed and patched all day. Geo mixed feed.

June 1948

Tues 1 – Fair. I patched all day. Geo worked about the place. 4H meeting in evening.

Wed 2 – Fair, hot. I ironed.

Thurs 3 – Fair, warm. Helped Clara in morning. Went to Red Bud church in afternoon.

Fri 4 – Fair, hot, 90 by afternoon. We took 2 hogs to Belleville early in morning. They weighed 440 lbs. Got $24.60.

Sat 5 – Fair, very hot, 93. We cleaned the church hall and prepared for our strawberry festival and dance. Rained & hailed hard by night.

Sun 6 – Cloudy all day, cool. We had a nice crowd at our Grange festival. Sold 5 trays of berries with 15 gal ice cream.

Mon 7 – Fair to cloudy. We took the ice cream tubs to Millstadt. Also went to Mrs. Seib's and paid for the berries, $16.25 in all, $3.25 per tray.

Tues 8 – Fair, cool to cloudy. I worked in garden, then we cleaned the brooder house and the chicken house.

Wed 9 – Fair, cool. I worked in garden and yard all day. Planted butter beans.

Thurs 10 – Fair. We worked about the place. Were to our Grange meeting in evening.

Fri 11 – We took 3 hogs to Streck's. Got $24.60 for 2 which weighed 590 lbs together, one weighed 190. We got $25.10 for it.

Sat 12 – I was to Ruth Gass wedding. Shower in afternoon.

Sun 13 – Fair. We spent the Sunday at home. Had our 4H dance show and dance in the church hall.

Mon 14 – Fair. I cut weeds. Geo hoed in his corn. Afternoon I went to Clara to get my 2 gal of cherries. Canned them.

Tues 15 – Fair. I picked and canned beans & beets. Geo worked in his corn.

Wed 16 – Fair. I washed and ironed and cleaned the flower beds. Geo hoed corn.

Thurs 17 – Cloudy, shower by afternoon. Geo crushed corn and mixed feed. I baked cookies.

Fri 18 – Fair to light showers, hot. Took 2 hogs to Belleville, 380 lbs. 4H meeting in evening. Bill & Anita brought Franklin & family out here.

Sat 19 – Fair, cool. We got things ready for our trip. Johnny & Katie and Bill, Anita & June were here for supper.

Sun 20 – Cloudy, showery. We (*Franklin & Katie*) are leaving for Calif. this afternoon.

Mon 21 – (*Written by Gerry while Katie is away*) Very warm & humid. Pop worked in field. Showers in afternoon & heavy thunderstorm at night.

Tues 22 – Hot and humid. Thunderstorm at night but not much rain. Aunt Katie, Johnny, Pearl, Melvin & Sharon were here.

Wed 23 – Hot and dry. Started combining wheat on the Gundlach farm. Leo Schilling brought 60 bus. Pop weighed it at 65 lbs per bu.

Thurs 24 – Hot & dry. It was 90 by 10 o'clock. Went to Floraville & got milk in evening.

Fri 25 – Hot and very close. I washed & got most of things dry. Went to Floraville, paid electric bill. Went to Smithton for feed for young chickens. I & M called from Calif.

Sat 26 – Hot and humid. Pop worked in field while I cleaned house & baked. Got letter from F & Mom written in Texas. Very bad wind & rain storm about 3 p.m. Very bad & more rain in thunderstorm late in the night. Boobe & Marcella were here.

Sun 27 – Hot. Went to church, also to Sophia Fischer's funeral. Uncle Will, Mr. Cook, Bill, Anita & June here for supper. Bad rain & electric storm in evening. Still raining, cooler.

Mon 28 – Hot & humid. Rain, thunderstorm in afternoon. Caught Uncle Henry & Harold here, had to stay inside. Orville & Marie over in evening. Rain late, all night.

Tues 29 – Cloudy & rain in morning, clearing by afternoon, warm & moist. Went to Belleville in evening with Marcella & Boobe to see Mrs. Poetgar.

Wed 30 – Clear & drying. Started combining again. Went to Millstadt. Edgar, Toddy & kids visiting Katie's. Cool by evening & windy.

July 1948

Thurs 1 – Cool & windy, drying fine. Went to Smithton to take chickens to Swiegel's. Also attended funeral of Mrs. Poetgar.

Fri 2 – Cool at night, warmed up to 89 in afternoon. Pop fertilized corn. Everyone is combining every minute.

Sat 3 – Cool in morning, very hot by afternoon, over 90.

Sun 4 – Mom & Frank returned from Calif.

Mon 5 – Hot, hard rain by night. I was tired, didn't do much.

Tues 6 – Cloudy to fair. We took 2 hogs to Belleville, got $29.35 a 100 weight, was 455 lb for the 2.

Wed 7 – Fair, hot. Schillings combined again. Geo worked in corn. I canned pickles and beets.

Thurs 8 – Fair, not so hot. I helped Clara dress chickens today.

Fri 9 – Fair, hot, 95 at noon. Schillings finished combining wheat on our ground, 879 bu. I washed. Geo put fertilizer in his corn field.

Sat 10 – Fair, hot, shower by noon. Katie & John were here in evening. I ironed for Mrs. Westerheide. Geo finished corn.

Sun 11 – Fair, very hot. We were at church. Then I walked over to Marcella's. Bill, Anita & June Ann were here in evening.

Mon 12 – Fair, very hot. We were at Ed Sander's for dinner. Then went to Millstadt to get Howerton's washer. I canned 6 quarts of pickles in evening.

Tues 13 – Fair to thundershowers, no hard rain tho. We didn't do much of anything. I baked 2 pies. Two 4H girls were here to talk about picnic.

Wed 14 – Very foggy, then fair, sorta hazy all day. I made sauerkraut, ironed, washed a few pieces, and picked about 1.5 gal blackberries.

Thurs 15 – Very foggy, then fair. Weeded garden & patched. Pop worked on the pond dam and mixed feed. Rained hard by evening.

Fri 16 – Fair, hot. I mowed lawn and canned pickles. Were to the 4H meeting in evening.

Sat 17 – Fair, not quite so hot, west wind. I dug my potatoes in garden, weeded flower beds, and mowed lawn. Geo worked by the pond.

Sun 18 – Fair to partly cloudy, hot. We had company all day and evening. Willie picked blackberries.

Mon 19 – Very hard rain in morning, then fair, but plenty rain again in the night. I washed & ironed.

Tues 20 – Cloudy all day, thundering all day, not too much rain tho. I helped Clara patch. I picked 1 gal blackberries for Marcella.

Wed 21 – Very hot and humid. We were at Millstadt in morning. Then I patched. Geo mixed feed. Showers now and then.

Thurs 22 – Fair, not quite so hot. I picked blackberries, canned some pickles, and helped Clara dress chickens and baked 2 cakes. Grange meeting.

Fri 23 – Fair, very cool. Pop & I were at Turkey Hill Grange 4H clothing show and judging, 6 of my club were there, got 3 blue, 4 red, and 1 white ribbon.

Sat 24 – Fair, 57 degrees. Canned 11 quarts peaches which I bought at Eckert's yesterday. I'm going to help at Paderborn picnic today.

Sun 25 – Fair, getting warmer. I was to the consistory meeting. In evening Boobe & Marcella took us along to the hospital to see Frank Klein.

Mon 26 – Rained hard last night, fair & hot today. We had feed ground at Smithton.

Tues 27 – Fair, very warm, around 93. We were at the Belleville Fair all day.

Wed 28 – Partly cloudy to a hard rain by 4 o'clock, also some storm. Henry Lang, Mrs. Westerheide and Mrs. Rauch were here in morning.

Thurs 29 – Fair, very hot and humid. We got feed crushed at Smithton. Then Geo chopped trees along the branch. I mowed lawn.

Fri 30 – Fair to partly cloudy, light drizzle. I washed. Then I went along with Mrs. Westerheide to see their lot on St. Louis Road.

Sat 31 – Fair, cool. I cut the lawn and did my Saturday baking. Geo worked by the branch.

August 1948

Sun 1 – Fair, cool. We were at the Smithton picnic a little while.

Mon 2 – Fair, cool. Iron peddler was here. We sold 18 dollars worth. It was close to 1800 lbs. Then we cut weeds in chicken yard.

Tues 3 – Cool, fair, 65 degrees. We chopped more weeds.

Wed 4 – Fair, very cool, 60 in morning. We chopped weeds and I baked cake.

Thurs 5 – Fair, cool, 58 degrees, stayed cool all day. I helped Clara dress chickens. In evening Henry Langs and Albert Hoffmans were here.

Fri 6 – Fair, cool, 53 in morning, warmer during the day. We chopped weeds.

Sat 7 – Fair, cool. I baked cake and prepared for Sunday dinner.

Sun 8 – Fair, cool. Lottie & Eddie were here for dinner. In evening we were at Frank Klein's.

Mon 9 – Cool, nice to work about outside.

Tues 10 – Fair, cool. We chopped weeds.

Wed 11 – We were at picnic at Millstadt a little while.

Thurs 12 – Fair. Langs plowed and filled in our bridge in the woods. Schillings started to plow here. Grange meeting in evening.

Fri 13 – Fair, hot. Langs finished filling up our bridge in the woods.

Sat 14 – Fair. We worked around the place. Geo chopped off brush along the branch.

Sun 15 – Fair, cool to hot by afternoon. We were at church and afternoon at the Hecker Church picnic with Metzgers. In evening at Clara Schilling's birthday.

Mon 16 – Fair, cool. We went to our home bureau meeting at Herr's, also had our 4H achievement day there, 9 of my girls were there.

Tues 17 – Fair, hot around 90. Bill, Anita and June came and June stayed here. We baked 2 angel cakes for Anita.

Wed 18 – Fair, hot 90. June & I walked to Westerheide's but they weren't home so we came back and baked doughnuts.

Thurs 19 – Fair, hot. We all went to Mrs. Ida Pinge's for home bureau meeting and 4H meeting.

Fri 20 – Fair, getting hot, 93. We worked around the place. June & I washed a few clothes and ironed.

Sat 21 – Fair, hot 95 by afternoon. We took June along to Freeburg Homecoming and Elsie Hesse got her there.

Sun 22 – Fair, very hot, 103 degrees. It is Sunday so we just stayed home and rested.

Mon 23 – Hot, 98 by noon. I pulled weeds. Geo got some feed ground & mixed feed.

Tues 24 – Hot, around 98. We took 2 hogs to Belleville early in morning. Hogs weighed 475, got $30.10. Paid our fertilizer, $219.00 for 5.5 tons @ $41a ton. 5% off for cash.

Wed 25 – We took eggs to Millstadt, got 42 cents a doz at Krogers. It was very hot around 100 by 3 p.m. Pop & Koerbers left for Urbana today.

Thurs 26 – Fair to partly cloudy, 102 degrees. I helped Clara peel peaches and patched some. In evening the girls & I went to Grange with Metzgers. It was their silver wedding celebration.

Fri 27 – Fair, hot, 101 by noon, hard rain by evening. Orville Koerbers and Geo came back from Urbana.

Sat 28 – Not quite so hot, around 92. We got 10 feeder pigs from Herman today at $80.00.

Sun 29 – Fair, around 94 today. We stayed home all day and rested.

Mon 30 – Fair, cooler. I worked in the yard. Geo chopped trees in the branch.

Tues 31 – Fair, cool. Geo made firewood. I worked in my yard and did some sewing.

September 1948

Wed 1 – Fair, very cool, 58 degrees. I worked about the yard. Geo cut off trees by the branch.

Thurs 2 – Fair to very cloudy, 60 degrees, light drizzle by nite. I washed today. Rollie, Barbara & children here in morning to get eggs. Alma was here in afternoon.

Fri 3 – Fair to partly cloudy, hot. I was at the guild meeting in evening.

Sat 4 – Fair to cloudy. We went to Millstadt Homecoming and got Franklin. Bill & Anita got him at East St. Louis.

Sun 5 – Rained all day. Bill, Anita, and June were here. We saw the Calif. pictures on screen.

Mon 6 – A good shower in morning, then it cleared up. We took Franklin to Millstadt bus so he could get to East St. Louis.

Tues 7 – Fair, warmer. We took 14 hens to Millstadt, got 28.5 cents a lb. I also put 5 spring chickens in locker.

Wed 8 – Cloudy, good shower by afternoon. I baked cookies. Pop crushed corn and mixed feed. Got much cooler by night.

Thurs 9 – Fair, cool, 52 degrees. We built a new pig pen for the 10 red pigs we bought from Herman. Grange meeting in evening.

Fri 10 – Fair, cool, 55 degrees. We took 2 hogs to Streck's, weighed 520 lbs @ $28.85. In afternoon I went to Marcella's.

Sat 11 – Fair, cool, 58 degrees. I pruned some peach trees. Geo went grinding. In afternoon Mr. & Mrs. Wimmer were here.

Sun 12 – Fair to partly cloudy, 60 degrees, 85 by noon. We moved things out of the old brooder house into the granary.

Mon 13 – Fair, 60 early in morning, 80 by afternoon. We were at church then from there we went to Robert Probst's for dinner.

Tues 14 – Fair, cool, 65 in morning, warmed up to 85. We took 2 hogs to Belleville, weighed 525 lbs @ $28.85. Afternoon I helped Clara patch.

Wed 15 – Fair, cool, 62 degrees, got up to 80 by noon. I helped Marcella quilt today. We got one load of lime dust to mix with fertilizer.

Thurs 16 – Fair, cool, 50 degrees, 85 in afternoon. I helped Marcella finish her quilt.

Fri 17 – Fair, cool in morning 60, 87 by noon. I worked about the yard and washed chairs. Geo made firewood.

Sat 18 – Fair, hot winds all day. We were to the Kempf, Gass wedding. 90 by afternoon.

Sun 19 – Fair, hot winds. Viola had the Reisses today for dinner & supper. I potted some flowers in the morning.

Mon 20 – Fair, hot, 95 by noon. I washed. Pop mixed fertilizer. Schillings & Langs started to spread fertilizer today.

Tues 21 – Cloudy, rained a little in morning. Langs finished the fertilizer. I painted the porch floor and some chairs.

Wed 22 – Cloudy, cooler, 68 in morning, warmed up to 75. Schillings finished spreading fertilizer. Clara helped me stipple my porch floor.

Thurs 23 – Fair, cold, 50 in morning. I painted chairs & waxed porch floor. Geo mixed feed. Broad Hollow Grange put on program here.

Fri 24 – Cold, 49 in morning. Clara came and we finished painting the porch floor and some chairs. Also mowed lawn.

Sat 25 – 50 degrees, very cool all day. I painted the porch bench and more chairs. Wimmers were here in afternoon.

Sun 26 – 50 degrees and cool all day. Had fire in the stove to keep warm. Herman & Frank were here. F. Schilling's birthday in evening.

Mon 27 – Partly cloudy, 50 degrees. We worked around the place. I put coal and wood in the basement. Were at Westerheide's a while.

Tues 28 – 52 in morning, cloudy all day, rain by night. I was at church meeting at Waterloo today. Got 6 baby pigs off the second sow.

Wed 29 – Cloudy, light drizzle during the day. We paid our taxes for 1947, $277.66. Also got some wheat grinding done.

Thurs 30 – Fair. I cleaned upstairs. Geo chopped more trees. Had our booster night in evening.

October 1948

Fri 1 – Fair, very pretty day. Geo & I fixed up the corn crib and moved chickens in. Moved our pullets into the hen house.

Sat 2 – Fair, 60 degrees. We tore down that old corn crib shed and patched the roof. I mowed some weeds.

Sun 3 – Fair, cold 43 in morning, NW winds, didn't get above 65 all day. We were at Margaret's birthday party in the evening.

Mon 4 – 48 degrees. We got our first rent corn from Kaubreck and Sensel today. And we sorted it.

Tues 5 – Fair, 37 degrees. We are still sorting corn. They finished picking today. They brought us about 200 bus from Crooks land.

Wed 6 – Fair to cloudy, rain by night. We finished sorting corn. Got about 210 bu, third from Sensel & Kaubreck renters.

Thurs 7 – Rained all night, then turned colder and stormy. We chopped trees & brush at the 7 acres branch.

Fri 8 – Light drizzle in morning, cold all day. Afternoon Geo & Ludger made the dam out south of orchard. We were in Belleville in morning.

Sat 9 – Fair, cool all day. Schillings sowed some wheat in the 20 acres. We put up our storm windows today.

Sun 10 – Cloudy all day. Franklin, Gerry, and the boys came to stay this week with us.

Mon 11 – Fair, very pretty day. We are enjoying to have the children with us.

Tues 12 – Fair, very pretty day.

Wed 13 – Fair, warm.

Thurs 14 – Fair. Franklin, Gerry, and the boys were at Millstadt and Lang's and Herman & Frank's.

Fri 15 – Fair, warmer. Franklin & I were at Belleville to get some sausage.

Sat 16 – Cold, very stormy and raining all day. We stayed in the house and looked over the old pictures.

Sun 17 – Cloudy to clearing. Bill & Anita and June Ann came for dinner, then they took Franklin, Gerry, and the boys to the station.

Mon 18 – Fair, heavy frost, 27 degrees. I washed, then went to the home bureau meeting.

Tues 19 – Frost, fair. I ironed then Pop & I went to Floraville to the hall for cleaning it for our supper this Saturday.

Wed 20 – Fair, warmer. We made and brought in firewood. Also sorted pears.

Thurs 21 – Cloudy, light rain thru the day, clearing by night. We made more firewood.

Fri 22 – Fair, getting colder. We were at Millstadt to order ice cream for our church picnic.

Sat 23 – Fair, very chilly. Had a nice crowd for our church supper.

Sun 24 – Fair, very pretty day. Irwin arrived from Calif. at 11:30 a.m. Took me to consistory meeting and then to Progressive Grange supper.

Mon 25 – Fair to hazy, no frost. Irwin & Pop went to Smithton. I sorted the limes & oranges.

Tues 26 – Very foggy till 10:00 a.m. Pop & I and Irwin took 3 hogs to Belleville. Then went shopping. Then we took truck to Mertz to have motor put in.

Wed 27 – Fair. Yesterday afternoon Irwin & we went to Carlena & then to Pearl & Melvin's. Got $25.60 for hogs. They weighed 740 lbs.

Thurs 28 – Fair. Schillings were here last night. Irwin showed his pictures. Tonight we all were at our Grange meeting.

Fri 29 – Fair. Woodland, Ridge Prairie, and Turkey Hill Grangers were at our Grange last night to put on degree work.

Sat 30 – Fair. Marcella & Boobe and children were here last night. Irwin worked about the place during the day.

Sun 31 – Cloudy to rain all afternoon. Bill, Anita, and June were here yesterday. In the evening Irwin packed his clothes to go to Indiana in the morning. We & Metzgers were at Dora Mueth's.

November 1948

Mon 1 – Cloudy and warm all day. I cleaned out closets and brushed off walls. John & Katie were here in evening.

Tues 2 – Rain all day. Election day. Dewey lost, Truman won. Did some cleaning in the bedrooms.

Wed 3 – More light rain. I washed windows. Geo mixed feed.

Thurs 4 – Very windy, fair to very cloudy, hard rain by night while we were at Gus Metzger's birthday party. Lightning & thunder.

Fri 5 – Cloudy to fair, cooler. I ironed. Ludger came and fixed our water system foot valve. Henry & Lavern were here a while too.

Sat 6 – Fair, cooler. I did my Saturday work. Geo & Ludger made a dam in the pasture.

Sun 7 – Fair, cool. Metzgers took us along to Hecker church women's guild diamond jubilee. Had supper there.

Mon 8 – Fair. In evening we went to Frank Klein's to get my quilt marked. Irwin was here when we came back.

Tues 9 – Cloudy, rain turning to snow, cold 33. Irwin took us to Farm Bureau dinner and then left for Calif. to get Mary & children.

Wed 10 – Cloudy to fair, cold. I quilted all day. Mrs. Hatter was here.

Thurs 11 – Fair. We had 3rd & 4th degree work at our Grange. Shiloh Valley and Emerald Mound also some of Ridge Prairie Granges.

Fri 12 – Cloudy, rainy all day. In evening we went to Belleville to the hospital to see Marcella and the baby.

Sat 13 – Fair, pretty day, cool. We worked about the place.

Sun 14 – Fair, beautiful day. We were at church. Afternoon at Rapp's. Bill & Anita were here in evening.

Mon 15 – Fair, warm, beautiful day. Geo hauled ashes and I quilted.

Tues 16 – Fair. I took sick with chills last night and feeling very badly now. Geo went to doctor for me.

Wed 17 – Fair. On this day I went to the hospital with 104 fever.

Thurs 18 – No entry.

Fri 19 – No entry.

Sat 20 – No entry.

Sun 21 – No entry.

Mon 22 – No entry.

Tues 23 – No entry.

Wed 24 – No entry.

Thurs 25 – No entry.

Fri 26 – No entry.

Sat 27 – No entry.

Sun 28 – No entry.

Mon 29 – No entry.

Tues 30 – No entry.

December 1948

Wed 1 – Fair, cold to warmer. Anita came to the hospital and got me and took me to their home.

Thurs 2 – Fair. June Ann's birthday.

Fri 3 – Franklin & Gerry stopped in at Bill & Anita's to see me.

Sat 4 – June Ann had a birthday party in the afternoon. Franklin, Pop, Mary & Mary Kay came to see me.

Sun 5 – Fair, very stormy, cold. Afternoon Bill, Anita, June, and I drove around and stopped to see Wimmers.

Mon 6 – No entry.

Tues 7 – No entry.

Wed 8 – Very cold, 24. Anita took me home today. Schillings came in the evening.

Thurs 9 – Fair, cold, 18 degrees. We could only do our house work.

Fri 10 – Fair, cold. Frank Kleins were here in evening.

Sat 11 – Fair, cold.

Sun 12 – Fair, warm. Bill & Anita & June were here for dinner. We had lot of company in the afternoon, also in evening.

Mon 13 – Fair, very warm, 68. Mary dug dahlia bulbs and cleaned the corner by the feed house.

Tues 14 – Rainy all day and heavy fog. Mary & Eileen Klein washed.

Wed 15 – Fair, very warm. Mary & I were to see the doctor.

Thurs 16 – We baked some cookies. Cooler, 28 in the morning.

Fri 17 – Fair, cold, 27. We baked cookies. In evening Clara and Ludger were here. Irwin came home.

Sat 18 – Cloudy, warmer. Mary, Irwin, and Stevie went to Indiana early this morning.

Sun 19 – Fair. Albert & Elsie Hoffman were here. Irwin was home over the weekend. Cold raw wind.

Mon 20 – Fair, warmer. Pop & I went to the home bureau meeting at Ed Barthel's.

Tues 21 – Fair, warm. Mary & Pop were at Belleville to the oil meeting.

Wed 22 – Fair, cooler. We washed today and set up our Xmas tree.

Thurs 23 – Cloudy, snow by 3 o'clock. Irwin came home at 4:00 o'clock and took us to the Grange meeting in evening. Xmas party.

Fri 24 – Cloudy and snow during the day. Mary & Irwin and boys went to Millstadt to get groceries.

Sat 25 – Fair, very cold, 17 degrees. Bill, Anita & June were here. Left for home early as it was getting colder and such icy roads.

Sun 26 – 6 below zero, fair, warmed up to 30 by noon. I went to the consistory meeting in afternoon. Mary, Irv, Pop & I played cards in evening.

Mon 27 – Cloudy to fair, warm. Irwin & I went to East St. Louis, then to Belleville to exchange my dress. Played cards in evening.

Tues 28 – Rained slowly all day. Mary & Irwin moved to Indiana today. 34 degrees.

Wed 29 – Cloudy, strong west winds, getting colder. Elmer, Carlena & Christian were here today. I cleaned my cabinets.

Thurs 30 – Fair, cold, 22, ground thawed during the day. I ironed and cleaned. Geo cut firewood. John & Katie were here in evening.

Fri 31 – Fair, 22 degrees. Geo cut firewood. I cleaned the bedrooms & I ironed some.

Matriarch #1 – Margaret Basler Reiss Ebert

Dear Will, Kayla, and Ava,   August 18, 2014

Your great great great great grandmother Margaret Basler was born on 10/22/1818 in this picturesque Swiss village of Niederzeihen (lower Zeihen). She was the second of ten children

and the oldest daughter. Her father Johann Basler was the village mayor, burgermeister, or gemeindeammann about 1823. The second photo is their house near the village center.

Johann, his wife Katharina, and eight of their surviving children arrived in New Orleans on 11/28/1839 from Le Havre, France on a ship called Salem as family number is 292308. Their oldest son Nicholaus had previously arrived in New Orleans on 12/3/1836 and settled in Louisville, Kentucky.

The Basler family quickly moved north to settle in the German community of Paderborn, Illinois about two miles from the 40-acre farm which Johann Adam Reiss had purchased from Thomas Houghan on 9/1/1838. Adam built his log cabin that fall and moved in with his pregnant wife Mary. He also built an adjacent log granary. Both measured about 15 feet by 18 feet and had stone foundations. Their son John was born soon

on 12/11/1838 but sadly Mary died during that childbirth.

Adam hosted Catholic church services on his farm in his log cabin, his log granary, or outdoors as the seasons allowed. He did that for about two years and may have started that practice with Mary. Anyway, those church services may have been where the Basler and Reiss families first met in late 1839. So here was Margaret age 20 and the oldest Basler child in the area. And here was Adam Reiss age 34, new landowner, handyman farmer, and widower with an infant son.

Margaret and Adam were married on 9/10/1840. In less than a year she had gone from an upscale house with wooden floors in Switzerland, to a very small log cabin with a dirt floor in Illinois, to a wife and homemaker, and to a step-mom with an infant son. Awesome lady!!!

- Her father Johann Basler bought a 40-acre farm northeast of Paderborn on 12/13/1841.

- Her next younger sister Sophia married nearby farmer Frantz Stauder on 3/28/1842. He was also a recent widower and was raising two small children under age 5.

- Her third son Charles Joseph Reiss was born on 2/17/1843.

- Her father Johann Basler sold his farm on 11/2/1843 and moved with his unmarried children to Louisville, Kentucky.

- Her fourth son Martin Charles Reiss was born 6/19/1845.

- Her first daughter Catharine Reiss was born 3/23/1847.

- Her second daughter Barbara Reiss was stillborn sometime in 1849.

- Her husband Adam Reiss died of cholera on 5/23/1849. Margaret is now a widow, age 30, five children ages 2 to 10, living in a small log cabin with dirt floor, on a 120-acre farm. Can you imagine!!!

The next decade of the 1850s were kinder to Margaret but still had major highs and lows.

- Margaret married Conrad Ebert on 4/2/1850. He was born in Germany on 5/11/1811 so he is seven years older than Margaret. He arrived in New Orleans on 6/7/1847.

- Her third daughter Anna Maria Ebert was born on 9/14/1851. She did not reach adulthood because she is not mentioned in the 1860 census.

- Her two younger brothers moved to California in 1852. George Anselm Basler took a steamship from New York to Panama, crossed the isthmus, and took a second steamship to San Francisco. He later participated in gold rushes in Nevada and British Columbia. Martin Basler, his wife Anna Maria, and two month old son John took a covered wagon for 105 days along the California Trail from St. Joseph, Missouri to Sacramento.

- Her fourth daughter Louisa Ebert was born on 12/??/1853.

- Margaret and Conrad Ebert bought 40 acres on 1/5/1854 to square off their farm at 160 acres.

- Her father Johann Basler died in late 1854 in Louisville, Kentucky.

- Her fifth daughter Margaret Ebert was born on 10/29/1856.

- Her last child with a name we don't know was born about 1859 but did not survive because there is no mention in the 1860 census.

The next four decades of the 1860s through the 1890s included additional joys and sorrows –

- Brother Nicholaus Basler died on 4/11/1860 in Louisville. Margaret is now the oldest of seven surviving Basler siblings.

- Son John Reiss married Maria Josephine Gass on 10/22/1861 and had ten children but lost four of them the week of 5/10/1888 to disease.

- Fighting in the Civil War with four different Illinois regiments were Margaret's brother George Basler with the 22nd, son John Reiss with the 43rd, son Frank Reiss with the 31st, and son-in-law Charles Max Wittig with the 82nd. All returned but two were wounded.

- Margaret and Conrad were subpoenaed on 4/18/1865 by the widow of Thomas Houghan over her dower rights to three 40-acre tracts sold by her husband to Adam Reiss in 1838, 1839, and 1842. The Eberts traveled to Springfield and were excused from the suit.

- Younger sister Sophia Basler Stauder died on 7/25/1865. Margaret is now the only Basler living in Illinois. Her parents are deceased. Two brothers are in California. Two sisters are in St. Louis. One brother is in a Civil War veterans' home in Dayton, Ohio. And one brother is in Sullivan, Indiana.

- Son Frank Reiss married Anna Antonia Syvilla Feder on 4/9/1866 and had eleven children but only seven reached adulthood.

- Daughter Kate Reiss married Charles Max Wittig on 4/9/1866 in a double ceremony with her brother Frank and Anna. They had five daughters with four reaching adulthood.

- Son Charles Reiss married Eva Dintelmann on 11/15/1866 and had seven children with all seven reaching adulthood.

- Margaret and Conrad bought 20 more acres on 5/13/1868 on the northeast corner of their farm.

- Her younger brother Ferdinand Basler died on 12/15/1873 in Sullivan, Indiana.

- Daughter Louisa Ebert married George W. Neff on 11/6/1873 and had one son before she died on 5/21/1875 when her clothes caught fire while making apple butter.

- Daughter Margaret Ebert married Conrad Charles Neff (George's younger brother) on 9/7/1877 and had five children who all reached adulthood.

- Margaret's husband Conrad Ebert's died on 7/23/1880 at age 69.

- Her younger brother Martin Basler died on 1/25/1881 in Sacramento, California.

- Son Martin Reiss married Margaret Williams in 1883 and had three children but only one reached adulthood. Margaret died in 1891 and Martin in 1898.

- Her younger brother George Anselm Basler died on 11/??/1888 in San Francisco.

- Her older brother Johann Jakob "George" Basler died on 9/7/1897 in Dayton, Ohio.

- The 1900 census shows Margaret with five of ten children still living. Stepson John was the first born, then five children with Adam Reiss, and four more with Conrad Ebert.

- Margaret saved 780 letters written to her or her neighbor son Frank Reiss between 1852 and 1888. They were written by her siblings and spouses, children, grandchildren, and friends. Only 22 of these letters were written by Margaret while she was visiting her daughter in Davenport or son in O'Fallon. Most were written in "old" German and were translated between 2004 and 2008. About 20% of the letters are in phonetic English and are just plain fun to read.

All these letters with some linking italics to make them more self-explanatory were published by Author House in 2009 in a book titled It Takes A Matriarch. There are 412,000 words, a dozen photos, and 600 pages.

These letters show a consistent and very conscientious pattern of caring, leading, counseling, listening, sharing, and compassion. Margaret Basler Reiss Ebert was an outstanding matriarch, patriarch, and big sister. She was my great great grandmother and simply a great person. I hope to meet her in heaven some day!!! Here's her book and her obituary on the next page.

Love, Granddad

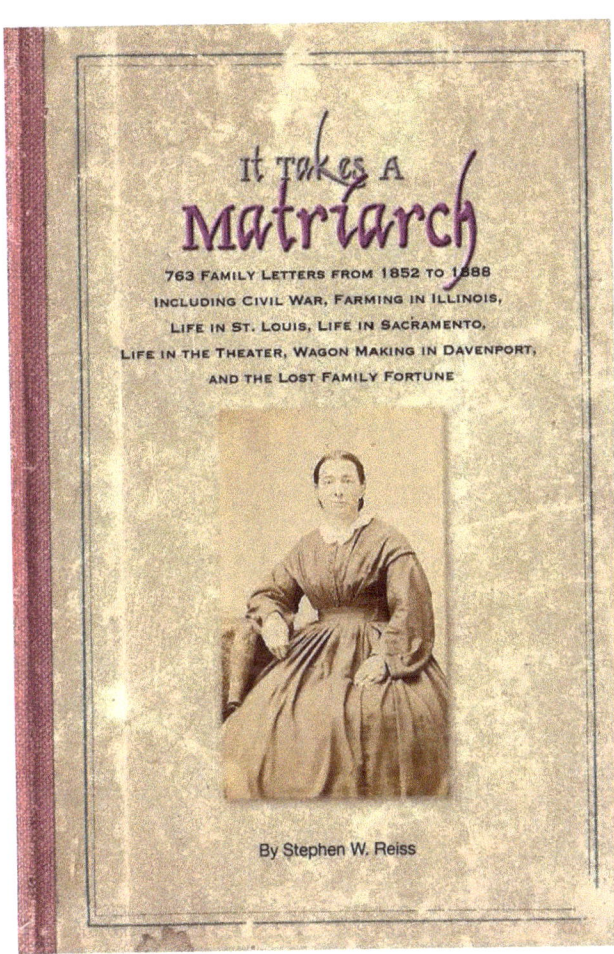

Below is Margaret's obituary as translated from a local German newspaper –

In the Prairie du Long Township died on Sunday morning Mrs. Margaretha Ebert at an age of 84 years and 9 months. Mrs. Ebert's maiden name was Margaretha Basler, she was the widow of Mr. Conrad Ebert. At the time of her death, Mrs. Ebert was living on the farm of her daughter, Mrs. Conrad Neff, 2 miles north of Hecker.

Mrs. Ebert was born in Switzerland and came to the United States in the year 1839. Her first husband Mr. Adam Reiss died in 1849. Her second husband Mr. Conrad Ebert died in 1880.

Mrs. Ebert is survived by her children: John Reiss in Belleville, Frank Reiss in Floraville, Charles on the Ridge Prairie, Martin in Missouri, Mrs. Max Wittig in Davenport, Ia. and Mrs. Conrad Neff as well as 31 grandchildren and 3 great grandchildren. Also her sisters Mrs. Charles Krone and Mrs. Samuel Perrow (*who died a week apart in July 1907*).

The funeral service has been on Wednesday morning at 8:00 o'clock in the Catholic Church in Hecker and the burial took place right after the service at St. Augustine Cemetery.

Matriarch #2 – Anna Antonia Sybilla Feder Reiss

Dear Will, Kayla, Ava,   August 18, 2014

This lady is your great great great grandmother. She was born in Popendorf Landgericht, Bordenstein Koenigreig Bayern, Germany on 9/26/1844 so next month she would be age 170. Her parents were George Feder who was born in 1817 and Anna Sybilla Rau Feder who was born in 1825. They were married in 1845. We think they adopted infant Sybilla who may have been a niece so they could all make a new home in the United States. **Immigrations Records** show a George Feder age 27 as Family Number 46250 arriving in New Orleans on 10/28/1845 from Bremen, Germany on a ship called Rajah. Included in his extended family were Johann age 23, John age 13, and Catherine age 9. Another George Feder was on that same ship at age 55 and Family Number 46135. This double family settled on a farm about two miles north of Belleville, Illinois in 1846.

The **1850 Census** under <u>Fader</u> shows a double family living together in Ridge Prairie in St. Clair County as George age 61, Anna age 60, George age 32, <u>Sevilia</u> age 27, John age 27, John age 18, Catharine age 15, <u>Sevilia</u> age 6, John age 2, and Anna age 1. Underlined names are misspellings.

A dozen or more years later, young Sybilla somehow met Frank Joseph Reiss who was born on 9/27/1841 so he was one day short of three years older than her. Their farms were 14 miles apart so they weren't neighbors, school friends, or church friends. Frank was away serving in the Civil War with the 31st Illinois Infantry Regiment from 12/2/1864 to 7/17/1865 as part of the Army of General William Tecumseh Sherman. Maybe they exchanged letters or maybe they met after he returned. We just don't know.

Anyway, here is their wedding picture when Sybilla and Frank were married on 4/9/1866 in a double ceremony when his sister Kate Reiss married Charles Max Wittig who had also served in the Civil War with the 82nd Illinois Infantry. Sybilla and Frank moved into this log cabin on the Reiss family farm where he had been born. Here's how it looked in 1957.

Frank's older and younger brothers had already moved out on their own and his sister was newly married to Max. Frank's mother Margaret and step-father Conrad Ebert had already built their new home on the southeast corner of the Reiss family farm. This log cabin had been built by Frank's father Adam Reiss in 1838 and measured 15 by 18 feet. It had a dirt floor. You can see a brick chimney for heat from a stove rather than a fireplace.

Sybilla and Frank lived 23 years in this small log cabin where 10 of their 11 children were born and where 4 of them died. Those four share this tombstone in St. Augustine Cemetery in Hecker where each child has a side. Their last child was born in a new house next door which they built in 1889. Sybilla and Frank raised seven children to adulthood who all did very well in life. Here are the details on all 11 children –

- Charles Martin was born on 10/17/1867 but died seven years later on 11/18/1874.

- Adam Joseph was born on 9/25/1869 but died two years later on 11/5/1871.

- Catherine was born on 11/11/1871 but died seven months later on 6/16/1872.

- George William was born on 4/22/1873. He bought 160 acres of land in Lamb County, Texas on 10/18/1907, married Catherine Luetzelschwab on 4/16/1911, they raised three sons, took over the family farm, and doubled its size. They were my grandparents.

Tombstone of Adam, Charles, Catherine and Lizzie Reiss, four very young children of Frank and Anna Reiss. There is one name on each side.

- Anna Margaret was born on 9/20/1875. She married George Dintelmann in 1908.

- John Jacob was born on 11/4/1877. He married Mary Etta Sellards in 1907. They founded the Reiss Dairy in Sikeston, Missouri.

- Henry William was born on 3/30/1880. He married Emma Caroline Eberlein in 1906 and Bertha Richards in ?? He was a pharmacist in St. Louis.

- Louis Phillip was born on 9/7/1882. He married Harriet "Hattie" F. Wright on 1/7/1904. He worked as a refrigeration engineer in Texas.

- Louisa Kathryn was born on 9/22/1884. She married Philip Heinrich Petry on 6/2/1909.

- Elizabetha (Lizza) was born on 7/1/1888 but died nine months later on 3/2/1889.

- William Martin was born on 9/17/1890. He married Mabel Golden in 1913 and Rose Freant on ?? He was a professional portrait photographer.

Here's a photo of the 1838 log cabin at left and the new 1889 house at right. Notice the log cabin chimney is at the side instead of on top like the newer photo above. Notice also that the front and side porches on the new house are not yet enclosed like they are today.

Here are Sybilla and Frank celebrating their golden wedding anniversary. April 9, 1916 was a Sunday so that's probably the exact date of this photo. Their hair and beard styles did not change in 50 years, only the color!!! I like her smile.

Notice in the birth summary above that George is the oldest surviving child and the next to the last one to get married. He was obviously a very busy and successful farmer, a strong handsome guy with a good tan, but he was also kinda shy. He didn't get out much. So in 1910 Sybilla had a plan to find a wife for her son. Besides, Sybilla was age 65 in that spring and all her other children had left home. She needed help around the homestead. Shortly before the Census on 4/25/1910 she hired attractive 20-year old Catherine Luetzelschwab as a live-in domestic to help with chores like laundry, cooking, cleaning, quilting, chickens, etc. Katie

appeared in that census but they butchered her last name as Luietcelschwab. Well, 37-year old George was no dummy so it didn't take him long at all to realize that <mark>Katie was a keeper</mark>. She maintained a good house, was outgoing and social, spoke German like he did, was very comfortable living on a farm, and would make an outstanding wife and mother. They were married a year later, on 4/16/1911 which is one week and 45 years after Sybilla had married Frank Reiss. Sybilla and Frank were married for 55 years and Katie and George were married for 53 years. <mark>Sybilla gets an A+ as wife, mother, and matchmaker!!!</mark>

New Subject – The deathbed will of Adam Reiss on 5/23/1849 gave 1/3 of his 120-acre farm and homestead to his wife Margaret Basler Reiss. That meant his sons John, Frank, Charles, Martin, and daughter Kate inherited the remaining undivided 2/3 share. Those children came of age 15 and more years later and married. Frank and Sybilla eventually negotiated to buy out his mother and his siblings to consolidate the farm ownership under their names. In the meantime, Margaret married Conrad Ebert on 4/2/1850 and had two more daughters who reached adulthood and married the Neff brothers. Margaret and Conrad also bought adjacent 40- and 20-acre farms. Conrad Ebert died on 7/23/1880 without a will. Frank and Sybilla negotiated to also buy out his mother again and his step-siblings. All these buy-outs happened over a 37-year period. Here are more details –

12-18-1869   Warranty Deed from Chas. Reiss and wife to Franz Joseph Reiss for $1,000 as heirs of Adam Reiss deceased for the northeast quarter of the southwest quarter, the southeast quarter of the northwest quarter, and the southwest quarter of the northeast quarter of Section 7, township 2 south, range 8 west. This is Charles' share of the 120 acres he inherited from his father.

11-4-1872   Indenture between Martin C. Reiss of the County of Buchanan, State of Missouri and Franz Joseph Reiss for $670 for Martin's share of the 120 acres he inherited.

7-31-1880   Letters of Administration whereas Conrad Ebert died intestate 7-23-1880 therefore Margaretha Ebert became administratrix.

5-12-1884   Quit Claim deed made 4-13-1875 and filed 9-9-1875 from Catharina and Charles M. Wittig to Frank J. Reiss for $950 for her share of the 120 acres she inherited.

7-15-1887   Letter to Margaretha Ebert from attorneys Dill & Schaefer saying her son called on them with her power of attorney to sell 20 acres instructing her to sign a petition to the County Court.

12-9-1887   Administrator's deed from Margaretha Ebert administratrix of the estate of Conrad Ebert to Charles J. Reiss, made 11-25-1887. Defendants named were Margaret Neff, Conrad Neff, George Neff, and George Neff, Jr. for $555 for the 60 acres she and Conrad Ebert had purchased.

1-12-1888   Quit Claim deed from Charles J. Reiss and wife Eva who had bought the Ebert 60 acres at an estate auction signing it back to Margaretha Ebert.

9-15-1900	Warranty deed from Adam Rapp and Jacob Rapp to Frank J. Reiss for $40 for a strip of land 16.5 feet wide which became the west entrance lane.
8-11-1906	Warranty deed from George Neff Jr., Margaret Neff and her husband Conrad Neff Sr. (heirs of the late Margaret Ebert deceased) for $500 to George W. Reiss for the 20 acres the Eberts had purchased.
8-11-1906	Warranty deed from George Neff Jr., Margaretha Neff and her husband Conrad Neff Sr. (heirs of the late Margaret Ebert deceased) for $800 to Frank J. Reiss and Anna S. Reiss for the 40 acres the Eberts had purchased.

Our story continues with Sybilla and Frank living on the family farm with Katie and George from 1910 onward. They were big helps when their three grandsons were born – William on 5/6/1912, Franklin on Halloween night of 10/31/1915, and Irwin on 9/18/1917. As live-in grandparents they were both blessed and a blessing. Frank died on 11/21/1921 and Sybilla on 5/14/1930. They are buried in Franklin Cemetery in Smithton. They have a tombstone together and Frank also has this Civil War stone.

Here's a family photo probably taken at Frank's funeral. Back row left to right is William, Louis, Henry, and John. Front row is George with the tan, Sybilla with the same smile, and Margaret. Kate is missing.

Will, Kayla, and Ava, you can easily see why I consider your great great great grandmother Sybilla a matriarch. She was an outstanding mother and wife nurturing a young family under very challenging living conditions. She was a farm business partner, a teacher for her children, and an astute matchmaker. I'm sure you are all equally impressed and very proud.

Love, Granddad

Cousin Richard's 1968 Letter to Grandma

Dear Will, Kayla, Ava, and Blake,   February 4, 2013

Grand DD and I were in Oxford, England this past September to visit Christ Church College which is one of 39 colleges that make up the University of Oxford. That's where John Wesley was a student before he became a famous preacher and founded the Methodist Church about 1750. We were on a pilgrimage of Wesley sites in London, Bath, Bristol, Oxford, and Epworth. It was a fascinating tour and we learned a lot about Wesley and the Methodist Church which we joined in 1976.

In Oxford we also walked past Queens College where my cousin Richard Reiss was a student for a year or so in 1968. He was a smart guy and already had a degree in economics from Yale University, a year as a Fulbright Scholar in Berlin, and eventually most of a doctorate from Rockefeller University in New York. While he was at Oxford, he wrote the letter on the next page to our Grandmother Katie Reiss at the family farm south of Belleville, Illinois.

Here's what I found on Google about Oxford and Queen's College. The **University of Oxford** is the second oldest university in the world after the University of Bologna founded in 1088 in Italy. Although its exact date of foundation is unclear, there is evidence of teaching as far back as 1096.

Most undergraduate teaching at Oxford is organized around weekly tutorials at self-governing colleges and halls, supported by classes, lectures and laboratory work organized by University faculties and departments. Oxford consistently ranks among the top five universities in the world. For more than a century, it has served as the home of the Rhodes Scholarship, which brings students from a number of countries to study at Oxford as postgraduates or for a second bachelor's degree. Famous American alumni include President Bill Clinton and NBA basketball star and US Senator Bill Bradley.

Queens College was founded in 1341 by Robert de Eglesfield, chaplain to Queen Philippa, the wife of King Edward III of England, hence its name. Two of their more famous alumni are Edmund Halley who discovered the comet that bears his name and King Henry V of England. It has a beautiful campus with several old buildings.

Dear Grandma,   February 6, 1968

Sorry I've been negligent in my letter writing. I certainly did get your birthday present and letter. Thanks.

I like England very much, and the English people have been very nice to me. I know several families and have been often invited to dinner, etc., so I have been able to get a change of pace from straight school work all the time.

Oxford is a very demanding school and I have to work very hard. The school system is very different from ours in America, and it took me a while to adjust to what they wanted. There are few regular classes and lectures. I'm studying philosophy and psychology and I have one teacher for each subject for which I must write one essay a week. I have to take the essay and read to my tutor, as the teacher is called here, and then we discuss what I've written for an hour or so. To write this essay, I have to read many books and articles, which means that I have to spend lots of time in the library.

Oxford is a very lovely town and very old. My college, the Queen's College, was first started in 1341, more than six hundred years ago. Consequently, they have lots of old traditions, like you're supposed to wear a robe each time one goes to the tutor or when one eats dinner in the college. Most of the students live in the college itself, but since I already have a degree from an American university, I don't; so I'm living now in a house with two other Americans, one of which I knew when I went to school at Yale. I like Oxford very much and I'm very interested in what I'm studying, so I don't really mind having to work so hard. I'm actually working harder, I think, than I've ever worked before, even at Yale.

The town Oxford is not so big and has lots of lovely countryside around it, so I can get to go out and take walks and things through lovely farm villages. Some friends of mine from London were here last weekend, and we drove out and saw a beautiful old English castle.

I can't write much more now, as I'm still in process of moving into this house and I also have to write an essay in philosophy for my tutor tomorrow.

I hope things are all right with you and the farm. Mom and Dad have been writing me about it and all the traveling you are doing. I think that's wonderful. I hope I can do that when I'm your age.

                                                          Love, Richard

So, Will, Kayla, Ava, and Blake, never underestimate the value of a good education from a good school. It opens many doors for career opportunities as well as eventual networking with high-end fellow students and professors. The other lesson here is to write often to your grandparents so you don't have to start your letters with an apology.

Love, Granddad

Reiss Family Farm History by Richard Reiss in 2009

Dear Will, Kayla, Ava, and Blake,   March 6, 2023

My first cousin Richard Reiss wrote the following history for his children, Jesse and Rebecca, two years before he passed away on 3/4/2011 at age 66 from cancer. Maybe he knew he was sick and really wanted to create this document for his family. Here is what he wrote.

Love, Granddad

LETTERS TO MY CHILDREN

by Richard Reiss, March 2009

My very dear children,

I am afraid this chapter will be more of a test of true interest and patience as I anticipate it to be longer than the first chapter. Also I will be including more boring details and dates and names and who needs all that?

One strategy is I am NOT going to try to repeat all the early stories that have been told and retold and are amply included in GG's [Grandma Gerry] memoirs of Grandpa Frank as well as her own memoirs plus all the data and history being competently accumulated by cousin Steve, for which we all owe him a major debt of gratitude.

For example, I am not bothering to re-hash the story of Grandpa Frank's birthday cake which was a pumpkin covered with icing, or the time he grabbed a skunk by the tail and ended up having all his clothes burned and having to take a bath when it wasn't even Saturday.

The Grandpa Frank I knew was the *master* of the woods and fields of the farm. He could identify every tree, every plant and flower. He knew where to find an owl in a tree and he even ferreted out a gopher for us one time. If there was one thing he knew how to do, it was farm! And he was the farm manager for the Home farm, a job he took over from his mother once she and my Grandfather stopped farming.

This year, as you well know, is the 175th year of the Reiss Home Farm, having been in continuous ownership by Reisses since its inception in 1834. We have all made the little trek, even you two, to the little catholic cemetery in Hecker where an old weather beaten gravestone marks the grave of Johann Adam Reiss, the very first of the Reisses to come to America from Germany.

He went by boat to New Orleans in 1833 and then up river as far as Natchez and then in 1834 purchased the original 120 acres for $1.25 an acre. The log barn still on the farm dates from 1834 and according to Steve was even once used as a place of catholic worship in 1840, before Paderborn had its catholic church.

Adam died in 1849 in a cholera epidemic, but not before he had twice married and had fathered both sons and daughters. The main protagonist here, being the second son, Franz Josef, born in 1841. This was my father's grandfather who I never personally knew but I frequently heard the story that my father had been christened and had it on his birth certificate that his name was Frank Jacob Reiss. Well, your great-great-grandpa Frank decided that one Frank was enough and so our Grandpa Frank became "Franklin" or "little Frank." And so it stuck.

The story that always fascinated me about great-grandpa Frank was that he had fought in the Civil War in Sherman's army. Fortunately, he was *not* on that devastating march of destruction from Atlanta to the sea where the army destroyed *everything*. Rather he caught up with them after the army had reached the sea and were being transported north to South Carolina to march north through the Carolinas destroying what was left of the Confederate armies there.

Eventually they were given a victory march through Washington DC in front of President Lincoln, but the story told to me was that Franz Josef was looking the wrong way to see Lincoln and so missed him!

After the war, Frank got married and he and his wife, Anna Sybilla Feder Reiss, had eleven children, seven of which lived to maturity, the oldest being George William Reiss the father of our Grandpa Frank.

As a young man he had a thriving hog farm and was an enterprising go-getting farmer. He was into buying pieces of land. Sight unseen he bought 160 acres of land in Texas when some of the large Texas ranches, like the King Ranch, were being broken up and sold. It then wasn't until over 30 years later that finally Grandpa Frank went down to Texas to find out what this land was and what was being done with it. He later took "Pop" down so he could see his land also.

The Texas land is high plains and very dry unless you have a well for irrigation. Grandpa Frank had wells sunk and suddenly the land blossomed and produced large yields in cotton and sorghum. I tell you there was one thing Grandpa Frank could do, and that was farm and he could make things grow and he knew how to make something into a going enterprise that paid for itself and produced income for the rest of the family. And so it was with the Texas land.

"Pop" bought other pieces of land, too. He married Catherine Charlotte Luetzelschwab in 1911 when he was 38 and she was 21. At the time she was being a domestic servant in the home of Frank and Anna Sybilla, although the story I always heard was that she had first seen George when he was driving a team of horses to St. Louis, taking hogs to market. Apparently, he cut a dashing figure with the horses and caught the eye of Catherine or "Katie."

Their wedding photo was always on the wall of the house whenever we visited and I used to marvel at this photograph. There was "Pop" looking stiff and staring into the camera all dressed up and looking most uncomfortable. "Mom" on the other hand, looks beautiful and serene as she *stands* next to the sitting "Pop." I always looked at it as the classic wedding photo. I believe Steve now has it up in his house.

Well, buy land they did. They first bought about 160 acres of adjacent land from the Schaeffers, before even buying the original home farm from Frank and Anna. Well, it was great-grandma Reiss who scrimped and saved and paid off every debt they had, to the point the whole 360 acres is freehold, with no lien or claim by anyone else on any of it! Quite an achievement, especially when you also have to live through the Depression and a few other catastrophes that life threw in the road.

One such catastrophe was religious conflict. My father told me that the Reiss home was known for its discussions and that they had a reputation for deep conversations and thinking. Originally the family was Catholic. Then one day the local priest came to "Pop" and said he wanted one of his sons for the church to become a priest. "Pop" was not in agreement and his answer was to leave the Catholic Church at Paderborn and join the protestant German Evangelische Church in Floraville.

Then disaster. "Pop" had a large going hog farm that he was doing well with. But one night there was a disturbance and it was found that someone had thrown a cholera-infested chicken into the hog pen. The herd was basically wiped out and Grandpa Frank says that "Pop" never really recovered from it.

Still "Mom" scrimped and saved and paid the debts and the taxes and the bills. Then Grandpa Frank made the Texas land into an income producing operation. He created the Smithton Sportsman's Club. And Grandpa Frank took over general management of the farm and then at least things were in the black again.

So much for history. Are you still with me? One of my earliest memories this life is getting put on a train along with GG and Uncle George to go down and stay on the farm while our 601 E. Washington house was being built. I was probably around 3 years old. The farm was always a place we could go. And it was always going home.

The three brothers loomed large over everything. First there was Uncle Bill and his wife Anita. He somehow worked for Secony over in East St. Louis which is not something I understood. Anyway, the important figure was always, June Ann. Number one, she was taller than any of the rest of us and that gave her automatic status. Number two, the

Reisses have always had a reputation for smarts and June Ann was certainly held up for the rest of us to emulate as she won citywide scholarship exams getting her a full scholarship into Washington University, etc. etc. June Ann won this and she won that and we all admired June Ann! We really did!

Then there was Grandpa Frank. He not only won scholarships to the University of Illinois, he also held down two jobs to pay for his room and board while doing 4 years of university classes in three and a half years, not to mention getting straight A's in every subject so he finished university in the top 1% of his class as a "bronze tablet scholar" whose name can still be seen in the great library of the University of Illinois.

And so the pressure was on. You are a Reiss. Of course, you are smart. Look at your father. Look at your cousin. Of course, you have to get straight A's. That would lead to its own set of problems but that is not the story line we are following here.

I must say, we loved going to the farm. The food would be terrific, from the fried chicken to the pork sausage (I did not care for the "blutwurst") and all the German coffee cake you can eat. All the cousins you could want to play with. Woods and fields to go tramping through and in all the different seasons!

One activity was looking for arrowheads! There were two places on the farm where it was supposedly good to look. It was also good to look after there had been some fresh ploughing that turned up new earth. Both were places where it had been said that an arrowhead maker had had his teepee. Well, I never found much as I never really knew what to look for, but Uncle George turned up a major portion of a spearhead and I think someone else found something of an axe. The stuff was there to be found!

Then there was the time someone decided to seine the old pond near the farm buildings. The net was dragged across the pond, which netted three very large fish that had obviously lived there, avoiding being caught by us boys for years and one *very* big snapping turtle that had already taken a large bite out of one of the three fish. It was a very impressive sight for a young boy.

For a young boy, the farm was a place of abundance and no lack of things to do. I could go help Grandma Reiss collect eggs out of the henhouse (except I was always afraid of the hens pecking me as I was taking their eggs). I will never forget Grandma Reiss taking slops out to the hogs and calling them to eat it. If you've never heard a real hog call, it is like nothing else you have ever heard and to hear out of my sweet little grandmother's voice!

In the fall there were tons of nuts to gather – walnuts, hickory nuts, etc. There was always a large bowl with a nutcracker and "help yourself." And then after the first freeze, you went and found the persimmon trees where the fruit was now sweet and succulent to eat. Try it before the first freeze and you will not make that mistake again.

A trip to Millstadt was a trip to the German bakery shop there and cream horns for each of us! Friday and Saturday nights at Smithton were the fish fries and we all enjoyed fresh fried fish sandwiches.

There was one other thing that going to the farm meant, because the farm is only 35 miles outside St. Louis and all that affords. As a result we could to go to Cardinal baseball games. We frequently went to the zoo in Forrest Park which was famous for its chimpanzee act. Plus we could take trips on the Admiral up and down the Mississippi. The trip I remember most, the Mississippi was actually flooded on the Illinois side and the Admiral could go only so far on the river because the water was so high it wouldn't be able to get under the Bridge.

Then there was more baseball, the Arch, the confluence of the Missouri and the Mississippi and the launching of the Lewis-Clark expedition, the Cahokia Mounds, etc.

1959 the family went ancestor hunting. Grandpa Frank took a sabbatical year and planned a tour of farms and estates through Germany, Holland, and the United Kingdom. This is not the story of that trip, but there was one small portion that is relevant. Back in that Catholic cemetery in Hecker, the weather-beaten stone of Adam Reiss said that he emigrated from Germany from the little village of Obernau, near to Aschaffenburg which is in Hessen, just north of Bavaria. I looked it up in my atlas. You can find Aschaffenburg but Obernau is too small to note.

Apparently, the year before, Uncle Louis had been there to try and trace ancestors. The day we arrived in Obernau, there was a polka band contest going on with large steins to be awarded to the winners. We joined the festivities and enjoyed dancing polkas while noticing that there were a fair number of people named Reiss in the village. Reis is very common in Germany, but Reiss is nowhere near as common. We found one man who had helped Uncle Louis and he introduced us to a girl who said that her great-great grandfather was Anton Reiss and he had had a relative who had emigrated to America! Later Grandpa Frank got a copy of the church records and they clearly show that Anton had a brother, Johann Adam who had emigrated to America. We had found them!

The farm was a great wonderful playground for me. It is hard to imagine what it must have been like to grow up on the farm and experience all its privations. When I first went to the farm there was electricity but I don't know how long it had been there. The stove that Grandma Reiss used to cook on was a wood burning stove. I remember the big day she got a new stove, that was half-electric but also still allowed you to cook over a wood burning fire too!

I remember the hand crank for the phone and the party line where you had to know what your ring was (two longs and a short as I remember). The house was also filled still with kerosene and oil lamps for when the electricity went off. I could tell that indoor plumbing was a total luxury, and we still saved on hot water by having baths in large washtubs with water heated from a pot on the stove.

But you could see the stars from that farm and more than one night we lay out on the lawn to watch for the meteor showers at night.

I admire those three boys who grew up on the farm. They made the daily trek to Floraville to go to school, a one-room schoolhouse with eight grades packed into one room and one teacher, Oscar Probst. Not to mention the fact that you came into the school speaking only German and had to learn and speak only English at school. I guess you had to want to learn and do something to improve your life.

I have given you this much picture of the farm as it is part of your legacy too. Grandpa Frank put it there and it is more there now than it has ever been. The Smithton Sportsman's Club was my father's creation and brilliant one as well. I, for one, really like having my own state park on the farm. The farm is today, more beautiful than I have ever seen it. For this I credit Bret Cude and the management by Farmer's National who have done a lot to clean the place up and get rid of all the liabilities it was carrying. I can't tell you how relieved I am that the liabilities are gone now.

My father talked to me many times about the future of the farm. For one thing he had long since wanted to sell the Texas land while he had it as a going concern, but that was not to be. As I have told you both, Uncle Irv never sold a piece of land in his life. He only bought land. It is possible that Steve has a similar record but I don't really know other than I do know he does have land around Peoria, plus he is the trustee for the land Uncle Irv owned.

I am delighted that both of you have been able to connect up more to the farm and appreciate just what a beautiful creation it is, thanks mainly to Great-Grandma Reiss and Grandpa Frank.

Ultimately the two of you will have to decide what you will do with the farm. My own recommendation is that whatever arrangement is ended up with, that it contains a proviso for the upkeep and maintenance of the memorials. Meanwhile I think we all should support Steve in his efforts to preserve the farm and organize the family history. It is a great favor to us all what he is doing!

Well, are you still reading or did I lose you somewhere? Let's just consider it one of those chapters that had to be written. . . . . . . Love, Dad

Richard Reiss in Yale Alumni Magazine

Richard Franklin Reiss was born November 21, 1944 and raised in Urbana, Illinois. He graduated from Yale University in 1966 with a degree in economics. He studied in Berlin for a year on a Fulbright Scholarship and then graduated from Oxford University with a degree in philosophy. Richard was working on his PhD at Rockefeller University in New York when he discovered and embraced the writings and philosophy of the Church of Scientology. He devoted himself fulltime to that ministry in 1973 and eventually became the senior minister of the church's headquarters in Clearwater Florida, a position he held for a quarter of a century. His primary duty was to oversee the spiritual counseling by church ministers worldwide. He was personally known and loved by tens of thousands. Richard died on March 4, 2011 and is survived by his wife of 36 years Cala, son Jesse, and daughter Rebecca.

Grandma's Sausage and Eggs

Dear Will, Kayla, Ava, and Blake,   July 8, 2013

My grandmother Katie Reiss would be your great great grandma. She was the matriarch of our extended family even before she married my grandfather George "Pop" Reiss on April 16, 1911. That's because she was a domestic housekeeper living on the Reiss farm with the Frank Reiss family (including bachelor son George) when the Federal Census was taken on April 25, 1910. They misspelled her last name as Luietcelschwab instead of Luetzelschwab. That's how/where she met Pop in the first place. They married a year later and raised three sons who married and raised six grandchildren. Grandma was a saint to all those descendants. You have two of her five-year diaries in book form as <u>Granger, Quilter, Grandma, Matriarch</u> (1944 – 1948) and <u>Quilter, Granger, Grandma, Matriarch</u> (1949 – 1953).

Grandma's world-class breakfast that we had almost every morning during our quarterly visits was pork sausage and scrambled eggs. Yummy, yummy, yummy!!! She cooked that on a kitchen stove which burned corncobs and small bits of wood that Pop cut and split. Later on Grandma got a new stove but still one half of it was a wood fire and the other half was electric. She preferred the wood side.

BURGERSANDBOURBON.COM

I remember we occasionally had Cheerios for breakfast on the home farm. I thought they were tasty and special but my mom apparently didn't care for them and never bought them back home in Sullivan, Indiana. So I grew up thinking Cheerios was a local breakfast cereal available only in the Belleville and St. Louis area. Wrong!!!

Anyway, I remember making trips to two butcher shops in Belleville and later to one in Millstadt to buy pork sausage, summer sausage, blood sausage, head cheese, and other German meats to be eaten at the home farm or taken back to our home in Sullivan. My favorite butcher shop was Weyhaupt's and then Streck's, both in Belleville. My ranking was based on the smells, sawdust on the floors, and the friendliness of the butchers rather than on the quality of their German meat products. Decades later Schubert's in Millstadt became my favorite.

I couldn't find any history on Weyhaupt's other than their address of **Weyhaupt Brothers Packing Company** at 1510 Lebanon Avenue, Belleville, IL 62221.

Streck Packing Company is at 401 W. Washington Street, Belleville IL, 62220. Not much history here either except this advertisement in the 1956 Floraville Telephone Directory. Three brothers, Ernest, Clarence and Adolph Streck, many years ago entered into a partnership to engage in the meat packing business in and about Belleville, Illinois. On January 31, 1928 the three brothers, together with their wives, executed a written partnership agreement that provided for the partnership to continue in case of the death of one of the brothers. Well one of the brother's wives died and he remarried. Then he died and that second wife initiated a lawsuit which got kinda messy. No thanks.

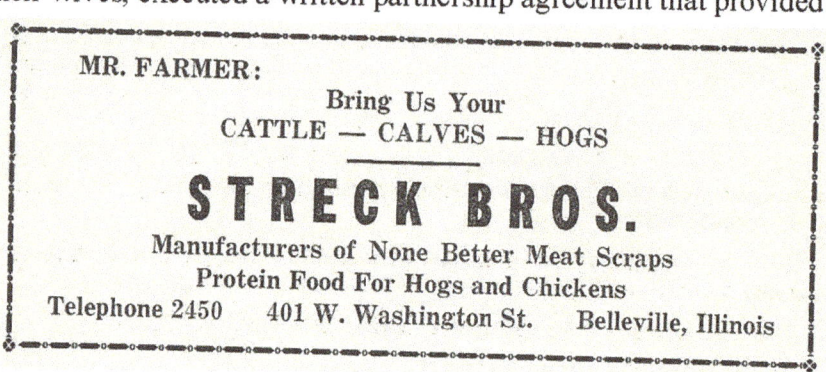

MR. FARMER:

Bring Us Your
CATTLE — CALVES — HOGS

STRECK BROS.

Manufacturers of None Better Meat Scraps
Protein Food For Hogs and Chickens

Telephone 2450   401 W. Washington St.   Belleville, Illinois

Schubert's Packing Company is at 700 S Breese Street, Millstadt, IL 62260. Their website has the following paragraph – Schubert's Packing Co., Inc., Millstadt Illinois owners Larry and Marlene (Mabel) Schubert have been in the meat processing business for 29 years. Their wholesale and retail operation starts at slaughtering and includes fresh and cured meats, homemade sausages, German style specialty meats and sausages, and deer processing. State and national award winning products include country style smoked hams (bone-in and boneless) and bacon, summer sausage, smoked jerky, bologna, braunschweiger, smoked turkey, bratwursts, and Schubert's Smokies. Their Hermann, Missouri Wurstfest award winners include braunschweiger (2 time winner of the Best of the Show), head cheese, liver sausage, blood sausage, smoked jerky, bratwurst, summer sausage, and Schubert's bockwurst (an old German favorite). As a result of Larry's achievements, in the summer of 2004, Larry and his son Bryan, were invited to Gross Bieberau, Hessen, Germany to prepare meat products such as bratwurst and cut pork steaks for an 'American Festival in Germany'.

Here's another tidbit from the obituary of Larry Schubert's father, Walter: Walter Kermit "Red" Schubert, 88, of Millstadt, IL, born Sept. 29, 1923, in Millstadt, IL, passed away Thursday, July 26, 2012, at his residence. Walter had worked for 40 years as a foreman/meat cutter at **Streck Packing Company in Belleville, IL, then he worked at Schubert Packing Company** in Millstadt, IL. Walter was a member of the Meat Cutters Local 545, Modern Woodmen, and Zion Evangelical Church in Millstadt, IL. Walter was an avid coon hunter. He and his friends were the charter members of the Millstadt Coon Hunters Association. He loved gardening and nurturing his pecan and walnut trees, and if you needed a well "witched", "Red" was the one to call. He enjoyed watching the St. Louis Cardinals and he loved visiting with his grandchildren and great-granddaughters.

Maybe it's obvious now that good German pork sausage was the foundation of Grandma's special breakfasts. She taught me how to use a fork to make lots of holes in the pork sausage as it was cooking so the oils could drain out. She taught me how to make scrambled eggs by not turning them until bubbles half an inch in diameter started rising from the egg/milk slurry. She was adamant that stirring or turning scrambled eggs too soon would lead to watery eggs that kinda looked like yellow cottage cheese. Not good. I have followed Grandma's scrambled egg advice for 60 years now and received lots of compliments, mostly from friends who didn't think I could do anything in a kitchen, let alone make good looking and tasty scrambled eggs.

So, Will, Kayla, Ava, and Blake, that's my story and I'm sticking to it. I'm very pleased that Grandma taught me how to make great sausage and scrambled eggs breakfasts and that I paid good attention as an eight-year old. An hour after I sent this Granddad's Mondays this morning, Will and I were busy on his first lesson cooking scrambled eggs. The photos below tell the story.

Love, Granddad

Harvesting Wheat on the Reiss Family Farm

Dear Will, Kayla, and Ava,   July 15, 2013

Exactly 130 years ago yesterday on July 14, 1883 your great great great grandfather Frank Reiss received 46 pounds of binder twine that he had ordered the previous month. Price was $0.20 per pound.

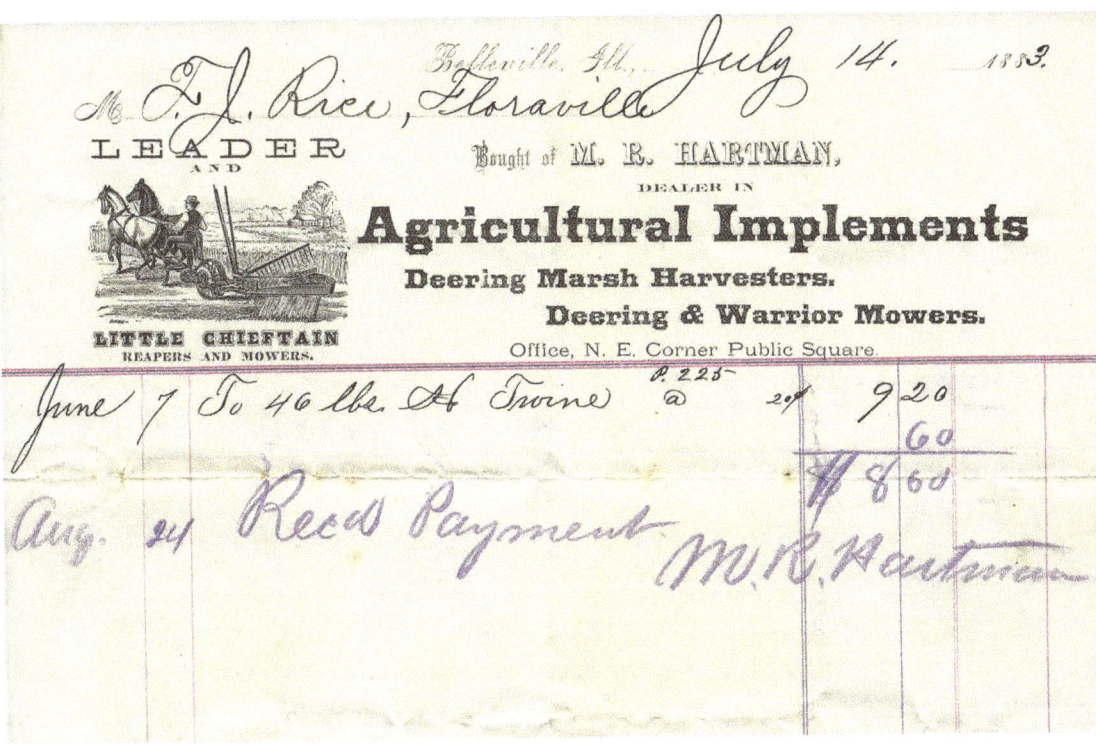

The **reaper-binder**, or **binder**, was a farm implement that improved upon the reaper. The binder was invented in 1872 by Charles Withington. In addition to cutting the small-grain crop, it would also tie the stems into small bundles, or sheaves. These sheaves were then 'shocked' into conical stooks, resembling small tipis, to allow the grain to dry for several days before being threshed. Refer to my Granddad's Mondays of 4/29/2013 about "bringing in the sheaves."

Withington's original binder used wire to tie the bundles. There were various problems with using wire and it was not long before William Deering invented a binder that used twine and a knotter (invented in 1858 by John Appleby).

Early binders were horse-drawn and powered by a bull wheel. Later models were tractor-drawn. The implement had a reel and a sickle bar, like a modern grain head for a combine harvester, or combine. The cut stems would fall onto a canvas, which conveyed the crop to the binding mechanism. This mechanism bundled the stems of grain and tied a piece of twine around the bundle. Once tied, it was discharged from the back of the binder.

With the replacement of the threshing machine by the combine harvester, the binder became almost obsolete. Some grain crops such as oats are now cut and formed into windrows with a swather. With other grain crops such as wheat, the grain is now mostly cut and threshed by a combine in a single operation, while the binder is still in use at small fields or outskirts of mountain areas.

Here's Frank Reiss and his son George harvesting wheat with a reaper-binder about 1910. My grandfather George is walking with a sheave of cut and bound wheat in his hands. He is piling a dozen or so sheaves into stooks or shocks. Below is what the fully harvested field might look like while waiting for the wheat to dry before it is hauled to the threshing floor in a barn.

Frank Reiss and son George harvesting wheat on Reiss Farm about 1910

Here are the Reiss brothers, Frank on the left and my dad Irwin on the right, after a hard day in the wheat field stacking sheaves into shocks behind them. The picture dates from about 1927. Notice the bib overalls and straw hats to create a little shade.

Franklin and Irwin Reiss about 1927

Below are two modern binders. The one on the right is pulled by a tractor instead of horses. There is a sickle bar cutter along the front edge of those white canvas panels. The cut wheat falls backward and the canvas belt rotates toward the binder operator where it is automatically tied into bundles or sheaves which fall out the right side.

That binder operator is probably not actually needed since the whole machine should be automatic. Here is one old farmer's interesting story - About 1905 an Illinois farmer commented that when he first began farming, "It took ten men with cradle scythes to cut and bind my grain. Now our hired girl gets on the seat of a self-binder and does the whole business." Will and Kayla, refer back to my Granddad's Mondays of April 29, 2013 to learn about cradle scythes.

Will, Kayla, and Ava, the binder below is used in small rice paddies in Asia. It harvests one row of rice at a time. The operator walks behind the machine and the bound sheaves are ejected along his right side.

Oh, and binder twine – today you can buy it from Shenzhen, China at $2.00 for a 2.5 kilogram spool FOB the US. That's $.36/lb instead of the $.20/lb it was 130 years ago. Just click on "add to cart" and buy it with Paypal. How times have changed!!!

Love, Granddad

One-Room School in Floraville, Illinois

Dear Will and Kayla,

September 16, 2013

This coming Wednesday would have been the 95th birthday of your great grandfather, Irwin H. Reiss. He and his two older brothers, Bill and Frank, were all very smart young men thanks in large part to their outstanding teacher, Oscar Probst. Irwin and Frank had Mr. Probst as a teacher for all eight years but their older brother Bill who started school in the fall of 1918 had a different teacher for the first two years. All three boys walked 1.7 miles from the Reiss family farm west to Floraville for instruction in a one-room school. My dad used to boast that it was uphill both directions and really cold in the winters.

This August 4, 1955 newspaper article from the *Millstadt Enterprise* mentions an upcoming celebration for Oscar J. Probst who taught at the Floraville School for 17 years from 1920 to 1937. Mr. Probst retired 58 years ago this coming Wednesday on September 18, 1955. He was a highly regarded public servant. Notice that Frank Reiss is mentioned in the fifth paragraph as a professor at the University of Illinois.

This Floraville School is also where your great great grandfather, George Reiss, was educated as a youngster as were six of his ten siblings. The other four died before they reached school age. My grandfather served as the clerk of the Floraville school board for over 20 years so you know that education was a big priority in his family.

The photo below was taken by Frank Reiss in 1962. A few years later the building was sold to a family who converted it into a private home. Several rooms were added in the front and along one side but the original structure still survives.

Floraville Community to Honor Oscar Probst, Retired Teacher

Floraville is getting ready for a homecoming that will be unusual in its aspect as to what such affairs represent. This will be a reunion of students of four schools in the Floraville area. In reality it will be Oscar J. Probst Day and the committee in charge expects to make it the biggest homecoming ever held in the little burg in the south end of Millstadt township.

The reunion was suggested by a number of former pupils of the Floraville School and it immediately met with favor resulting in a committee of five being selected to plan the affair.

Oscar J. Probst had taught for thirty-five year and retired several years ago. He resides in Floraville where he delights to meet his friends and is especially fond of reverting to former days of his teaching career. In that time there were hundreds who entered school under him and were followed by their children.

His first position was at the Robertson School where he taught in 1902-03 and 1904. Then he had charge of the Saxtown School 1905-7; Vogel School 1908-9; Floraville 1910-11; Vogel 1913-17; Saxtown 1919-20 and again at Floraville where he finished in 1937 after seventeen years of continuous service.

During these years many students received their fundamental education who have found high places in the educational field. Among these are outstanding, Dr. Wm. Schneider, now instructor at Southern Illinois University, Carbondale; Prof. Franklin Reiss, an instructor at University of Illinois; Norman Boeker, Principal of Canteen School and many more who have made their mark in Engineering, industrial and agricultural fields. His influence has remained with the youngsters as is shown in the social life as it is lead in Floraville. They have live organizations such as Granges, 4-H Clubs, Fraternal, Musical Groups and Church organizations and they are very active. Musically inclined, Oscar Probst taught all his students the rudiments of music and for many years directed the Community Band.

The committee is somewhat handicapped in their search for names of pupils of the various schools which Mr. Probst taught in that some of the records are lost or incomplete. They will appreciate

OSCAR J. PROBST

assistance from former pupil spreading the news of the reu to their classmates. Leroy Fra 911 Wabash avenue, Belle Phone ADams 3-5793 is the retary of the committee.

The date set for this big O J. Probst Day is September 18 friends and the general public cordially invited. It will be in form of a basket picnic at M.V Park, Floraville. No special gram will be arranged althol some of his friends will be ca upon for short talks. Most of day will be spent in the spiri homecoming and renewing pleasant school day memories.

Below is an article from the *St. Louis Post-Dispatch* on June 14, 1964 about the closing of the Floraville one-room school –

The school bell has tolled for the last time in Floraville. Residents of the Illinois community will no longer hear the sonorous summons to study nor see the students scurrying from the playground into the brick building. The bell will be replaced next fall by the toot of a horn as school busses transport the youngsters to a consolidated school at nearby Smithton.

The children were generally happy about the change as they look forward to the newness and excitement of a larger school. One girl, however, who had attended several large and small schools, said she preferred the smallest of them all – Floraville. She enjoyed being able to know all the other students and to study under a "real ding dong teacher – the best."

One-room schools were once the backbone of rural education in the United States. In them, one teacher had to work long and hard to teach 20, 30, or more pupils in all eight grades. In past decades, before the push for consolidation, the county and state fortified the country schools with roving specialists – county nurses, music and art teachers, audio-visual specialists – and with radio programs directed at the one-room schools. As the number of these schools dwindled, however, these services were dropped.

In Floraville, local sentiment backed by the fear of higher taxes in the consolidated districts helped the one-room country school to survive as long as it did. In 1963, however, the state did not issue its usual certificate of recognition to Floraville, thus posing the threat of the end of state aid. Floraville residents decided it was time to give up their school, which had flourished for over 50 years.

The one-room school has its disadvantages. Small classes eliminate much of the competition between students that educators feel is important. Classes are necessarily short and study projects limited because of the many demands on the lone teacher. Yet, an inquisitive youngster could obtain an excellent education in a one-room school. There was always the intriguing opportunity to eavesdrop on class discussions of the upper grades or to browse among the histories, novels, and anthologies meant for the older students.

Undoubtedly, much has been gained by the consolidation of rural schools, but just as certainly something has been lost. A one-room school was always a family affair – especially during the Christmas programs, the Arbor Day outings, the spring picnics. The big disadvantage of a one-room school – its smallness – was also its charm.

The last recess of the last day of school is a joyous occasion for the boys, girls, and a tag-along dog at the Floraville School, 10 miles southwest of Belleville. It was a sad day, however, for the lone teacher who had worked for 15 years in the little brick building and the many alumni of the school who still live in the tiny Illinois community. Floraville, the last of the one-room schools in St. Clair County (once there were about 100), will not re-open in the fall. Its 17 pupils will ride busses to a nearby consolidated school. As elsewhere in rural America, the one-room school will become merely a nostalgic memory. In 1945, before the push towards consolidated districts began, there were 8,045 one-room schools in Illinois. In the 1963-64 term, there were only 15.

So, Will and Kayla, one-room schoolhouses had their place in history. They were effective and practical for small and somewhat isolated communities before the days of school buses. Some parents today choose to home school their children which is kinda like a modern version of a one-room school but without all the friendships and memories from recess and special programs.

Love, Granddad

161

George Reiss Penmanship Lessons

Dear Will, Kayla, and Ava,   September 16, 2013

Your great great grandfather, George Reiss, was an intelligent man and a very successful farmer in St. Clair County, Illinois. He doubled the size of the Reiss Family Farm and was an astute businessman and community leader. You would be impressed and proud if you met him today.

George accomplished much even though he had only four years of public education. That was at the one-room school in Floraville, about 1.7 miles west of where he was born in a log cabin on the family farm on April 22, 1873. He was the fourth of eleven children but the oldest to reach adulthood.

Here are two of 109 pages where young George practiced penmanship by carefully writing 21 copies of the first line which had been written by his teacher. He would have used a quill pen possibly made from a turkey feather and liquid ink. The year was about 1883 when George was age 10. He would have officially been in the fourth grade but since it was a one-room school he probably eavesdropped on the higher grades. I'm sure he was "smarter than a fifth grader" to quote that popular television show.

His pages were 7" by 9.5" but I shrunk two of them for this story. It looks like they were also practicing capital "M's" on both pages because that letter is repeated at the end of each line.

Some of the other phrases which were copied appear below. They were used to teach young minds about more than just penmanship.

Many men have many minds, Today will never be tomorrow, Strike while the iron is hot, Penmanship is an art, Contentment leads to happiness, We live in the state of Illinois, St. Clair is the name of our county, Reading makes a versed man, Always have a plan to work by, Never go to extremes in anything, Floraville is a small village, Do not lose nor sell your books, A good son will help his father, Never come tardy to school, Aim at improvement in writing, From nothing, nothing comes, Good manners procure respect,

Make hay while the sun shines M. *(repeated in cursive handwriting, many times down the left column)*

Kindness comes from the heart, Much depends upon promptness, Nothing ventured, nothing have, Occupation prevents temptation, Sell not virtue to purchase riches, The honest man need not repent, Ches. Arthur is president of the US, Washington was our first president, Daniel Webster was a great orator, Today will never dawn again, Christmas will soon be here, Tomorrow may be never, May is the month of roses, Our earth is a great sphere, Every beginning is different, We do not like to see our own sins, Live coals of fire glow with heat, Never stop trying to improve, Our time is worth a good deal, Use one kind of ink for writing, Tea is the leaf of a bush, Gentle means are often best, Children should not whisper in school

Grand DD and I were in Scotland last year and visited the Highland Folk Museum near Kingussie and Newtonmore. It was a series of buildings that had been moved to a 40-acre site. My favorite was a one-room school which was full of visiting fourth-graders like your grandfather George above.

We paid very special attention to what the teacher was saying and to what the students were doing. We even did the same penmanship lesson ourselves with a quill pen. Here are the pictures. Notice the old school desks and the small slates the children are writing on. The blackboard behind the teacher has the plans for the day. Notice there is both a recess and a physical education lesson.

The last picture below is my penmanship lesson where the teacher gave me a grade of 7.5 out of a possible 10. He didn't like that ink smudge in the upper left which was caused when Grand DD tried to write on my paper. I told the teacher it wasn't my mistake so he wrote in red – "blames wife!"

Will, Kayla, and Ava, we already have old school desks for you in our basement and in our log cabin. I even have a real turkey feather found in our yard which we'll make into a quill pen. Grand DD used to teach fourth grade so some day soon you two will have your own authentic penmanship lessons here. Be aware that you'll have to do it without spell check, texting, and Google. Your great great grandfather George would have been very proud!!!

Love, Granddad

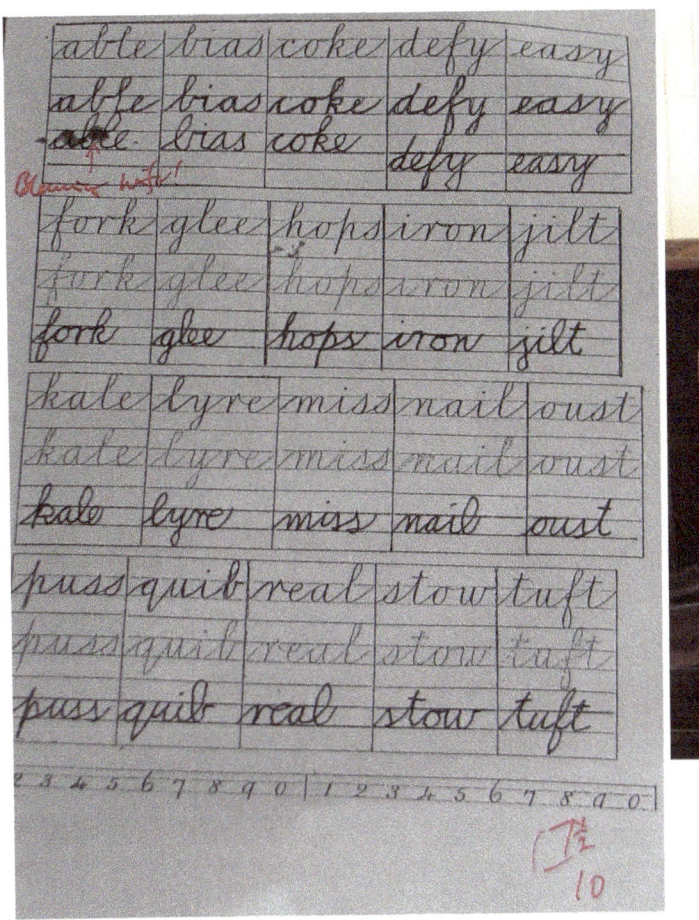

DC Electricity Comes to the Reiss Farm in 1940

Dear Will, Kayla, Ava, and Blake,   December 9, 2013

My Uncle Frank Reiss took this picture in 1948. The caption on his slide mentions the wind charger which is the taller of two electrical poles on the center right. You can make out a large propeller on the top which is turned by the wind to generate 6-volt electrical current that goes to a rechargeable battery inside the house. This home was built in 1940 and was partially wired for DC and then AC electricity.

Our family had traveled from Sullivan, Indiana to the home farm to celebrate Grandma's 60th birthday on March 25. Here are two entries from my Grandma Katie's diary in March 1950.

Fri 24 – Cold winds, fair. Henry and the boys worked on the yard fence, tore down the old brooder house, and set new posts. Irwin & Mary and family came.

Sat 25 – Fair, windy, and getting warmer. Henry, Harold, and Lavern cut down the big wind charger pole and put up a telephone pole for the private line.

I remember this day in 1950 because all the big people wanted all us little people to stand way back when they cut down the pole. That's because the wind charger had not been used since late

1945 when AC electricity was brought to the home farm via the other tall pole in this picture with the connecting wires coming from the left.

By the 1930s windmills were widely used to generate electricity on farms in the United States where distribution systems had not yet been installed. Used to replenish battery storage banks, these machines typically had generating capacities of a few hundred watts to several kilowatts.

The brand name of my grandparents' wind charger was Wincharger. Here's what I found on Google. The most widely-used small wind generator produced for American farms in the 1930s was a two-bladed horizontal-axis machine manufactured by the Wincharger Corporation. It had a peak output of 200 watts. Blade speed was regulated by curved air brakes near the hub that deployed at excessive rotational velocities. These machines were still being manufactured in the US during the 1980s. In 1936, the US started a rural AC electrification program that killed the natural market for wind-generated DC power, since network power distribution provided more dependable usable energy for farms. Funny thing, now we're going back to monster wind farms to help power the grid!

Albers Propeller Company – In 1927, John and Gerhard Albers started experimenting with wind driven generators and eventually established the Albers Propeller Co. in Cherokee, Iowa. They developed a small wind generator called the "Wincharger" to charge 6 volt radio batteries. The Wincharger was a local hit and the company grew to three employees and production increased to 6 units per day.

Wincharger Corporation – In December, 1934 the Albers brothers together with two partners formed the Wincharger Corporation to manufacture their wind chargers at the former Hawkeye Truck plant in Sioux City, Iowa. Later that year, executives from the Zenith Radio Corporation visited Wincharger unannounced, placed an order for 50,000 Winchargers, and took a 51 percent stake in the company. The small Wincharger radio unit would become the most produced wind generator over the next 60 years and the Wincharger name would immediately become an important force in the wind electric plant business. The new larger 30,000-square-foot manufacturing plant had 52 full time employees, the product line was expanded to include larger full home units, and daily production increased to 200 units. Zenith bought the remaining 49 percent of Wincharger, and sales of radio and full home power plants were maintained under the difficult market circumstances resulting from federal rural electrification.

Wincharger Radio Plants – In time, production of the radio charger soared to 2,000 units a day at a price of $44 apiece, or even better at $15 per unit with the purchase of a special Zenith radio with a single rechargeable 6 volt battery. The unit was a two-blade, upwind, direct-drive design.

A tail vane was fixed in place by a length of angle iron to the back of the generator to point it into the wind. A small four-post tower with a turntable, slip ring assembly, and mounting feet for easy installation on the roof of an outbuilding were included. It was not a good idea to mount the Wincharger on the roof of the house since the roof would act as a sounding board to the point of being intolerable. Wires connected the generator to a simple relay panel in the house and to the radio battery. When the wind blew, the battery would charge and the radio would provide continuous entertainment on demand. Since the battery was usually kept charged, the owner would frequently add a few light bulbs to make good use of the abundant wind energy.

Wincharger Power Plants – Before too long, a larger 32-volt, gear-driven "Famous" model with a 10-foot diameter propeller rated at 650 watts was offered to the farm electric plant market. This model was similar to the small model in that it was a 2-blade design with the Wincharger patented air-brake governor. It sold for $69.95, plus tower and battery when it was first introduced.

Will, Kayla, Ava, and Blake, isn't this a fascinating story? The wind made it possible to listen to a radio and do your school homework after dark. In 1940 you would have used a pencil, quill pen, or fountain pen because ballpoint pens we're really perfected until 1943. There were no televisions or computers or heated wet ones. How times have changed!!!

Love, Granddad

AC Electricity Comes to the Reiss Farm on November 17, 1945

Dear Will, Kayla, Ava, and Blake,   December 9, 2013

You know from my other Granddad's Mondays story of today that the Reiss farm home was built in 1940 and was partially wired for DC electricity from a 6 volt rechargeable battery. That battery was charged by a wind charger on a tall pole about 50 feet southeast of the house. You see large wind farms in many places around the country today. It's the same idea as before except that modern wind farms generate AC electricity. The wind charger my grandparents had generated DC electricity which is the same current stored in your car battery. DC stands for "direct current" and AC stands for "alternating current."

Limited DC electricity was the way it was for my grandparent's first five years in their new house until late 1945. Here are entries from Grandma Katie's diary about the coming of AC electricity.

February 1945

Sat 3 – We were at Electric meeting at Waterloo.

September 1945

Fri 7 – The Schilling boys wired our basement today.

Wed 19 – Ludger Schilling was here all day to put in switch box and wire basement and tested all lights.

October 1945

Mon 29 – The Illinois Power men staked off our line today.

November 1945

Wed 7 – The poles for our electric line came today.

Thurs 8 – The electric men brought the hole digger and things.

Fri 9 – The electric men dug the hole for the pole.

Sat 17 – Mr. Lane hooked up our electric this morning. Lights are fine.

January 1946

Mon 7 – Romuald Schilling was here to put in our front porch light.

March 1946

Wed 20 – The boys finished wiring the house and Mr. Dengler brought the pressure pump and connected the sink.

May 1946

Thurs 2 – Rain. Geo was grinding a lot of corn with his electric motor.

July 1946

Tues 30 – Hot. We were at Belleville to get electric stuff for the other house. Towards evening. Ludger came and did the wiring.

March 1948

Fri 12 – Ludger put a light above my sink today.

March 1950

Sat 25 – Fair, windy, and getting warmer. Henry, Harold, and Lavern cut down the big wind charger pole and put up a telephone pole for the private line.

Will, Kayla, Ava, and Blake, now you know the electrical history of our home farm. The tall pole in this picture is DC and the shorter one is AC. The next page shows my grandparents application for AC service. Note my grandfather's robust signature.

Love, Granddad

Aerial Photo of the Reiss Family Farm, Circa 1941

Dear Will, Kayla, Ava, and Blake,   December 16, 2013

Happy Birthday, Ava. You were born yesterday at 3:45 this afternoon. Welcome to your first of many Granddad's Mondays stories.

Here is an aerial photograph of the Reiss Family Farm looking southeast that was taken in the fall of 1941 to 1944. There is no snow and no leaves on the trees which mean it was taken either in the fall, winter, or spring. You can see a white sheet on the ground east of the right side 1940 house which is covering parts of Grandma Reiss' garden against frost which probably means the time is fall rather than spring. There is smoke from a wood-burning kitchen stove or furnace coming up from that roof. The AC electricity lines arrived in late 1945 so this picture was taken before then. The grass yard looks fully established on the 1940 house so at the earliest the picture was taken in 1941.

A month ago I showed the original 11 by 14 colorized print to Lavern and Lucille Lang for their input. They started as our farm tenants in 1954 so everything you see here predates them. They said the angled roof on the west side of the log cabin was a brooder house where hatchling chicks are kept warm and fed. They saw the outhouse but said they always had indoor plumbing. They said the partially visible building on the near right corner was both a hog house and a chicken house during their tenure. You can see hogs at the left end of the dark strip across the bottom.

I also showed the original print to Marcella Klein whose son Al is now our farm tenant. Marcella was born on 2/20/1920 so she is 93.5 years old and still as sharp as a tack. Her parents were Frank and Clara Shilling who lived a quarter mile south on the adjoining farm which you can barely see at the top of this photo. Marcella married Ignatius "Boobie" Klein in 1940 and moved half a mile to the adjacent farm west. The Kleins, Shillings, and my grandparents were all the best of friends. When I showed the print to Marcella, the first thing she immediately said is, "Yes, I can see it." She was referring to a small window box in the north wall of Grandma's summer kitchen (balloon 4) where Pop had built a little rack for short term storage of milk, meat, and cheese since that was the coolest side of the summer kitchen. Here's a fuzzy blow up of that window box.

Here's the same aerial photo but with callout balloons for these captions.

1. Log cabin built in 1838 by Adam Reiss
2. Brooder house for young chickens on the back side of the log cabin
3. Old house built in 1889 by Frank and Anna Reiss
4. Summer kitchen attached to the 1889 house

5. Old chicken and hog house built by Frank Reiss and his son George
6. Outhouse for the 1889 house
7. Log granary built in 1838 by Adam Reiss
8. Two story barn built about 1920 by George Reiss
9. Wooden storage shed
10. Corn crib
11. Machine shed
12. New house built in 1940 by George and Katie Reiss
13. Wind charger which generated 6 volt electricity at about 200 watts
14. Grain grinding shed and single garage for Model T car
15. New brooder house
16. New chicken house
17. Fruit orchard

Besides the photograph, there is significant people history in four of these buildings. Here's a summary using the same balloons.

- 1. This is the log cabin where Adam died in 1849 and his first wife Mary died in 1838. It is where six of Adam's children were born and where the last one died. It is where ten of eleven children born to Adam's son Frank Reiss and his wife Anna were born and where four of them died.

- 1. and 7. These are the log cabin and log granary where Adam Reiss hosted Catholic worship services from about 1838 to 1841. My guess is they switched between buildings depending on the season and number of worshipers. They may be the "church" where Adam married first wife Mary in 1838 and married his second wife Margaret in 1840.

- 3. This is the 1889 house where the youngest child of Frank and Anna Reiss was born in 1890. This home is where Frank Reiss and his wife Anna died. This is where three sons of Frank's son George and his wife Catherine were born. The last of those was my dad Irwin.

- 12. This 1940 house is where George Reiss died.

- There is no callout balloon but the far upper left is the southeast corner of the 160-acre farm as it existed in 1854. That corner is where Margaret Reiss and her second husband Conrad Ebert built a small house such that her son Frank and his expanding family could take over the 1838 log cabin.

Will, Kayla, Ava, and Blake, our extended family is very fortunate to still own this family farm after nearly 180 years and to have lots of original documents and family correspondence. I'm trying to make all that available to relatives through a series of family history books. Hopefully the next milestone event for all of us is a bicentennial family reunion in 2034. You guys are in charge!!!

Love, Granddad

Log Cabin and Log Granary in 1838

Dear Will and Kayla,   April 23, 2012

This is a picture of the log cabin built on the Reiss Family Farm south of Belleville, Illinois in 1838 by your great great great great grandfather, Johann Adam Reiss. He is your grandfather's grandfather's grandfather. He went by Adam instead of by Johann.

Adam was born on May 7, 1804 in Obernau, Bavaria, Germany which today is a suburb of the much larger city of Aschaffenburg. He sailed for America in 1833 and landed in New Orleans. Economic and political times were difficult in Germany so he was striking out on his own for farming opportunities in the new world. He worked his way north along the Mississippi River and may have spent his first winter in Natchez, Mississippi. In April 1834 (178 years ago this month) he arrived in St. Clair County, Illinois and bought his first 40 acres of land from a famous speculator named Thomas Houghan, but that's the subject of another of Granddad's Mondays.

Adam built this log cabin for himself. Note the brick chimney above the roof which means there was a fireplace inside for heat. The cabin was about 15 by 18 feet so it was very small compared to modern homes. Adam married Mary Schuessler on May 15, 1838. She may have also been from Obernau so perhaps they were sweethearts back in Germany such that his coming to America to establish a farm and home (with her to follow when it was ready) was their joint master plan. But sadly Mary died in this cabin during the birth of their first child, John, on December 11, 1838. The baby survived despite having no mother to nurse him and the onset of winter.

Well, God provided another very nice woman who became Adam's second wife. Her name was Margaritha Basler, but she went by her Americanized name of Margaret. She was born in Zeihen, Switzerland near the Germany border on October 22, 1818 and immigrated to St. Clair County with her parents and siblings in 1839. Margaret married Adam on September 10, 1840. They both spoke German in this, their log home. Adam and Margaret had five children in the cabin but the last one died in infancy. Adam died in this cabin on May 23, 1849 of cholera which was an epidemic in the area.

On April 2, 1850 Margaret then married Conrad Ebert who may have also been a childhood friend of Adam's from Obernau who had also immigrated to St. Clair County and lived near the Reiss farm. Margaret and Conrad were probably already good friends because they married less than a year after Adam died and here was Margaret with five children under age eleven. Conrad must have been a real saint of a guy to take on an instant family and a farm which by then consisted of 120 acres.

To kinda wrap up the cabin history, Adam's and Margaret's oldest son Frank Reiss married Anna Syvilla Feder in a double wedding ceremony with his sister on April 9, 1866 (146 years and two weeks ago). Frank and Anna are the two oval pictures in my den. Margaret and Conrad built a new log cabin for themselves half a mile southeast so that Frank and Anna could have this older one. Here is where ten of their eleven children were born and here is also where four of them died of disease. Frank and Anna built a new house right next door in 1889 and that is where their eleventh child was born. His name was William Martin Reiss, almost like yours, Will. That new home is also where your great grandfather (my dad), Irwin Henry Reiss, was born on September 18, 1917.

Sadly this cabin was demolished in 1957 to make room for a new three-stall concrete block garage. Removing that historic cabin was a huge mistake in my opinion. On the good side, however, the log granary which was also built nearby in 1838 survives to this day. Maintaining that structure and its memories is now a major family priority.

Will and Kayla, I see major similarities between our original Adam Reiss and your mom/aunt Hany. Both left their native countries, families, language, friends, and comfort zone to strike out for America. Both had lots of energy, self-confidence, and determination to make things work in a new country over 8,000 miles from where they were born. And both were or are continuing to be very successful. Your mom/aunt is a pioneer and her husband Grant is a fifth generation descendant of one. I'm very impressed. You should be doubly proud. But, dear grandchildren, please don't take all this story as authority to leave Illinois and strike out for yet another country on your own!!!

Love, Granddad

Here's my aunt Katie Petri at the log cabin door about 1948. You can see some of the construction. Two more photos appear on the next page. The first one from 1950 shows the cabin at the far left. Farm tenants are living in that part of the homestead at that time so that's their child.

Original Log Cabin on Reiss Farm probably built in the mid 1830's

Four-Leaf Clovers

Dear Will and Kayla,   April 2, 2012

I made an April Fools Day resolution to send you two something of interest on Mondays from our yard, our travels, our memories, or something just plain goofy. So here is the first subject – **Four-Leaf Clovers**. The photo below is from our fruit orchard and shows two four-leaf clovers, one for each of you.

I learned about four-leaf clovers from my grandma Katie Reiss on the family farm south of Belleville, Illinois. She would find a few such clovers per week all summer long. She saved them between the pages of several books in her home. The books kept the clovers flat and let them dry out slowly. There were several hundred that she saved that way. I still have a few of them from her books that are now over 75 years old.

When I was about ten years old, I started looking for four-leaf clovers in Sullivan, Indiana where I grew up. I could usually find one good clover every five minutes or so. I learned that four-leaf clovers often grow in clusters about a yard in diameter. If you find one, you might find fifteen more in that same area. For every 50 four-leaf clovers, I could usually find one or two five-leaf clovers. For every 100 fours, I could usually find a six-leaf clover. Eventually I found two seven-leaf clovers. Most of these are still saved in various books from my younger days in Sullivan.

Anyway, I like looking for four-leaf clovers, mostly because it is something I learned from my grandmother Katie. She was a very kind and special lady. She had outstanding people skills. I know my dad who was her third son, really loved his mother. Grandma was born on March 25, 1890 and died on October 17, 1986 at age 96.

Here's some stuff on four-leaf clovers that I found on Google. The four-leaf clover is an uncommon variation of the common, three-leafed <u>clover</u>. According to tradition, such leaves bring good <u>luck</u> to their finders, especially if found accidentally. According to legend, each leaf represents something: the first is for <u>faith</u>, the second is for <u>hope</u>, the third is for <u>love</u>, and the fourth is for <u>luck</u>. It has been estimated that there are approximately 10,000 three-leaf clovers for every four-leaf clover.

Love, Granddad

Looking for four-leaf clovers on the southeast corner of the Reiss Family Farm about 1960. Grandma Katie is on the left. Mom and us kids are to the right. This corner is where the great great Grandma Margaret Ebert had her second home from about 1870 to 1880.

Pop's Pine Woods

Dear Will, Kayla, Ava, and Blake,   October 15, 2012

Here are three paragraphs which your great great uncle Frank Reiss wrote 61 years ago yesterday on Sunday October 14, 1951 after returning from a visit to the Reiss Family Farm 12 miles south of Belleville, Illinois.

We just returned from a trip down to the home farm. We arrived down there on Friday evening. Mother, Dad, and I immediately went to the Floraville Grange Booster Night. Saturday morning we all went to look at the new lake on Gundlach's land. It is really nice. About 5 – 6 feet of water in it already at the lower end.

We stopped in the long bottom and got two big sacks full of walnuts. They are large size and heavy this year. Took pictures of Dad and his planting of short-leaf pines. He planted them as seedlings in the spring of 1940.

Gerry and I drove the car back to the 8 acres and gathered hickory nuts. We found the ground just covered on top of the hill in the mailbox woods where the pigs used to be. We gathered about ½ bushel of shelled nuts. I have never seen them so plentiful.

This edition of Granddad's Mondays will concentrate on the middle paragraph which mentions your great great grandfather's planting of short-leaf pines. That was something that Pop, as we called him, was very proud of. That grove is about 200 yards northeast of the mailbox at the end of the woods lane. That new lake on the Gundlach land that he mentions is what we now know as the first lake at the Smithton Sportsman's Club.

From the photos below we can estimate these trees were on 10-foot centers and the rows were on 15-foot centers which is about 280 trees per acre and there is at least one acre of them. The spring of 1940 is also when Grandma and Pop broke ground for their new house. Perhaps there is a connection between the two projects or maybe Pop had long term plans for those trees. Here's what I found on Google about that species:

Shortleaf Pine is a species of pine native to the eastern United States from southern New York to northern Florida and west to eastern Texas. The tree is variable in form, sometimes straight, sometimes crooked, with an irregular crown. This tree reaches heights of 65 to 100 feet with trunk diameters of 1.5 to 3 feet. The leaves are needle-like, in

83

bundles of two and three mixed together, and from 2.7 to 4.3 inches long. The cones are 1.5 to 2.8 inches long.

This pine is a source of wood pulp, plywood veneer, and lumber for a variety of uses. The Shortleaf Pine is one of the southern US "yellow" pines; it is also occasionally called Southern Yellow pine or the Shortstraw Pine. Shortleaf Pine has the largest range of the southern US yellow pines.

I remember walking through "Pop's Pine Woods" dozens of times. One time when I was about 12, we found one particular tree with lots of white bird droppings under it. We looked up and saw a great horned owl looking down at us. This was obviously his home.

Over the years, some of these trees were harvested for fence posts and other farm uses. Some of the land was returned to farming so today Pop's Woods is about 40 trees. We call it the George Reiss Memorial Grove which we would like to preserve well beyond its current 72 years.

So, Will, Kayla, Ava, and Blake, trees are beautiful creations of nature. You can admire them from a distance, walk through them for special smells and discoveries, climb them for better views, or even build a tree house as we did in our back yard. Remember when walking through a woods to look in all directions including down and up. And thanks to Uncle Frank, we're finding it greatly helpful to future generations if you take pictures and keep a daily diary. A recently found photo album included the picture below from 1945 when Pop's trees were about five years old.

Love, Granddad

Gold Coins (1873 and 1890)

Dear Will and Kayla, April 16, 2012

Here are two $20 gold coins dated 1873 and 1890, the years that your great great grandparents, George and Katie Reiss, were born. George William Reiss was born on April 22, 1873 (139 years ago this week) and Catharina "Katie" Charlotte Luetzelschwab was born on March 25, 1890. He was almost 17 years older than her. They were married on Easter Sunday, April 16, 1911 (101 years ago today) at St. Paul's Church in Floraville, Illinois. I have their marriage certificate in a beautiful frame in our upstairs hallway.

I think George's parents were afraid their oldest surviving son, who was quite handsome, was never going to get married. So in 1910 when George was 37 years old, they hired attractive, young Katie Luetzelschwab to be their domestic worker to help with laundry, cooking, and light duty chores around the home farm south of Belleville, Illinois. Well, George was no dummy and he soon took proper notice of their live-in worker. He got over any bashfulness that might have existed and I'm sure Katie did her best to impress him with her cooking, darning socks, making quilts, and all that domestic stuff. It all worked and they were married about a year later. I'm sure many of their "dates" were long slow walks in the woods. Keep that domestic worker trick in mind as the ultimate matchmaker tool if your children are slow about spreading their wings. George gave this 1890 coin to his bride, Katie, as a wedding gift. I don't know where or when

he got the 1873 coin but I do know they gave it to their third son (my dad), Irwin Henry Reiss, and his bride, Mary Leone Stephenson, as a wedding gift on November 8, 1942. It was a real big hit with the wedding crowd in Atascadero, California. Irv's parents could not make the trip from Illinois for the wedding since the United States was in the middle of World War II and gasoline, batteries, car tires, and many other items were rationed or simply not available.

George and Katie were married for 53 years and 4 months. I remember going to their golden wedding anniversary celebration in 1961 at the Smithton Sportsmens Club on the Reiss Family

Farm. We six grandchildren always called them Grandma and Pop. They were outstanding grandparents and taught us how to play pinochle cards, find mushrooms in the woods, pick dewberries along the country lanes, fish in the farm pond, take care of baby kittens which were all over their farmstead, play in the hay mow in the old barn, go to the "fish place" in Smithton for weekend suppers, decorate a cedar tree cut from their pasture as our Christmas tree, sleep upstairs under feather blankets, take baths in a wash tub of cistern water warmed by the sun, feed the chickens and gather eggs, pick apricots in the orchard, eat Grandma's fruit pies where she used custard instead of corn starch for filling, cook with a kitchen stove that burned corn cobs or kindling, play with clay marbles and Lincoln logs on the living room carpet, butcher hogs, dig a cistern, look for arrowheads on their Indian mound, dismantle a 1932 Model A pickup truck, feed Pop's two horses that he farmed with until 1948, and do lots of other really cool things.

Will and Kayla, here is their picture from 1959. Pop died in August 1964 at age 91 when our family was on vacation in Europe. Dad flew back ahead of Mom and us three kids to go to his funeral. We had left our car in New York with Mom's brother so the rest of us drove back to our home in Sullivan, Indiana. Grandma died in October 1986 at age 96 two months before Caterpillar moved us to South Korea. I remember going to her funeral which was really sad for me because I don't do funerals very well and because I had so many fond memories of my grandparents. They are buried side by side in Franklin Cemetery in Smithton, Illinois. Their two gold coins are also side by side now in a plastic case in a safe in our home. They should stay in our family forever.

Love, Granddad

Growing Corn on the Reiss Family Farm in 1944

Dear Will, Kayla, Ava, and Blake,   October 10, 2016

This story is a sequel to "Growing Corn and Raising Hogs on the Reiss Farm in 1944" dated 2/24/2014. That story contained entries from Grandma Katie's 1944 diary which mentioned "growing corn" and/or "raising hogs." Well, I'm repeating just the 41 "growing corn" entries to make my point and to say that farmers are now in the middle of harvesting corn as you know.

Let me emphasize that my grandfather (Pop, Geo, Dad) turned age 71 on April 22, that he farmed only with horses, that he never owned a tractor or corn picker, that he had no electricity, and that he picked and husked all his corn by hand. No wonder he had such massive hands with a size 13 wedding ring. Shaquille O'Neal wears a size 17 but he's also twice as big as Pop was.

I'm now a year older than Pop was in 1944 when he's growing and harvesting all this corn. It absolutely blows my mind what he was physically able to accomplish. ABSOLUTELY BLOWS MY MIND!!! I AM SOOOOO IMPRESSED!!!

April 1944

Tues 4 – Geo husked corn.

Wed 5 – Geo disked corn land.

Thurs 6 – Geo plowed.

Tues 18 – Geo plowed.

Wed 19 – Pop plowed.

Thurs 20 – Pop plowed.

Fri 21 – Pop plowed.

May 1944

Thurs 4 – Geo got corn land ready.

Fri 5 – Geo planted first corn in Schaeffer's place.

Sat 6 – Geo plowed in back of barn for corn.

Thurs 18 – Geo disked the bottom land.

Sat 20 – Geo plowed in the bottom.

Mon 22 – Geo plowed in the bottom.

Wed 24 – Geo planted the long bottom in corn and harrowed it.

June 1944

Fri 2 – Dad finished planting corn.

Thurs 8 – Pop replanted corn in long bottom.

Fri 9 – Pop replanted corn.

Sat 10 – Dad hoed corn.

Mon 12 – Geo worked in corn. Stephen William Reiss was born today in California.

Tues 13 – Pop worked in corn.

Wed 28 – Hottest day so far, 100 degrees by 5 p.m. Geo hoed in the corn.

July 1944

Thurs 13 – Geo cleaned weeds out of the corn.

Fri 14 – Pop plowed.

Sat 15 – 90 degrees at noon. Pop plowed.

Wed 19 – Pop plowed.

Thurs 20 – Dad plowed.

August 1944

September 1944

October 1944

Sat 14 – Geo shucked corn.

Tues 17 – Pop husked corn.

Fri 20 – Geo husked corn.

Sun 22 – Brandenburger brought us corn.

Mon 23 – Geo husked corn. Westerheide brought us some of our third of the corn.

Thurs 26 – Then Geo husked corn.

Mon 30 – Geo husked corn.

November 1944

Wed 1 – Geo husked corn.

Thurs 2 – Geo husked corn.

Mon 6 – Geo husked corn.

Fri 10 – Pop husked corn.

Wed 15 – Geo husked corn.

Thurs 16 – Geo husked corn and brought in the pumpkins.

Sat 18 – Geo husked corn.

Mon 20 – Geo husked corn.

December 1944

Fri 8 – Pop husked corn.

Will, Kayla, Ava, and Blake, are you impressed by your great great grandfather George William Reiss, aka Pop? Wasn't he just absolutely awesome? Here's a letter that Grandma Katie wrote to my dad while he was serving with the US Army in Burma.

Our Dearest Irwin,   September 20, 1944

We are going thru such a busy time the last two weeks that we can hardly rest up any more. It's not all work, it's go here and go there and always company in between. Today we had a very nice day here on the farm. Uncle John and Aunt Etta and Audrey were here. Audrey was very much interested in seeing all the pictures from you and Mary and Stevie, also those of your camp life, those many nice pictures from Calif. and Camp Roberts. Audrey said I should say hello to you for her, she wishes so often that she could get to see you all sometime again. She hadn't been here for 10 years. She is 30 years old and is doing office work at some camp in Tenn. She still is very pretty. She liked the pictures of your wife and son. Everybody who sees Stevie's pictures thinks he looks so much like you.

I looked up your record of when you were a baby and saw that you also weighed 15 lbs. at 3 months old, so I guess Stevie is about your size. Irwin, thanks a million for the beautiful flower vases. My, they are pretty, they just came today and Etta and Audrey too think they are beautiful. Now I've got more to show people when they come.

Irwin it's very pretty on the farm now, the woods is turning all colors, wish Mary could see it once at this time of the year. Corn is mostly all ripe, in fact Shillings got one of our fields all picked already. It made 45 bu per acre, our lawn is beautiful. I have a million and one flowers. The people today just stood and looked at all those flowers. But all those things don't mean much to me. Sure I like to work with flowers, but what would be more beautiful than all those flowers, would be if you and Mary and Stevie and Frank & Gerry & Georgie and Bill, Anita and June all could be here and enjoy the farm together. So I hope things will soon take a turn for the better and that you could be with us all real soon.

Audrey brought me three quilts to quilt for her this winter, and Etta has three altho I finished one of Etta's last week and she took it along home today. Etta's are just common patch quilts, but Audrey's are fancy ones and need a lot of careful sewing so you see I'll be busy every day of the year. I love to quilt. I can rest my legs and feet when it's nice outside, then Pop and I are always working together fixing up things and so on. Good luck, dear son.   Love, Mother & Dad

Will, Kayla, Ava, and Blake, here's a chart showing various technical advancements in farm equipment, fertilizer, and seed in the last 100 years. Pop's 45-bushel corn in 1944 was just about average. Look at what it is now at 180 bushels per acre. Your Double R Farm made 227 bushels in 2014 and I'm sure the Petersons picked it in less than half a day.

Love, Granddad

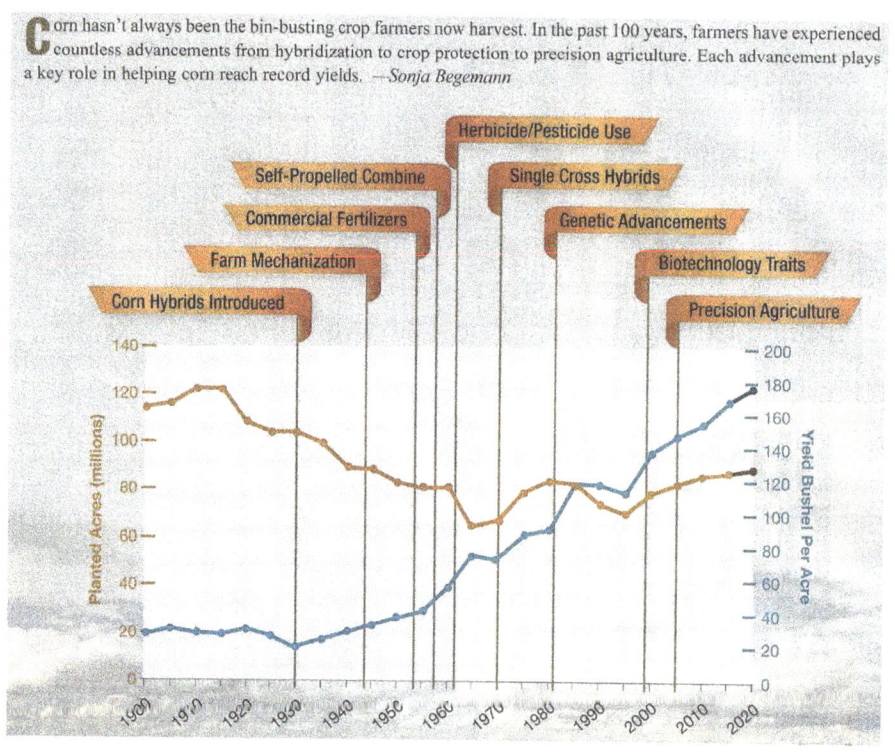

Corn hasn't always been the bin-busting crop farmers now harvest. In the past 100 years, farmers have experienced countless advancements from hybridization to crop protection to precision agriculture. Each advancement plays a key role in helping corn reach record yields. —*Sonja Begemann*

Pop's Grindstone Sharpening Wheel

Dear Will, Kayla, Ava, and Blake,   July 20, 2015

This tattooed young man wanted to grind an old railroad spike into a throwing knife. He could use that overhead can which held water to keep his work piece cool. The wheel could rotate in either direction depending on which way you initially pushed it by hand to get it started. Only problem for our young operator was that he couldn't reach the foot pedals to keep the wheel in motion. He also needs eye protection.

I have fond memories of sharpening my pocket knife on Pop's wheel. My brother and I would have contests on who could pedal the fastest. These wheels were outstanding for sharpening axes, hatchets, splitting wedges, garden hoes, stakes to play horseshoes, making bolts shorter, and just about anything you wanted. On the next page is an advertisement from 1910 by a company in Aurora, Illinois. We don't know the brand name of Pop's wheel.

I typed "pedal grinder" into eBay and got a dozen hits. Most were $150 to $250 but one was $850 and had 46 people watching. They also advertised "free shipping" which may have been a big perk. There was another internet story where a Boy Scout camp was looking for someone to donate their old wheel so the boys could have some unique fun and learn more about farm times.

Will, Kayla, Ava, and Blake, I don't want you to grow up too quickly because I enjoy you all so much just as you are. But if you do happen to grow taller such that your legs can reach these pedals, then we'll have fun sharpening and grinding something. But maybe not your moms' Cutco kitchen knives.

Love, Granddad

Driving Cross County in July 1943

Dear Will, Kayla, Ava, and Blake,   July 17, 2017

Seventy-four years ago yesterday my parents, Irv and Mary Reiss, departed from Mom's parent's home in Atascadero, California to drive to New Haven, Connecticut. Dad was in the US Army and was relocating there for three months to take a crash course in Chinese at Yale University. World War II was two years old and still had two years to go. Mom and Dad drove their own car and were reimbursed for expenses. Gasoline was rationed so the Army issued them gasoline ration cards or "gas rats" for the trip. Maybe they got military discounts on food and lodging.

With them was Mom's younger brother Andy Stephenson who celebrated his 19th birthday on July 17, 1943, the first full day of their travel. Here are entries from the travel log my parent's kept for their expense account. Andy would have paid his own expenses and was a huge help with driving. The first number on some entries is the odometer reading on their car.

July 16 – 40,316 miles – With Mom (my Grandma Daisy) in tears we left at 5:20 p.m. with a full tank and five so-called tires.

40,530 miles – 11.4 gallons of gas and 1 quart of oil for $2.52.

40,734 miles at **Madera, California** 11.0 gallons of gas and one quart of oil for $2.80, auto court for $2.35, dinner for $1.85

Merced, California for breakfast $1.20

Placerville, California for lunch $.80

Lovelock, Nevada dinner for $2.45 and one quart of oil for $.30, film $2.00, and miscellaneous $1.00

Winnemucca, Nevada motel for $3.34

40,975 miles at **Battle Mountain, Nevada** 10.6 gallons and one quart of oil for $2.94

41,161 miles at **Wendover, Utah** 8 gallons of gas and 1 quart of oil for $2.39

Lunch $1.60

41,374 miles at **Evanston, Wyoming** for 12 gallons of gas for $2.87, lube job for $2.53, and auto court for $3.34

Fort Bridger, Wyoming for breakfast $2.00

41,597 miles at **Rawlins, Wyoming**, 10.5 gallons of gas, $.15 for Cokes

Lunch for $1.05

41,772 miles at **Cheyenne, Wyoming**, 9.5 gallons of gas, dinner $1.00

Sidney, Nebraska auto court for $2.67, breakfast for $1.20

41,992 miles at **North Platte, Nebraska** 10 gallons of gas and one quart of oil for $2.19

Kearney, Nebraska for lunch $1.20, two quarts of oil for $.70

42,283 miles at **Nebraska City, Nebraska** 13.1 gallons of gas for $2.37

Mound City, Missouri tourist home for $1.50

St. Joseph, Missouri breakfast for $.90

42,561 miles at **Shelbina, Missouri** 12 gallons of gas and one quart of oil for $2.45

Hannibal, Missouri lunch for $.90

St. Louis, Missouri 8 gallons of gas and one quart of oil for $1.85

Millstadt, Illinois, hairdo for $.75, melons for $1.10, car grease for $1.75, miscellaneous for $.25. This is five miles from Dad's parent's farm so they stopped for parts of at least two days for a visit. From the left are oldest brother Bill, his wife Anita, Dad, Mom, older brother Frank, and his wife Gerry. It was the first time Mom had met any of them since all were unable to travel from Illinois to their November 1942 wedding in California. The next picture are Reiss brothers with their parents Katie and George. This was September 1943 so Dad had recently turned age 26, George was 70, Katie was 53, Bill was 31, and Frank would soon be 28. Each of the older brothers had one child.

42,929 miles at **Hamel, Illinois** 11.7 gallons of gas for $2.21

Urbana, Illinois, film for $1.00, Mrs. Evans for $1.50. This is where Dad's brother Franklin lives so they stopped for a visit.

43,162 miles at **Crawfordsville, Indiana** 11 gallons of gas for $2.13

Greenfield, Indiana lunch for $.90

Springfield, Ohio two quarts of oil for $.50

43,384 miles at **Columbus, Ohio** 10.5 gallons of gas for $1.87

Hebron, Ohio supper for $2.58

Cambridge, Ohio tourist home for $2.00

Cadiz, Ohio breakfast for $.90

43,574 miles at **Pittsburgh, Pennsylvania** 9.8 gallons of gas and one quart of oil for $2.23
Pennsylvania Turnpike lunch for $1.05

43,808 miles and Turnpike toll of $1.50, 11.4 gallons of gas and one quart of oil for $2.58

43,994 miles at **Easton, Pennsylvania** dinner for $1.30, watermelon for $.60 and 9 gallons of gas for $1.86, one quart of oil for $.31, headlight and paint for $1.70. This is where their log ends but they were only 158 miles from New Haven and would have arrived the next day.

None of their entries after departing California are dated so I highlighted overnight stays to see how long they traveled. It looks like nine nights and ten days on the road for 3,622 total miles.

My Granddad's Mondays story of 3/7/2016 says Dad's class in Chinese started on 7/15/1943 which was a day before they left California on this 10-day trip. Maybe they arrived late or maybe the class really didn't start until later in July. That story also mentions that Mom's younger brother Andy accompanied them on this cross-country trip. Perhaps he was the photographer.

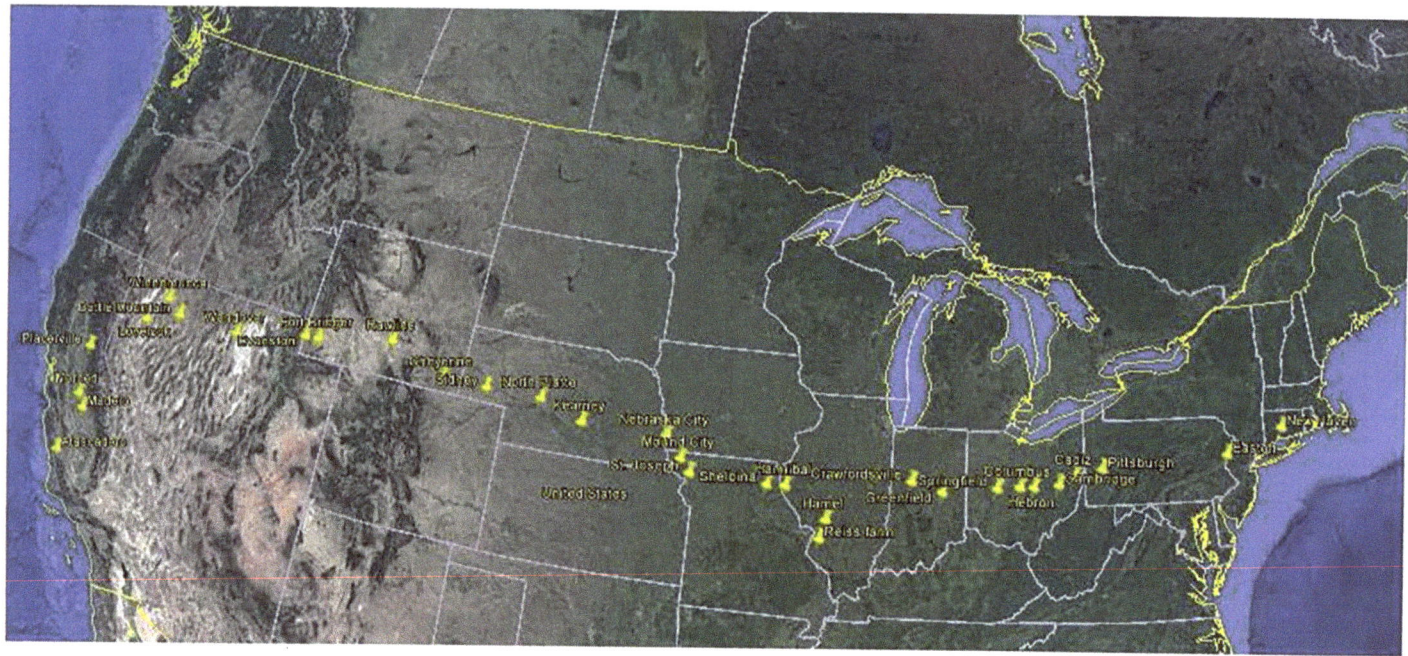

Will, Kayla, Ava, and Blake, Mapquest shows this trip at 3,036 miles and 44.5 hours which is 68.2 miles an hour average. Much of that route is along Interstate 80 which is 238 miles or 4 hours north of the home farm. The detour so Mom could meet Dad's parents, brothers, and their wives explains the mileage difference. Can you believe the prices they paid for food, lodging, and gasoline but maybe they were low because they qualified for military discounts.

Love, Granddad

My Dear Son

Dear Will, Kayla, Ava, and Blake,   July 4, 2016

Happy Independence Day!!! Here's a letter my dad wrote to me 72 years ago today which was shortly after I was born on 6/12/1944. He learned about my birth ten days later on 6/22/1944 via a telegram from the American Red Cross because he was away serving in India with the US Army during World War II. Dad's words were poignant and still apply for the next three and ongoing generations of both sons and daughters.

What the next generation will value most is not what we owned, but the evidence of who we were and the tales of how we lived. In the end, it's the family stories that are worth the storage.

Love, Granddad

Ramgarh, India
July 4, 1944

My dear Son,

How are you? I have never seen you. I don't even know how you look. All that I know is what the cablegram said – you arrived safely (on June 12) and you and Mother are doing fine.

I am very sorry that I wasn't there with your mommie to help welcome you into this world. But right now I am in the far away land of India doing a job which society has presumed upon me. But I want you to know that spiritually I was right there with you when you were born. I am very proud of you, Son, and your mother and I love you very much.

Sometime soon I am coming back home, Son, to make a happy home for you and Mommie. Your mother and I will give you the best of care. We will try and give you very good education. In return I want you to do something for us. Wherever you are and whatever you do, I want you to do it so that your mother and I can say with pride, "that is our son." In other words, Son, I always want you to be a man.

Every day here in India, I see thousands of boys and girls who don't have a chance in life. They have no food to eat or a place to sleep. They don't have an opportunity to get an education. They don't have the privilege of worshiping in Christian churches. You have every opportunity in the world to do some good for society. I want you to make the most of that opportunity.

One more thing, Son – when you were born, you made your mother and myself very happy. I want you to continue to make us happy the rest of our lives. Will you do that for us, Son?

Your affectionate father,

Irwin H. Reiss

199

National Grandparents Day

Dear Will, Kayla, Ava, and Blake,   September 4, 2017

Next Sunday is National Grandparents Day which has been celebrated in our country since 1978. Other countries have similar celebrations but sometimes have separate days for grandmothers and grandfathers.

Here's some history -- Marian McQuade of Oak Hill, West Virginia, has been recognized nationally by the United States Senate and by President Jimmy Carter, as the founder of National Grandparents Day. She made it her goal to educate the youth in her community about the important contributions seniors have made throughout history. She also urged the youth to "adopt" a grandparent, not just for one day a year, but rather for a lifetime.

The pictures below are Easter Sunday at the Reiss home farm on April 6, 1958. My Stephenson grandparents are outside of my Reiss grandparents. Hats for the ladies were customary back then. They're not quite the traditional Easter bonnets.

Will, Kayla, Ava, and Blake, if you have any special grandparents in Illinois, they may be expecting your call next Sunday. You could mention special artwork you've made, a Lego project, a 250-piece puzzle, or a school report card. You could also do a Facetime call and tell them all about your fun weekend. You could even mention which of the following pictures is your favorite.

Love, Granddad

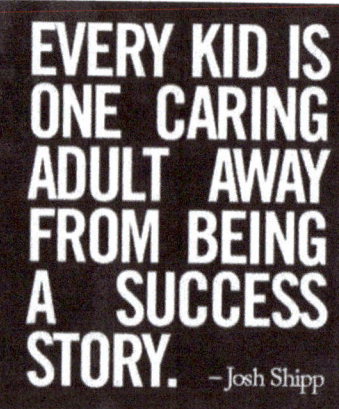

To Do List:

~~X~~ pick up grandchildren

~~X~~ spoil them

~~X~~ load them with sugar

~~X~~ send them home

GRANDPARENTS ARE THERE TO HELP THE CHILD GET INTO MISCHIEF THEY HAVEN'T THOUGHT OF YET.

Blessed are those **who** SPOIL and SNUGGLE hug and hope PRAY and pamper FOR they shall be CALLED GRANDPARENTS

GRANDPARENTS' HOUSE RULES
Kitchen open 24 hours
EXPECT TO BE SPOILED
DESSERT COMES FIRST
NO PARENTS ALLOWED
laugh - giggle - snuggle
Sleepovers Welcome
Storytelling
play lots of games
BED TIME NEGOTIABLE
ALWAYS HAVE FUN
...SS HUGS & KISSES
...for breakfast are acceptable
...T HAPPENS HERE
...AYS HERE

SLOW Grandparents AT PLAY

Solar Eclipse on August 21, 2017

Dear Will, Kayla, Ava, and Blake,   August 28, 2017

Last Monday was the first time in hundreds of years that the Reiss Family Farm south of Belleville experienced a total solar eclipse. That happens when the moon gets between the sun and the earth such that it's totally dark for a very few minutes. That complete central shadow is called an umbra where a partial shadow away from totality is called a penumbra. The maximum totality anywhere in the US this time was 2 minutes 41 seconds. For us it was dark for 1 minute, 48 seconds. You could have held your breath.

Maybe you remember my Granddad's Mondays story from 6/9/2014 about this upcoming eclipse. It started with a heads-up from cousin Jesse so we had three years to prepare. The next solar eclipse at the RFF will be April 8, 2024 so you have seven years to prepare. That's also a Monday so you'll just have to take a day off from school and be there.

Here are our relatives who made it this year. We're all wearing dark eclipse glasses so you may not recognize. All are Reisses after the first three on the left who are Mary and Greg Blitz from Indianapolis and Crystal Pritchard from Los Angeles. Next are four more from Los Angeles - George, Becky, Paula, and Jesse followed by Heather and Adam from Springfield, and Grand DD and me from Peoria. Our Farmers National manager Bret Cude was also with us and took this picture.

The Smithton Sportsmen's Club hosted a fabulous lunch for our group in their clubhouse. They were very generous. We enjoyed meeting their leadership again and hiking around the lakes and grounds. It was all very nice and a good and very filling time was enjoyed by all. Here's some public info leading up to last Monday's eclipse:

- Today a total solar eclipse will be visible from coast to coast, according to NASA. It will be the first total eclipse visible only in the USA since the country was founded in 1776. It will also be the first total solar eclipse to sweep across the entire country in 99 years. Not since 1970 has there been an opportunity to see a total solar eclipse in such easily accessible and widespread areas of the nation.

- At any given location, the total eclipse will last for two or three minutes. About 12 million people live within the path of totality.

- Outside the narrow shadow track, a partial eclipse will be visible from all of North America, parts of South America, Western Europe, and Africa.

- Although Monday's eclipse was peaking over two minutes in the path of totality, the April 8, 2024 eclipse will have peaks of 4½ minutes. It will be visible in a diagonal path crossing from Texas to Maine.

Here's what we saw and what the astronauts in the International Space Station saw:

Next page is a composite picture of all phases of the eclipse.

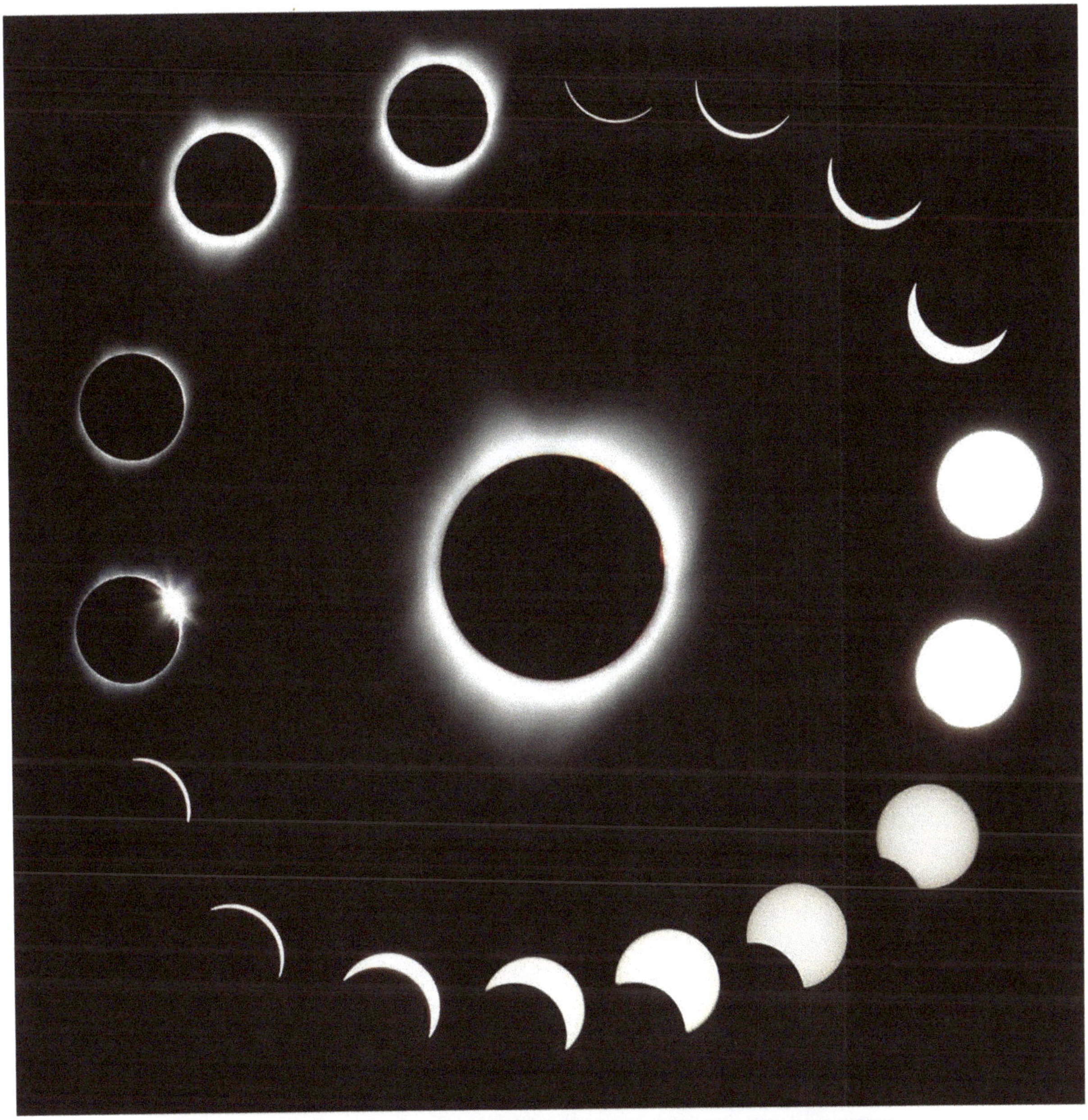

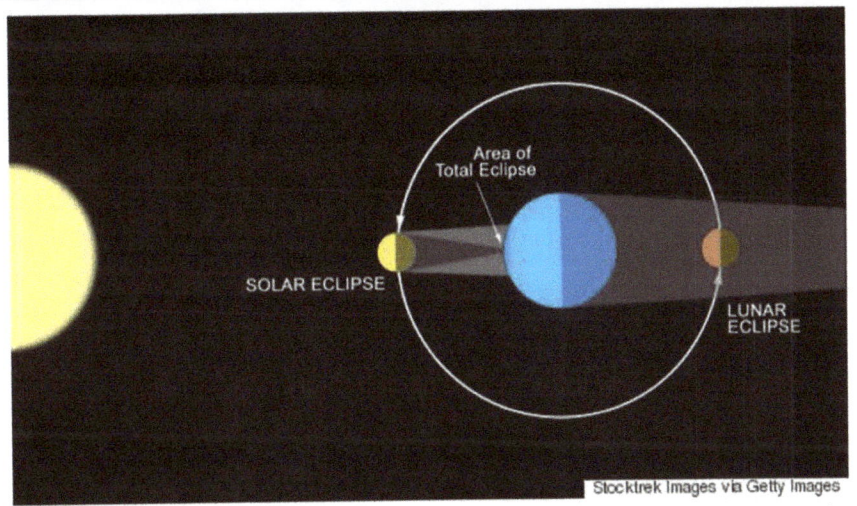

Area of
Total Eclipse
SOLAR ECLIPSE
LUNAR
ECLIPSE
Stocktrek Images via Getty Images

Here's how an eclipse happens. The sun is at the far left. It is 400 times bigger than the moon, but is also 400 times further away, which makes the two objects appear exactly the same size in the sky. We were in that area of total eclipse for 1 minute, 48 seconds.

Here's the eclipse shadow coming toward us. North is to the right. Our farm is between Hecker and Freeburg at the lower left edge of the shadow. The farm is under the "e" in Waterloo in the Illinois state map.

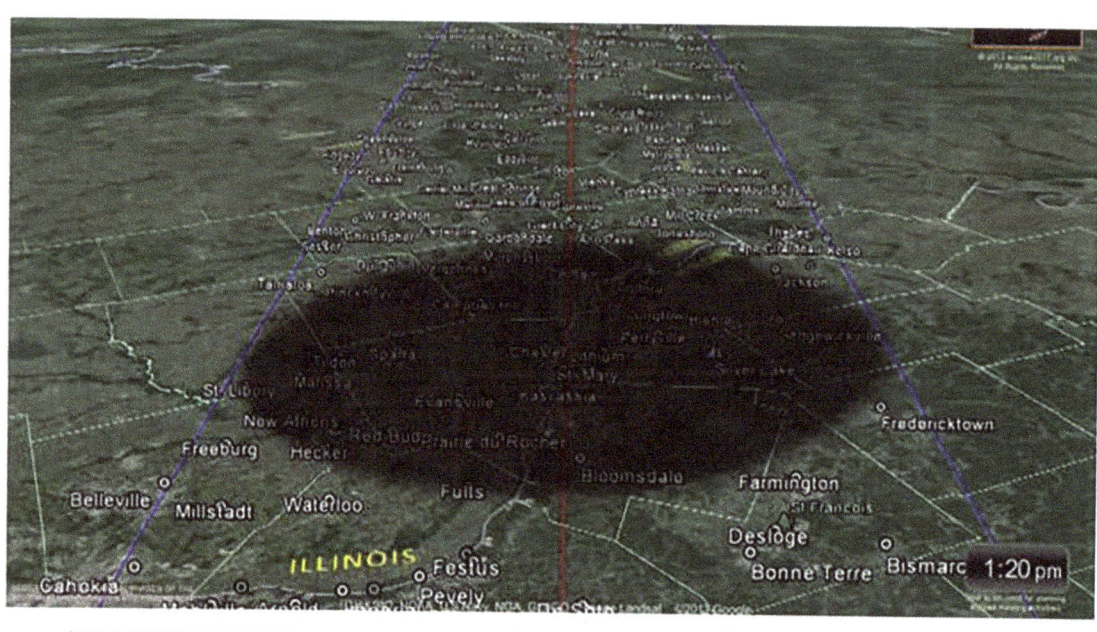

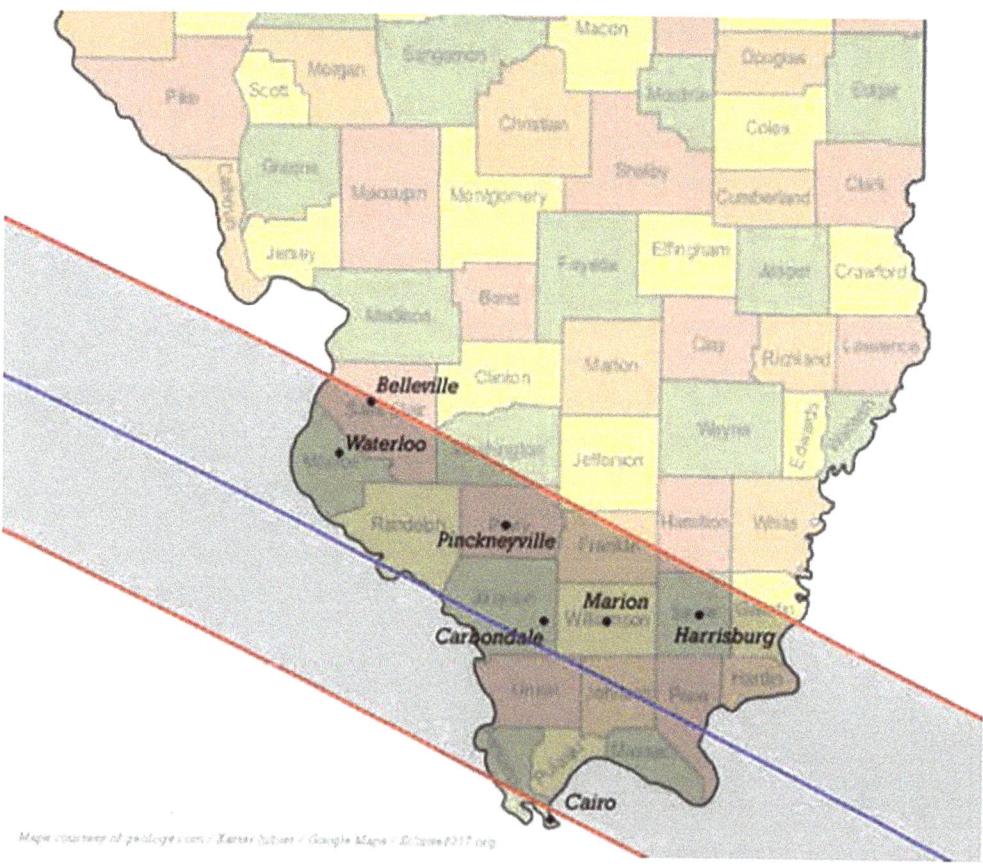

Maps courtesy of geology.com · Xavier Jubier · Google Maps · Eclipse2017.org

Will, Kayla, Ava, and Blake, here are paths of the 2017 and 2024 total eclipses. They almost cross right over our family farm. We will be a mile or two left of the 2024 path but that's close enough to gather together to celebrate again. We will save our two dark eclipse glasses.

Love, Granddad

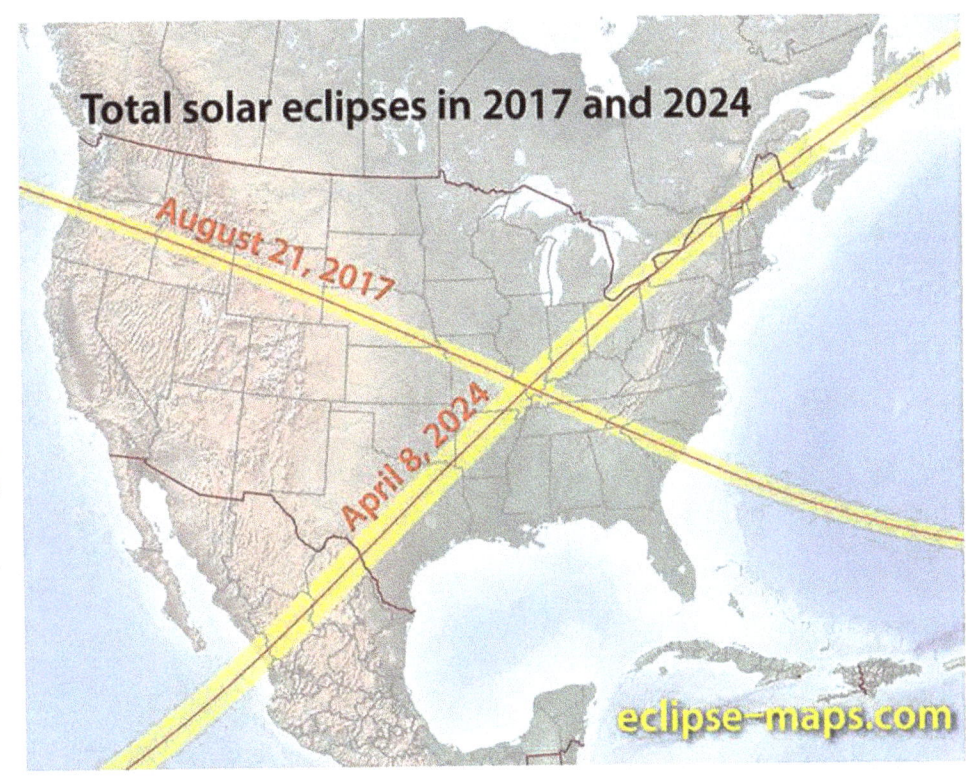

Total solar eclipses in 2017 and 2024

August 21, 2017

April 8, 2024

eclipse-maps.com

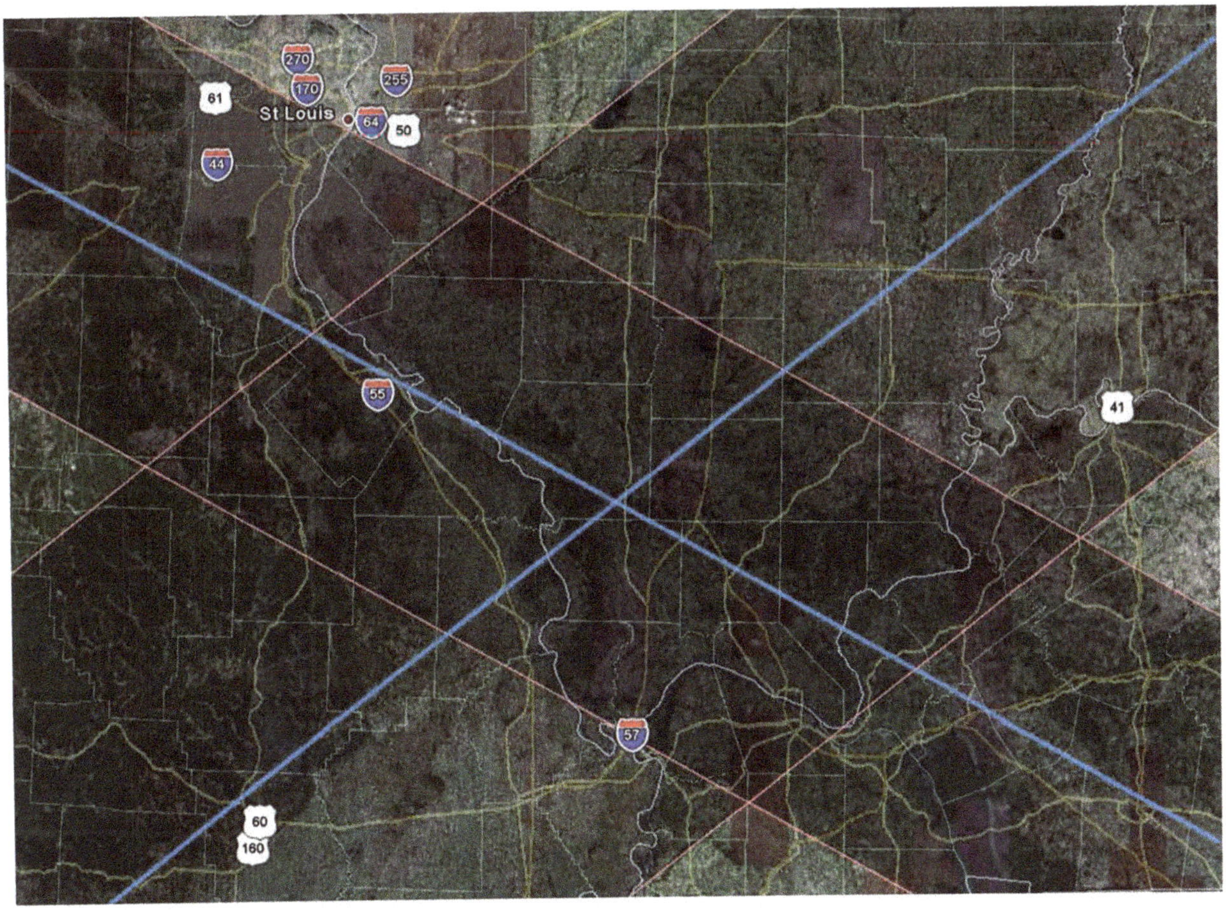

PS: I should have mentioned that we spent time with our tenants in both houses. They are all good people and appreciate the lifestyle of country living. I showed everyone this 1889 date that is carved into the cellar cornerstone of the older home. This home was built by my great grandparents Frank and Anna Sybilla Reiss. They had eleven children but lost four to disease. The oldest to survive is my grandfather George.

There have been several upgrades to this house over the decades. The summer kitchen is now the master bedroom.

Here are arc shapes of light under a tree next to our gravel driveway. They are created by the small gaps between leaves in the tree above which act like pin-hole cameras. The arc shapes reversed direction as the shadow of the moon passed.

It took us about 3 hours to drive from Peoria to the home farm last Monday morning. Southbound traffic was triple the northbound traffic. There was a surprise escort just south of Springfield when Jesse pulled up beside us with Paula, Becky, and Heather in his rental car. Adam drove separately after a business stop in Decatur. He arrived just 20 minutes before totality.

Returning traffic about 4:00 p.m. was slow bumper to bumper for the first 100 miles. Everyone was leaving at the same time. We arrived home about 8:30 for our second sunset of the day.

PPS: Check out the next two pages from young Will Reiss after seeing his first solar eclipse.

My first week of second grade was great. My favorite part was washing the solar eclips. I cant wait to learn more things.

Will

2017 ECLIPSE

my name is: Will

I was 7 years old.

I WENT TO School TO WATCH THE ECLIPSE.

IT WAS ABOUT 5 **MILES** FROM HOME.

IT WAS PRETTY **AWESOME!!**

I will always remember that it was on the 1st day of school

I WAS WITH: My second grade class

THE **WEATHER** WAS LIKE THIS: thunder and some clouds

WAS IT **TOTAL DARKNESS?** ☐ YES ■ NO

Here's what I learned. there are two different types of eclipses.

Crossing the Frozen Mississippi

Dear Will, Kayla, Ava, and Blake,   February 5, 2018

When I was a youngster a little bit older than you, I remember my grandfather "Pop" Reiss telling me about the time he drove a wagon and team of horses across the frozen Mississippi River at St. Louis. He had probably taken a wagonload of six hogs to the stockyards in East St. Louis. Maybe he needed to buy something in St. Louis for the return trip or maybe he said to himself, "Hey, I see hundreds of people walking across the river on the ice, I'm still single and don't have a wife to say I shouldn't do this, and finally, I need an impressive story to tell my grandchildren someday. Besides a unique memory, maybe he was also trying to save a dime on the bridge toll!!!

Pop was probably talking about February 1905 when he would have been age 31. Here's a photo from that time where you can see several hundred people on the ice far behind this lady. The ice was there to walk on, so they had to go. That's the Eads Bridge overhead which was completed in 1874, the year after Pop was born.

The **Eads Bridge** is a combined road and railway bridge. It was envisioned and financed by a young Andrew Carnegie. Opened in 1874, it was one of the earliest long bridges built across the Mississippi, the world's first all steel construction, and built high enough so steamboats could travel underneath. As such, the St. Louis Landmark is listed on the National Register of Historic Places as a National Historic Landmark. As of April 2014, it carried about 8,100 vehicles daily.

The bridge is named for its designer and builder, James B. Eads. When completed in 1874, the Eads Bridge was the longest arch bridge in the world, with an overall length of 6,442 feet. The ribbed steel arch spans were considered daring, as was the use of steel as a primary structural material. This was the first such use of true steel in a major bridge. The cost of building the bridge was nearly $10 million ($210 million with inflation).

Eads Bridge was recognized as an innovative and exciting achievement. Eads' secured 47 patents during his lifetime, many of which were taken out for parts of the bridge's structure and devices for its construction. President Ulysses S. Grant dedicated the bridge on July 4, 1874, and General William T. Sherman drove the gold spike completing construction. After completion, 14 locomotives crossed the bridge to prove its stability.

In 1949, the bridge's strength was tested with electromagnetic strain gauges. It was determined that Eads' original estimation of an allowable load of 3,000 pounds per foot could be raised to 5,000 pounds per foot. The Eads Bridge is still considered one of the greatest bridges ever built.

Will, Kayla, Ava, and Blake, what do you think about your great great grandfather driving a wagon and team of horses across the Mississippi River? I think it's pretty awesome. He could see that hundreds or thousands of people were safely crossing and that the risk to himself and his transport would be minimal. Maybe the coolest part of that whole experience is that he had a major story to tell his 10-year old grandson who would still be majorly impressed 63 years later.

Love, Granddad

Frank and Anna Sybilla Reiss Golden Wedding

Dear Will, Kayla, Ava, and Blake,   April 9, 2018

Exactly 152 years ago today my great grandparents Frank Reiss and Anna Sybilla Feder were married on 4/9/1866. It was a double ceremony with his sister Kate Reiss marrying Charles Max Wittig. They were married by a justice of the peace so it's highly likely that ceremony was on the north porch of the 1889 house on Reiss Family Farm. That home is where Frank and Anna would start a family of eleven children and spend the rest of their lives. Seven of their children reached adulthood and five are in the photo below.

That porch is where they celebrated their golden wedding anniversary 50 years later. Sadly Kate died just one week prior to that date. It would have been nice to have a double golden wedding anniversary celebration. Here's the group photo and attendees. Frank and Anna are front center. Looks like Frank had that same beard for those 50 years!!!

Bottom Row (left to right)

1. Son-in-law, George Dintelmann holding son George
2. Daughter, Margaret Reiss Dintelmann
3. Daughter-in-law, Etta Reiss holding daughter Audrey
4. Daughter-in-law, Katie Luetzelschwab Reiss holding son Frank
5. Anna Sybilla Reiss
6. Frank J. Reiss
7. Son, George W. Reiss holding son Bill
8. Son, John J. Reiss holding daughter Lillian
9. Son, Henry Reiss
10. Daughter-in-law, Emma Reiss

Second Row

1. Daughter-in-law, Mable Reiss, wife of son William nine to the right
2. Neighbor
3. Neighbor
4. Neighbor, Dominick Klein
5. Half-sister, Margaret Ebert Neff
6. Neighbor, Alma Probst Medsker
7. Elsie Weihl???, daughter of Mary and Jacob Weihl
8. Unknown
9. Neighbor, Mary Englerth Klein
10. Son, William Martin Reiss
11. Mary Luetzelschwab Weihl
12. Neighbor, Christine Fischer
13. Caroline Luetzelschwab Gummersheimer

Third Row

1. Frank Luetzelschwab
2. Jacob "Jakie" Luetzelschwab
3. Husband of half-sister, Conrad Neff

Fourth Row

1. Herman Luetzelschwab
2. Jacob Weihl
3. Neighbor Otto Fischer

The Luetzelschwabs are brothers and sisters of Katie Luetzelschwab Reiss, the celebration hostess who lived in this 1889 house with her husband George and his parents, Frank and Anna.

Will, Kayla, Ava, and Blake below are individual photos of Frank and Anna taken for their 50th wedding anniversary. They are your great great great grandparents. These original pictures in curved glass frames are now prominently displayed in my den. You've seen them hundreds of times. Smaller copies are in the bedroom at our Indiana lake house. Do you see any resemblance to your dads?

Love, Granddad

Postcards from George and Katie Reiss in 1911 and 1912

Dear Will, Kayla, Ava, and Blake,   September 2, 2019

Today is Labor Day as a run up to next Sunday which is **National Grandparents Day**. Let me tell you about my Reiss grandparents in the first 14 months of their married life. My visual aids are three postcards my grandfather George sent to his wife's oldest sister and her husband, Mary and Jacob Weihl. The maiden name for Katie and her sister Mary was Luetzelschwab which is often missspelled as you can see below. It was Mary's eventual granddaughter, Gladys Wittenauer Thiele, who gave me these postcards a few years ago.

Here are my family tree notes on my grandparents, George and Katie Reiss – Catherine (Katie) Charlotte Luetzelschwab (3/25/1890 – 10/17/1986) married George William Reiss (4/22/1873 – 8/16/1964) on 4/16/1911 at St. Paul United Church of Christ in Floraville, IL. Witnesses were Herman F. and Lottie H. Luetzelschwab. They are buried in Franklin Cemetery in Smithton. The **1910 Census** shows George 37 as head, his parents Frank age 68 married 44 years and Anna age 65 with 7 of 11 children still living, and servant Katie Lueteelschwab age 20 who he married in 1911. A 1919 auto-owners directory shows him driving a Ford. George's **9/12/1918 World War I Draft Registration Card** shows him as a self-employed farmer with height "tall", build "medium", eyes "hazel", and hair "dark brown". The **1920 Census** shows George age 46, Katherine age 29, William age 7, Franklin age 4, Irwin age 2, father Frank age 78, and mother Anna Syvilla age 75 living on the home farm. The **1930 Census** shows George age 56 owning his own farm, Katy C. age 40 married 19 years, William age 17, Franklin age 14, and Irwin age 12 living in Prairie du Long Township. George and Katie hosted the **1934 Reiss Centennial Reunion**.

Here are my notes on their firstborn son – William George Reiss (5/6/1912 – 8/29/1989) married Anita Theresa Hesse (8/12/1917 – 12/17/1960) on 6/9/1935. He was christened on 6/2/1912, weighed 9¾ pounds at birth, started to walk at 13 months, and started to talk at 18 months. His daughter June Ann (12/2/1936 --) married James McBrayer (7/7/1936 --) on 8/2/1958. They live in Oviedo, Florida.

Here are my family tree notes on Mary and Jacob Weihl and their first daughter Elsie – Mary (baptized Anna Maria Charlotte) Luetzelschwab (6/14/1882 –1/21/1971) married Jacob Weihl (3/7/1878 – 6/4/1937) on 5/8/1900 at home. They are buried at Kolmer Memorial Cemetery in Waterloo. The **1900 Census** shows Jacob age 22 working as a farmer and Mary age 17 as newlyweds living in Waterloo Precinct but outside the city. The **1910 Census** shows Jacob age 33 working as a farmer, Mary age 28 married 9 years with 1 of 1 children still living, and Elsie age 6 living in Waterloo Precinct. Nearby farmers include Conrad Weihl, Christian Weihl, Peter Weihl Sr. and Peter Weihl Jr. The **1920 Census** shows Jacob age 41 working as a farmer, Mary age 37, Elsie age 16, Melva age 5, Lilian age 2 11/12, and a hired hand living in Waterloo Precinct. The **1930 Census** shows Jacob age 52 working as a farmer, Mary age 47, Melva age 15, and Lillian age 13 living on their grain farm in Waterloo Precinct.

Here are my notes on their firstborn daughter – Elsie C. C. Weihl (1/30/1904 – 12/27/1979) married Albert Hoffman (9/25/1893 – 9/22/1979) on 7/31/1927 in Waterloo. They are buried at Kolmer Memorial Cemetery in Waterloo. The **1930 Census** shows Albert Hoffmann age 36 working as a fruit farmer and Elsie age 26 renting a house in Bluff Precinct of Monroe County. I wonder if her "C. C." middle names became my grandmother Katie's given names as well.

To summarize, George is five years older than Jacob and Mary is eight years older than Katie. The Weihls were married eleven years and had a child before George figured out that housekeeper Katie Luetzelschwab was a real keeper, that they should get married, and then play catch up having kids. The men must have been good friends which triggered these postcards.

The first card mentions George and Katie driving to his younger brother John's home in Sikeston, Missouri for their honeymoon trip nine days after their wedding. John eventually founded the Reiss Dairy which is one of our public books and soon to be a second edition. Notice the $.01 stamp on this postcard. Now those stamps are $.35.

The cards on the next page were written by Grandmother Katie whose handwriting is remarkably similar to that of her husband George. The first card mentions receiving a letter from 8-year old Elsie Weihl. The second card mentions her brand new 6-week old son William.

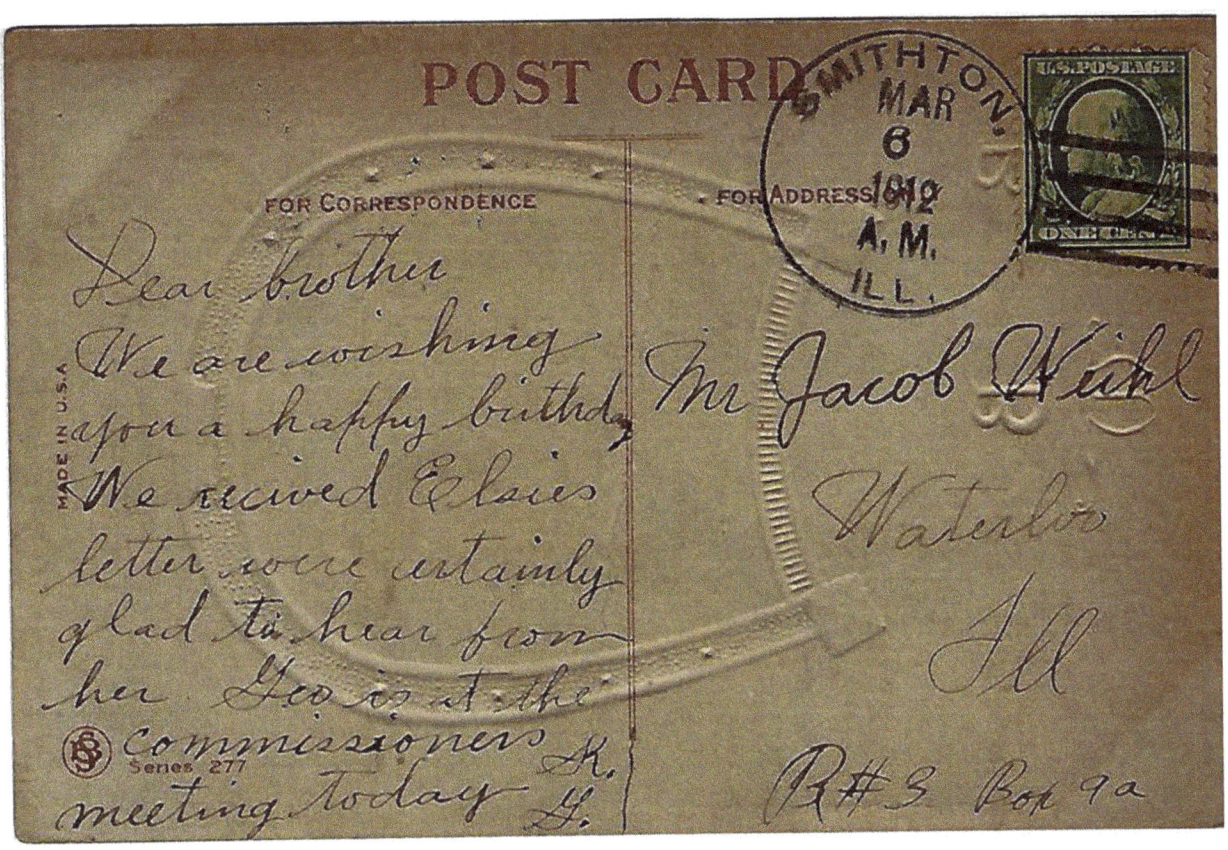

POST CARD

SMITHTON, ILL.
MAR 6 1912 A.M.

FOR CORRESPONDENCE — FOR ADDRESS

Dear brother
We are wishing
you a happy birthday
We recived Elsies
letter were certainly
glad to hear from
her. Geo is at the
commissioners
meeting today K.
R.

Mr Jacob Weihl
Waterloo
Ill

R# 3 Box 9a

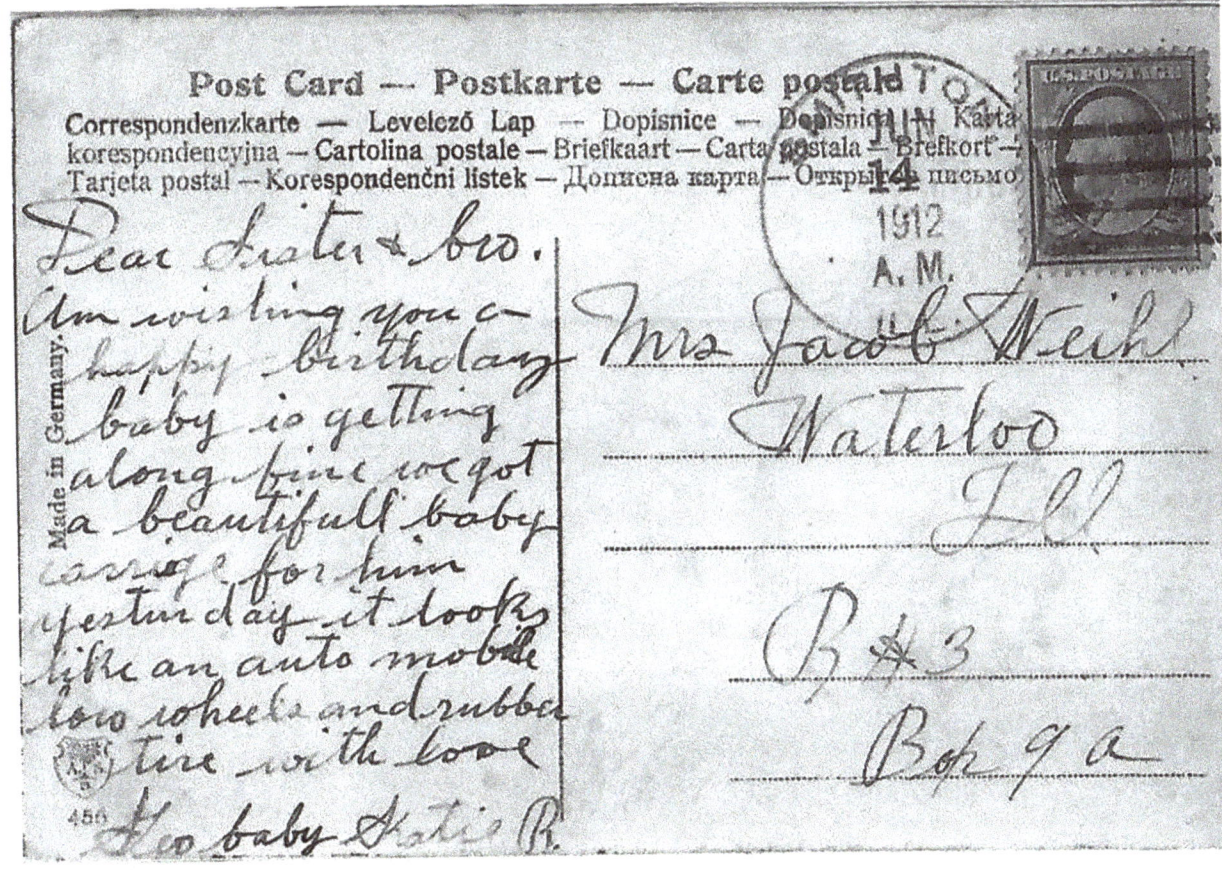

Post Card — Postkarte — Carte postale
Correspondenzkarte — Levelező Lap — Dopisnice — Dopisni Karta
korespondencyjna — Cartolina postale — Briefkaart — Carta postala — Brefkort
Tarjeta postal — Korespondenční lístek — Дописна карта — Открытое письмо

SMITHTON
JUN 14 1912 A.M. ILL.

Dear sister & bro.
Am wishing you a
happy birthday
baby is getting
along fine we got
a beautifull baby
carriage for him
yesterday it looks
like an auto mobile
low wheels and rubber
tire with love
Geo baby Katie R.

Mrs Jacob Weihl
Waterloo
Ill

R #3

Box 9 a

Will, Kayla, Ava, and Blake, it took me about two hours to write this story. I learned so much and identified a special connection between these two sisters and their families. That kind of thing is the real serendipity in putting these stories together for you. It's fun and probably a better use of my time than sleeping in till 8:00. It's sad that none of you could meet my Reiss grandparents because they were wonderful people. You may want to reread my Granddad's Mondays story of 8/26/2014 titled **Matriarch #3 – Catherine Charlotte Luetzelschwab Reiss.**

Love, Granddad

PS: Notice in the first paragraph on page 2 that Elsie C. C. Weihl has two middle names both starting with the letter "C". I became curious about whether those two names were also the first two names of my grandmother Catherine Charlotte Luetzelschwab Reiss. So, I wrote to my second cousin Gladys who gave me the three post cards. Here's our email exchange –

Hi, Gladys. I hope this find you two in good health and ready for a beautiful summer. I wrote the attached story for my grandchildren to go to them in September. Can you look at my notes in the green highlights and tell me what your mom's middle names were. Thanks,

Steve

Hi, Steve. It is always good to hear from you. We are doing well. My mother's middle names were taken from her grandmothers. Elsie C. C. Weihl. The two "C's" stand for Charlotte (Luetz) and Caroline (Keim) Weihl.

Also looking forward to the June 6, 2020 Luetzelschwab Reunion at the farm home of Leon Lang. Save the date cards will soon be in the making.
Gladys

PPS: If you four ever have another sister or a daughter of your own, you might consider naming her Charlotte to continue that family connection. Turns out my grandmother Katie even had a sister named Charlotte H. Luetzelschwab who went by "Lottie".

Put June 6, 2020 on your calendars for the next Luetzelschwab Reunion. They do that every five years. We'll make it into an extended weekend at our family farm and go to a baseball game in St. Louis to help convert your dads away from being Cubs fans!!!

Reiss Men at the Family Farm

Dear Will, Kayla, Ava, and Blake,   November 25, 2019

Here's my brother Ken and me with our dad in front of the home where he was born on September 18, 1917 on the Reiss Family Farm. This was probably Dad's last visit to the farm because he died less than two years later on April 11, 2007. Ken and I had previously taken Dad to the dedication of the World War II Memorial in Washington, DC on Memorial Day 2004.

Will, Kayla, Ava, and Blake, your great grandfather lived a long and very full life. His humble beginning on a farm with **no electricity or indoor plumbing until after he left home for college** is still amazing to me. He did his school homework by kerosene lamp or candles.

Our family farm was established in 1834 and is the oldest lineally owned family farm in all of St. Clair County, Illinois. We already appear in the 150-year sesquicentennial registry of family farms established by the State of Illinois. You four are in charge of the 200-year reunion coming up in less than 15 years. In the meantime, enjoy a bountiful Thanksgiving on Thursday.

Love, Granddad

Our Grapevine Swing

Dear Will, Kayla, Ava, and Blake,   April 14, 2014

Here is the extended Reiss family on the Friday after Thanksgiving in 1954 working off a big meal from the day before. The photo is by Frank Reiss. The head scarf ladies are Gerry Reiss at center and Grandma Katie Reiss at the lower right. George Reiss is on the swing, Ken Reiss has already swung across, Richard Reiss and I are next in line. Location is the east side of the woods lane halfway from the homestead to the mailbox on the Reiss family farm.

The only negative about making a grapevine swing is that you have to cut the grapevine off near ground level so it's free to swing out from a hillside or across a creek like this picture. That cutting kinda kills the vine such that it will only last another two or three years for safe swinging.

That cutting also stops the vine from making hundreds of pea-size grapes like this picture. These little grapes are quite small so it takes a lot to make a dozen. On top of that they are mostly skin and seeds such that you can't munch on them like the seedless kind your moms bring home from Krogers. These wild grapes however are good for making old fashioned wild grape jelly. Grapes ripen in late August. Get them ahead of the birds. Here is the recipe.

3 lbs wild grapes, stemmed
3 cups water
4 1/2 cups sugar. That's a lot of sugar to look into using honey.
1 (85 ml) package liquid pectin

Directions:
- In large saucepan, crush grapes with potato masher; pour in water and bring to boil.
- Reduce heat and simmer, covered, for 10 minutes or until fruit is very soft.
- Transfer to jelly bag or colander lined with a double thickness of fine cheesecloth and let drip overnight.
- Measure juice (you should have 3 cups) into a large heavy saucepan; stir in sugar.
- Bring to boil over high heat, stirring constantly.
- Stir in pectin.
- Return to full boil and boil hard for one minute, stirring constantly.
- Remove from heat and skim off foam with a metal spoon.
- Pour into sterilized jars, leaving 1/8 inch headspace.

Practicalities:
- Don't de-stem the grapes. It takes too much time and your fingers get all blue. Just pick out the unripe grapes and most of the spiders.
- Don't let your first slurry drip overnight. Just use that same potato masher to gently push the liquid through the cheesecloth and continue with the directions.
- That foam during the second and third boilings can be eliminated with a pinch of butter to break the surface tension. We know that from making maple syrup.
- If you made only enough jelly for one or two jars, keep it in the fridge for use over the next few months rather than messing with a water bath canning process.
- If even this practicalized jelly-making process sounds like too much work, make grape wine instead of grape jelly!!!

One question I try to answer when I see real old and loose grapevines is how they grew so high without being attached to anything closer to the ground. There might be 20 feet before their smaller tentacles attach to nearby tree canopies. I think the answer is that both the vine and the tree started out small and grew up together. Maybe the tree died and rotted away.

Will and Ava, one time your dad and I sawed through a poison ivy vine that had grown up a white oak tree in our front yard. We counted the growth rings and found there were 35 that were each less than 1/16th of an inch thick. That vine was about 1.5 inches in diameter. Those numbers would also apply to grape vines.

Will, Kayla, Ava, and Blake, we have lots of grapevines in our yard for harvesting grapes and making jelly. I don't recall any, however, that are on a hillside for making a swing. Plus I'm not real keen about cutting them off because that would make the grapevine sad. We'll make rope swings on those hillsides instead. Check out the grapevine swing poem on the next page.

Love, Granddad

PS: Here's a poem from 1892 by Samuel Minturn Peck from his book of poems called <u>Rings and Love-Knots</u>. He was Alabama's first poet laureate. It's written from a southern perspective about plantations and cotton but it does a good job expressing the fun and unique memories of swinging on a grapevine swing.

Swinging on a Grapevine Swing

When I was a boy on the old plantation,
Down by the deep bayou -
The fairest spot of all creation
Under the arching blue -
When the wind came over the cotton and corn,
To the long, slim loop I'd spring
With brown feet bare, and a hat-brim torn,
And swing in the grapevine swing.

Swinging in the grapevine swing,
Laughing where the wild birds sing,
I dream and sigh
For the days gone by,
Swinging in the grapevine swing.

Out o'er the water lilies bonny and bright
Back to the moss-green trees;
I shouted and laughed with a heart as light
As a wild rose tossed by the breeze.
The mocking bird joined in my reckless glee;
I longed for no angel's wing;
I was just as near heaven as I wanted to be
Swinging in the grapevine swing.

Swinging in the grapevine swing,
Laughing where the wild birds sing -
Oh, to be a boy
With a heart full of joy,
Swinging in the grapevine swing!

I'm weary at noon, I'm weary at night,
I'm fretted and sore of heart,
And care is sowing my locks with white
As I wend through the fevered mart.
I'm tired of the world with its pride and pomp,
And fame seems a worthless thing.
I'd barter it all for one day's romp,
And a swing in the grapevine swing.

Swinging in the grapevine swing,
Laughing where the wild birds sing -
I would I were away
From the world today,
Swinging in the grapevine swing.

Last Will and Signature of Adam Reiss

Dear Will, Kayla, and Ava,   May 19, 2014

Here is the last signature of your great great great great grandfather Adam Reiss –

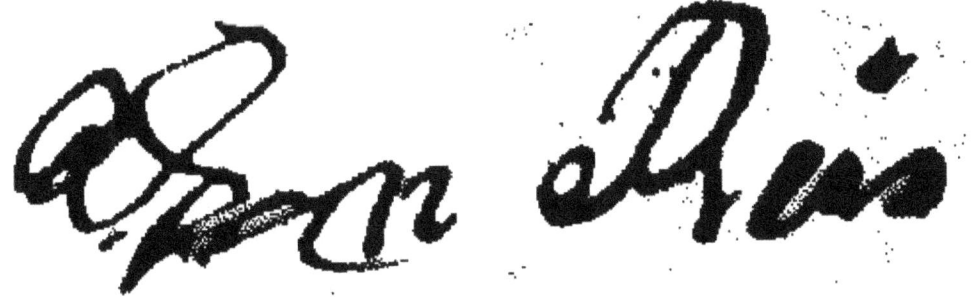

You can see it below at the end of his last will and testament that he signed on May 23, 1849, the day he passed away at age 45 years and 16 days which is 165 years ago this coming Friday. It was written in German and later translated into longhand English which I then typed.

Translation – Last Will & Testament

I the undersigned have come to the conclusion to make these presents my last will and testament to wit. My wife Margaret Reis alias Basler shall have and receive beforehand two hundred dollars. #2 I devise to my wife, one-third part of my farm as her absolute property for and during her natural life: which I have signed with signature in presence of witnesses.

County St. Clair this 23rd of May, 1849.

George Ritter
Franz Stauder
Dr. Peter Bauer
Adam Reiss

Will, Kayla, and Ava, above is the last of three signatures we have of our patriarch Adam Reiss who established the family in 1838 in Prairie du Long Township of St. Clair County, Illinois. A lot has transpired in the 165 years since his passing. He left behind his wife Margaret age 30 and 5 children under age 11. Worse yet, Margaret lost their sixth child who was stillborn sometime in 1849. They all lived in a one-room log cabin and would have been extremely challenged to eke out a living on the family farm. Can you imagine what they had to endure?

Love, Granddad

The Reiss Family Farm Pond

Dear Will, Kayla, Ava, and Blake,   June 9, 2014

Here is the 70-year history of the home farm pond which lies west of the 1889 homestead and between the north and south rows of cedar trees. It starts with three entries from my Grandma Katie's diary – three days after I was born in 1944 followed by two entries in 1948.

June 1944

Thurs 15 – State men were here to measure and outline the pond or lake.

July 1948

Thurs 15 – Pop worked on the pond dam and mixed feed.

November 1948

Sat 6 – Geo & Ludger made a dam in the pasture.

March 1949

Fri 4 – Fair very pretty day no frost. Henry Lang brought some fish for our pond.

Here's what the farm pond looked like in the fall of 1949 when my cousins George and Richard were throwing mud balls and sticks to make ripples. You can see there isn't much water because the drainage area that fed this pond was too small. Notice the north row of cedar trees in the distance. Next page has two photos from 1955 – one before a major bulldozer renovation and one after. Still not much water before the grading.

That's my 82-year old grandfather "Pop" in the second picture. That brown cylinder in the middle of the second photo is a 55-gallon steel drum full of rocks which was part of the overflow which established the maximum water depth.

Pond in 1955 before and after renovation.

Here's the pond in 1960 with a field of mature wheat to the south and the Klein farm in the distance. The two rows or cedar trees are out of the picture to the right and left.

Photos from 1964 on the next pages are of Lavern and Harold Lang seining for fish and turtles with a long net. Their families and other relatives are helping. You can see the top of that overflow drum in the foreground. I remember seeing all these huge fish being caught and then butchered for a big fish fry. It was really a lot of fun. I remember Lavern's brother Harold somehow catching a large snapping turtle which became tasty soup.

Here's the pond in 1974 full of water and hosting several families of ducks.

Here's the pond in 2013. It had been bone dry for several years. You can also see how what water it occasionally held would have contained lots of fertilizer runoff from fields to the left.

We asked our crop share tenant, Al Klein, and our farm manager, Bret Cude, about the viability of bulldozing the pond half of that field back into agricultural production. We asked that same question of the area where the question marks are on the other side of the

woods lane. Both men thought both ideas were good. Al even mentioned that he had a bulldozer and did that kind of work himself. He gave us a price and estimated we could pick up five acres of cropland. He added that his wife Ann sat on the local environmental board that would have to first approve such work because it was a watershed issue. We owners voted for that bulldozer work to proceed. Below are several photos from 2014 where that work was completed except for burning five large brush piles. Those two areas are now in soybeans for this year's crop. Only problem was that Al's earthmover was a Deere instead of a Caterpillar.

Will, Kayla, Ava, and Blake, this ends the 70-year history of the family farm pond. Biggest problem besides many years of insufficient water is that we ran out of grandchildren who greatly enjoyed quarterly weekend visits to the home farm to stay overnight with Grandma and Pop. That's a huge frustration for me but that's simply how time moves on.

Love, Granddad

Farming with Horses

Dear Will, Kayla, Ava, and Blake,   July 14, 2014

I think you know by now that your great great grandfather, George Reiss, farmed the home farm in St. Clair County with horses. Pop never owned a tractor. He used only horses until 1948 when he retired at age 75. His horses also retired then but they were probably only 20 years old. I remember feeding them handfuls of grass through the fence boards. They liked that.

I am totally totally totally blown away by how labor intensive it is to farm with horses. We know from Grandma Katie's two diaries which covered 1944 through 1953 how hard her husband worked to first plow his fields, then smooth the ground with a disk or harrow, then plant his crop, then cultivate for weeds, and finally harvest with horse-drawn equipment or a wagon he loaded with hand-picked corn.

Grand DD and I wanted Will to see what's involved in plowing with horses, so we traveled 20 miles north of Springfield in the spring of 2013 to see lots of demonstrations in a 40-acre field. There were about 30 teams of horses, mules, and ponies. All pulled one-bottom plows which would make furrows about two feet of width and five inches of depth. You can do the math and see that a one-acre field that was only two feet wide would be four miles long. So, plowing one full acre of any shape was considered a full day's work for one horse and operator whether that man was walking or riding. Plowing a 40-acre field would take a month so no wonder farms were much smaller than they are now. Check out our photos below.

Here's are three paragraphs I found on the internet – The question of how many horses to keep was tied closely to the value of the tractor when the farmer considered the most hectic stage of production: springtime plowing. Without a tractor, plowing created a temporary large demand for horses. After the ground thawed, farmers had only a few weeks available to break and disk their fields. Plowing was a time-consuming job: a single horse took a full ten-hour day to break one acre.

A single draught horse can normally pull a single-furrow plow in clean light soil, but in heavier soils two horses are needed, one walking on the land and one in the furrow. For plows with two or more furrows more than two horses are needed and, usually, one or more horses have to walk on the loose plowed sod – and that makes hard going for them, and the horse treads the

newly plowed land down. It is usual to rest such horses every half hour for about ten minutes. Amish farmers tend to use a team of about seven horses or mules when spring plowing and as Amish farmers often help each other plow, teams are sometimes changed at noon. Using this method about 10 acres can be plowed per day in light soils and about 2 acres in heavy soils.

Will, Kayla, Ava, and Blake, the letter below was written 145 years ago by your great great great great uncle Charles Reiss. He was the third son of Adam Reiss who established our family farm in 1838. Charles loaned his team of mules to a neighbor near his farm in O'Fallon, Illinois who severely overworked and underfed them. Charles was not happy and minced no words. His phonetic English is a challenge at times. German was his first language. Enjoy.

Love, Granddad

Jan the 7th, 1869
O'Fallon

Brother Frank,

I am giting consarn for not hearing anney news of Brother Martin or of anney one of yours. Martin I gas is not com & you I expected to com Chrismas or New Years but you dit not so, how ever the weder (*weather*) dus not alweys alou satch as travling wit familay.

Frank I will let you know to bee careful next time in loning your team. That fallow of corse went out the Collinsville Road. At least he was at his broter in laws & I think or have heard so that tha had a fallin out togater & so he come up to me yet after we hat spoken & he told me storey that tha hat been at the graveyard at her Faters so long. We knot (*knowed*) in the first quarter of an hour that the men drove them. The poor mules was awful hukray (*hungry*) and tursday (*thirsty*), but don't you tell him about it at least not of me. I gave him corn along & told him partickler to feed tham in Balleville. But it is doutful if he has dun it. I du dispice the fallow now. Some how I think he had to much back at home alltho that she is nothing but a little shiting liing bitch & dumhead.

Frank I wish you talk C. Armbruster. See wen my note is du, what day & month. I will send the interest, but see if I can have the money six monts or a year longer. Trey so if you can. We have a good prospect for next year. Our wheat looks splandant yet. Let me know in time of all quasttions. I think my mother in law is out there now. Have you seen one hurt of her? Are their anney thing new? News of Martin or Crone?

Come over hear some time yet if you can. If there should bee more satch nice weter, Mother & Ebert could come even too. I have my cyder tabt (*tapped*) now. Tell tham so & give my love to Mother & children. I also give my complaments to you & famlay and hope that this will find you all in good heald. My selve & famley have been pradey well ever sins William began to walk a little sins three days. He is very slow about it. Your Brother,

C. J. Reiss

PS: How dit Chrismas & Newyears pa of? Our Chrismas a friend of ours paid for a gallon of bear witch we drink in the eavning & lunsht (*lunch*) sassach (*sausage*) to it. A happy & lucke new year to you all in dat famley.

Pop's Hands

Dear Will, Kayla, Ava, and Blake,   September 29, 2014

My grandfather, George "Pop" Reiss, had the largest and strongest hands of any person I ever met. You can see that in the second and third pictures below where he is holding his first surviving grandson, George Henry Irwin Reiss, who was born on 2/26/1942. The first picture of the two was taken about 72 years ago. The second picture of them was taken less than a year later. Grandma and Pop did have an earlier grandson, William George Reiss, Jr., who was born on 11/4/1938 but he did not survive the day. That sad news made the 1942 birth even more special. Both grandsons had "George" in their name.

Pop was born on 4/22/1873 on the Reiss Family Farm and lived there until he passed away on 8/19/1964 at age 91.3 years. Here he is about age three in 1876 which is the oldest picture we have of him. I remember him telling me a story which happened when he was age five or six. He was at a general store with his dad, perhaps the one that used to be in Floraville 1.7 miles west of their farm. The storekeeper asked young George and other kids if they wanted some free candy. You know their immediate answer, but George had to first empty rocks and sticks out of his pants pockets to make room for that candy. George was eagerly throwing those sticks to the side and did not realize that he was standing close to an old German sword which was lying on top of a wooden barrel. The end of the middle finger on his right hand struck that sword with enough impact to split the fingernail back into the quick. From then on, George had two fingernails on that finger. You can see that in next picture below.

Pop and Grandma bought the 180-acre family farm from his parents in 1921. They had already bought 180 acres of adjacent farmland in 1917 so now he was farming 360 acres just as his three sons were born in 1912 thru 1917. So Pop and Grandma had their hands very full with three sons, church, one-room school, crops, chickens, pigs, horses, wood heat and cooking, no tractor, and no electricity until 1945. He worked as a farmer until age 75. No wonder Pop developed large, strong hands. Can you imagine!!!

Will, Kayla, and Ava, there is absolutely no greater joy for an adult than holding a new family baby, especially when it's your own grandchild who is named after you. Will, I know that feeling very well myself since you have been a huge joy in our lives for 4

243

years, 8 months, and 8 days. I'm also thrilled that you share your first name with your other grandfather, "Ba" Pottgen.

I have Pop's wedding ring which shows very little wear. I took it to a jeweler who measured it as size 13 which is the largest standard size available. Anything larger would have to be custom made for really big people like Shaquille O'Neal. Here's a full size chart of standard sizes. I don't see that ring on Pop's finger in the 1943 picture below. Perhaps he didn't wear it because it was too small and his ring finger was actually larger than size 13!!!

Size 5
15.7 mm

Size 6
16.5 mm

Size 7
17.3 mm

Size 8
18.2 mm

Size 9
18.9 mm

Size 10
19.8 mm

Size 11
20.6 mm

Size 12
21.3 mm

Size 13
22.2 mm

Will, Kayla, Ava, and Blake, here's Will "wearing"
Pop's ring on two fingers and Ava "wearing" it on three.
Below is a poem I found titled "My Grandfather's
Hands" which is very appropriate for this Granddad's
Mondays story. The poem even mentioned 91 years
which exactly matched Pop's life.

Love, Granddad

My Grandfather's Hands

Funny the things we recall.
Images that flash through our brain.
Some most vivid for me were of an old man.
Skin like creased parchment paper,
Lined and yellowed with age.
The veins visible just below the surface,
of a thin nearly transparent veneer.
Liver spotted flecks of red,
Charted paths from the toil of many years,
Palms callused forever from a life time of labor.
Big fingers knotted and misshapen.

Looking at those old hands, one could hardly guess
That still there remained gentleness in their caress.
For an old dog, or a little grandson in need of some
Companionable affection or parental love.

Those aged hands could also make things,
Toy sailboats, and wooden trains, complete with caboose.
A cool flute whistle that actually worked,
He said it was like the Indian's used out Oklahoma way.
And he would know, he'd cowboyed there.

His hands taught me to tie my shoes,
Open and close my first pocket knife.
Those same hands could become birds,
rabbits, butterfly's, all sorts of things.
When projected up on the wall,
Silhouetted by a naked back light.
His hands knew magic too,
Could pluck silver coins right out of my ears.

His tired face matched his hands,
visual weathered, creased, and wrinkled road maps,
Of 91 years of rugged life traveled.

Yet, his lively pale blue eyes remained
forever fraudulently youthful prisms,
Eyes and spirit of a much younger man within.

But it is his hands most of all I shall remember,
Their imposing look and their reassuring
touch of tenderness.

I shall never forget my Grandfather's hands.

Cisterns and Saturday Night Baths

Dear Will, Kayla, Ava, and Blake,   December 15, 2014

Maybe it's obvious but there is normally no city water when you live on a farm. It's just too far away and too expensive to lay water pipes. Farmers have several options – draw water from a nearby lake or stream, dig a well to reach underground water, dig a cistern to save rainwater from roof gutters, or stand in the rain with their mouths open.

Here are Grandma Katie's diary notes from 1953 when a new cistern was dug on the north side of their farmhouse. They already had a well and a cistern on the south side from when the house was built in 1940. Jakie and Johnny are Grandma's brothers Jacob and John Luetzelschwab. Lavern is the new tenant on the Reiss farm and Henry is his dad. George is Katie's husband and Bill is their son. Henry's wife is Katie's sister Edna so all of these people are relatives except Raymond who is a neighbor.

If this new cistern was 10 feet in diameter and 6 feet deep, that would be 471 cubic feet or 3,500 gallons of water. The house is 28 by 32 feet so with 1-foot eaves, the roof area is 1,020 square feet. That means it would take 41" of rain to fill the cistern. Average annual Illinois rainfall is 48" in the south to 32" in the north. A more likely scenario is that the cistern was maybe 8 feet in diameter and 4 feet deep which means it would fill on just 18 inches of rain. I called Lavern who dug the cistern and he said it was about 8 feet in diameter and 10 feet deep so it would take 45" of rain. In other words, it was probably never full, especially when rainwater was also diverted to the cistern on the south side of the house.

April 1953

Fri 17 – Jakie brought all the bricks for our new cistern.

June 1953

Mon 1 – Johnny & Jakie came to start on the cistern.

Tues 2 – Henry & Lavern Lang helped ½ day with the cistern. Raymond helped in the afternoon.

Wed 3 – Johnny, Jakie and Geo & I worked on the cistern.

Thurs 4 – Langs, Jakie & Johnny all worked on our cistern. All dug and started to lay bricks.

Fri 5 – Langs, Jakie & Johnny bricked the cistern today.

Mon 8 – Johnny & Jakie made the concrete slab for the cistern top.

Mon 15 – Lang's, Jakie & Johnny came and plastered the cistern & laid the slab on top.

Tues 16 – Johnny & Jakie finished the spouting for cistern.

July 1953

Sat 18 – Bill & Johnny set up our water system.

Rainwater is naturally "soft" because is has not touched the ground where it could absorb calcium and other elements which make it "hard." Hard water tastes "normal" but soft water is better for laundry and baths because it makes soap bubbles faster, easier, and bigger.

Here's my cousin George Reiss in 1945 taking a bath in cistern water that sat in this tub all day so it could be warmed by the sun. That means this is the south cistern which is in

the sun instead of the new north cistern which is in the house shadow. I remember taking lots of these cistern baths in the 1950s. The real challenge was to figure out which of us three kids went first because the same water was used for all. Maybe we flipped a coin or maybe whoever was dirtiest always went last.

Will, Kayla, Ava, and Blake, this coming summer we'll put our laundry tub on our back deck and let you fill it from the garden hose. There is lots of privacy there just like on Pop and Katie's farm so you four can take Saturday night baths. We'll let you figure out who goes first. Whaduyasay?

Love, Granddad

Cedar Row Farm

Dear Will, Kayla, Ava, and Blake,   October 13, 2014

Your great great grandfather George "Pop" Reiss planted two rows of cedar trees about 1900 on the Reiss family farm. You can see those two rows in the satellite photo below going left from the two yellow pins. This picture was taken on 11/12/2013 about 10:00 in the morning because the shadows angle off to the north northwest which makes the trees appear much taller. Kinda neat photo effect, don't you think?

The north row was probably intended as a windbreak to knock down storms coming from the northwest. The south row was planted right along the west farm lane probably as an accent effect. My guess is that trees for both rows were volunteer saplings which Pop simply transplanted from croplands where they would be destroyed by farming. These trees were planted well before the second homestead was built on the south side of the farm lane in 1940.

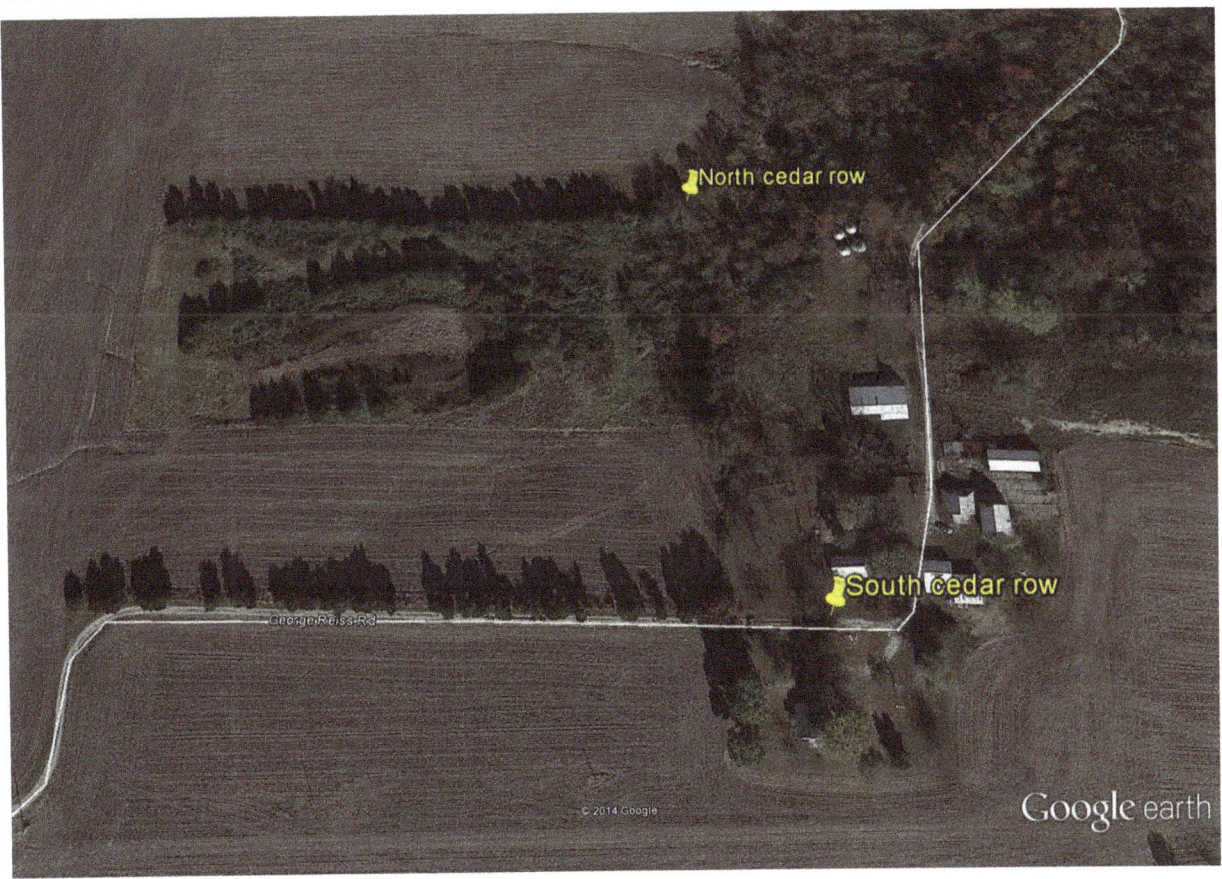

Pop was really proud of his cedar trees and eventually named his farm "Cedar Row Farm" which was part of his mailing address with the Post Office. I remember writing letters to my grandparents in the 1950s and my dad always made sure I included "Cedar Row Farm" as a separate line of the envelope address.

The first picture below is the north cedar row in 1955. It looks like Pop kept the lower branches trimmed. The second picture is the south cedar row in 2014.

Will, Kayla, Ava, and Blake, I'm proud to say your great great grandfather was a "tree guy." Not only did he plant these two rows of cedar trees but Pop also planted about an acre of pine trees in 1940 which is mentioned in my story on 10/15/2012. You might want to reread my cedar Christmas tree story on 12/17/2012. It will be a little difficult to collect a cedar "leaf" for your seventh grade science project, but we'll do our best since there is a long family connection.

Love, Granddad

A New House on the Reiss Farm in 1940

Dear Will, Kayla, Ava, and Blake,   October 6, 2014

Here is a construction view of the west side of Grandma and Pop's new house in the middle of 1940. The builder is John Luetzelschwab who is walking the roof getting ready to lay two more rolls of tarpaper and then five bundles of shingles. Johnny is Grandma's oldest brother by 6.5 years and made his living as a carpenter and general contractor. He was charging my grandparents $0.50 per hour for his time. I don't know the other worker but it might be one of Grandma's other brothers – Herman, Jacob, or Frank. He even looks a little bit like my dad who had that summer off from college.

In the doorway is my Aunt Anita Reiss and her daughter June Ann who is age 3.5. They belong to Bill Reiss who is my dad's oldest brother.

A faint copy of the first-floor blueprint appears on the next page. West is to the right and east to the left. Area is 896 square feet. The second floor has 3' knee walls so its central area is about 500 square feet. There is a full basement. Not shown is an enclosed porch along the east side which measures about 8 by 25 feet for another 200 square feet. It had windows on three sides and was a great place for fragrant geraniums which were always in bloom. The porch was often the lunch or dinner location for large family meals on holidays.

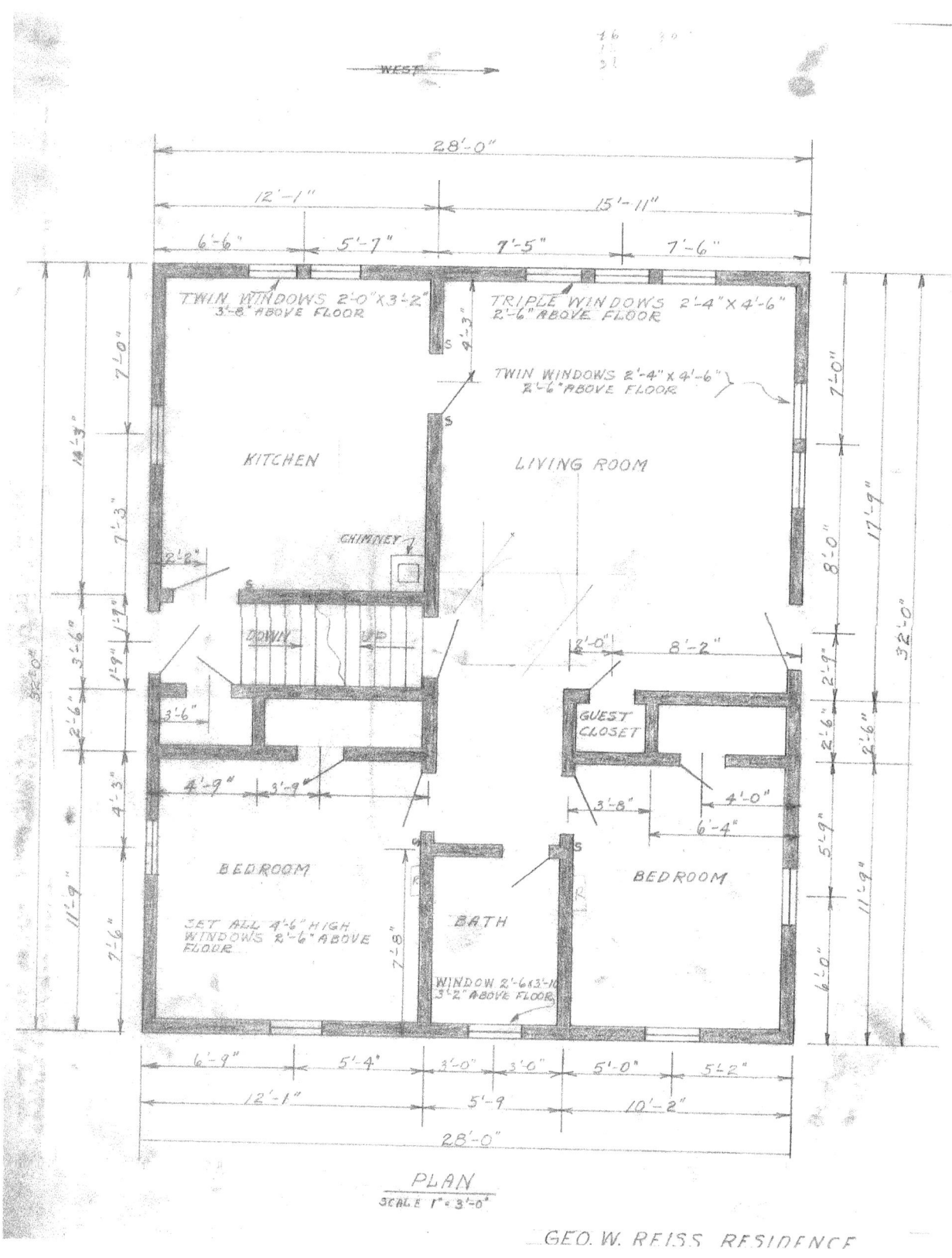

PLAN
SCALE 1" = 3'-0"

GEO. W. REISS RESIDENCE

Here's a tally of eggs Johnny was buying from his sister during August and September. It was written on the back of his letterhead which you can see in reverse. Notice the egg prices are per dozen. Ask your moms what they pay now for eggs. I'm sure it's more than a penny apiece.

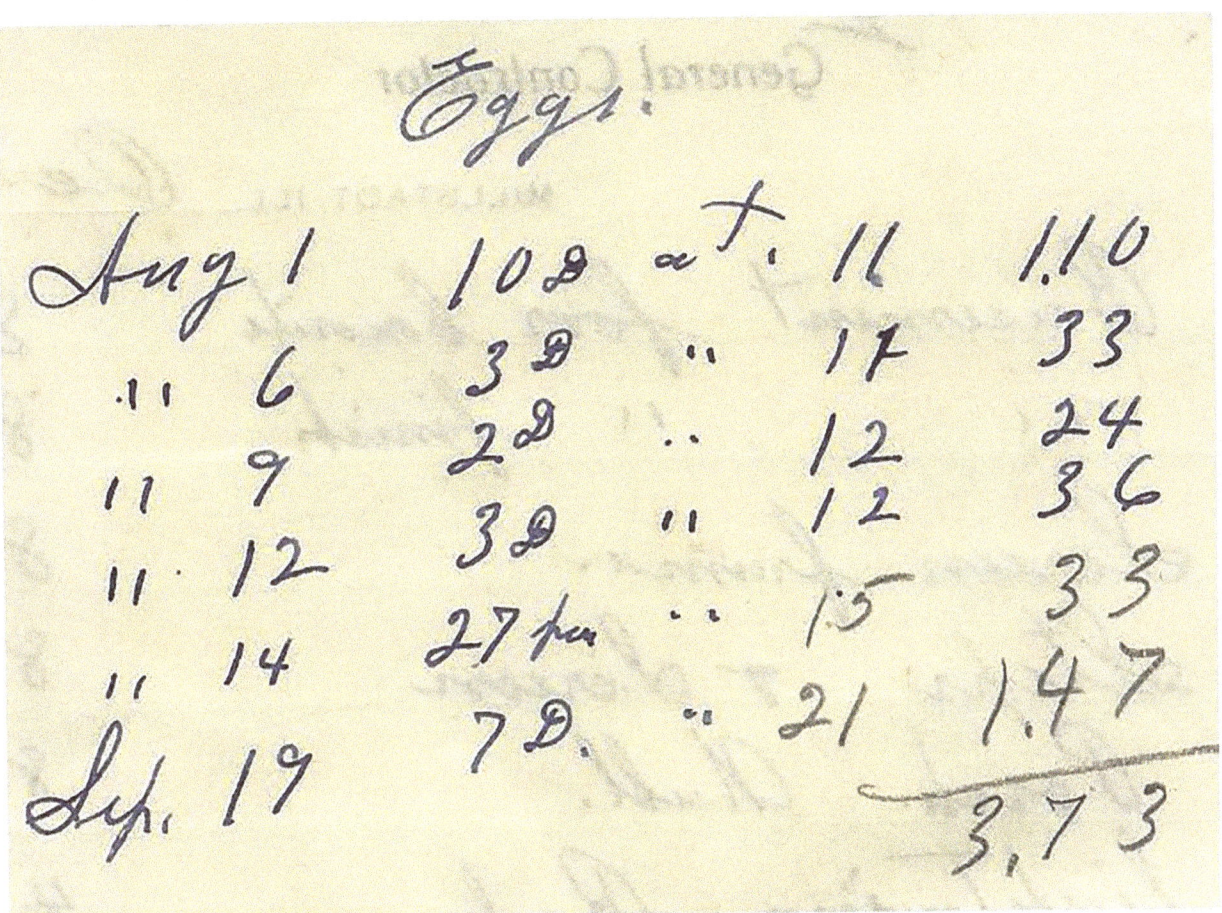

Will, Kayla, Ava, and Blake, the picture on the next page is my Grandmother Katie on her 53rd birthday March 25, 1943. She is standing outside the south porch door. That purse is probably a birthday gift. Notice that she is wearing an apron. That's not because she was cooking her own birthday dinner that Thursday. It's because she just liked to wear an apron, especially when going for walks with her grandchildren. Maybe it's a German or Swiss custom. That will be the subject of a future Granddad's Mondays story.

Love, Granddad

March 25, 1943

Grandma's Diary on Butchering Hogs, Preserving Meat, and Making Soap in 1944 – 1948

Dear Will, Kayla, Ava, and Blake,   February 15, 2021

I remember watching several hogs being butchered on our family farm in the early 1950s. These were semi-social events involving three or more neighbors and relatives who took turns doing this on each other's farms. The men did outdoor cutting and cleaning tasks and the women did meat preservation tasks including rendering lard. This was all 75 years ago, some of it without electricity which did not come to our farm until 11/17/1945.

Each of you has our family history book "Granger, Quilter, Grandma, Matriarch" which is your great great grandmother Katie Reiss' five-year daily diary for 1944 – 1948. Each of you also has the companion diary book for 1949 – 1953 titled "Quilter, Granger, Grandma, Matriarch".

Perhaps you remember my Granddad's Mondays stories of 2/10/2014 titled "Raising Chickens and Eggs on the Reiss Farm in 1944" and of 2/24/2014 titled "Growing Corn and Raising Hogs on the Reiss Farm in 1944". They were summaries of Grandma's diary entries on those subjects for that one year. Well, what follows below is a summary of Grandma's entries on the three title subjects above for all five of those diary years.

I want to explain several terms – rendering lard, sausage, fried-in, canning, and cooking soap. Remember, Grandma had no refrigerator but she did have access to a public locker or freezer in Millstadt which would store meat for a fee. They might have even made sausage for a fee from the raw meat Grandma provided because they had electric grinders.

1944

Jan 3 & 4 – We butchered a 450-lb hog, made summer sausage. We rendered the lard. It made 10 gals. I canned 7 quarts of liver sausage.

Feb 4 & 7 & 9 – We butchered a 300-lb hog. I salted and wrapped up the 2 hams and 2 shoulders. Fried-in sausage and canned ribs in evening.

1945

June 29 – Hot winds all day. I cooked soap and picked apricots.

Oct 4 & 5 & 13 – Fair. I cooked soap. Geo fixed his disk. I cooked soap. Geo husked corn. I cooked a kettle-ful of soap. Geo worked on his wheat land.

Dec 13 & 14 – Cloudy to fair, snowed 2 inches over night, 25 degrees. We butchered one 400-lb hog. I canned 12 qts liver sausage and rendered the lard.

1946

Mar 13 – We butchered 2 hogs today. One for Johnny & Katie and one for us. We put most of it into locker, 74 lbs.

1947

Jan 3 & 4, 8 & 9 – 13 above. Edna called up that Henry would come and get our hog and butcher it at their place so I went along & stayed overnight. After butchering, Henry took me home, went thru Millstadt and left 17 lbs pork sausage mix at the locker. Next day I smoked the pork sausage. Next day I fried-in 4 gals pork sausage and made brine for the ham & bacon.

May 2 & 3 – We butchered a 100-lb hog. We were at Millstadt, took 2 hams to locker.

May 12 & 13 & 14 – We went to see about a horse at Leingang's. The next day, Leingang brought the horse, 85 dollars, collar 3 dollars. Next day was fair, very hot. Geo disked with the new horse. *Pop retired from farming in 1948 at age 75. He never owned a tractor and farmed only with horses.*

1948

Jan 9 & 10 & 14 – Fair, colder. We butchered at Henry Lang's today and took 2 hams, 2 shoulders, and 2 backbones for pork chops to locker. I rendered the lard today, made 6 gallons. One inch of snow, cold, 7 above, I rendered the lard for Bill & Anita.

Pigs are usually harvested at the age of one year or less because feed conversion is faster and better. A 350-pound pig would yield about 175 pounds of marketable cuts.

- 90 lbs Sausage
- 40 lbs Ham roasts
- 15 lbs Shoulder roasts
- 15 lbs Ribs (with bone)
- 8 lbs Chops
- 5 lbs Shank (with bone)
- 4 lbs Tenderloin
- 42 Quarts stock
- 5 Gallons rendered lard

Rendering lard – This starts with chunks of fat from various parts of the hog which are put into a large pot on a stove top and heated until it becomes liquid. The lard would become solid again at room temperature. It can be stored in glass jars at room temperature for future use. But as a liquid it could be poured over cooked meat in glass jars or glazed

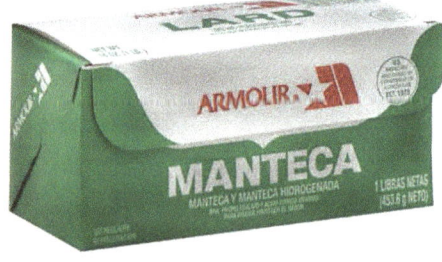

earthenware crocks to seal out the air. It could also be mixed with lye to make soap.   It looks just like Crisco which is made from vegetable oils instead of animal fat. Today you can buy lard in a grocery store on the baking goods shelf in a cardboard wrap.

Sausage – Grandma's pork sausage as patties or as brats is my all-time favorite food. It's better than Jimmy Dean and Johnsonville combined, especially when cooked with scrambled eggs on a woodburning stove in her kitchen. Grandma's sausage was even better than "pralines and cream" ice cream from Baskin Robbins. Anyway, you get the idea.

Look at the pounds per hog in the table above and see that over half of all the meat ends up as sausage. It's all the meat trimmings that are not made into larger cuts. Seasoning includes black/red pepper, paprika, fennel, dried parsley, etc.

Fried-in – This means to cook sausage patties or three-inch cuts of links until it's almost done and ready to eat. It's a way of killing germs, melting out a little fat, removing air trapped in links, and putting great smells in the kitchen. While that cooked meat is still hot it's transferred into glass jars or earthenware crocks for sealing with hot liquid rendered lard.

Canning – Grand DD and I can applesauce for you kids using the water bath process. I don't know if that's the process Grandma used or whether she used a pressure cooker. We prefer our process because the temperatures are lower and have less effect on the food. Here's a photo which shows sausage patties in a glass jar which was partially filled with liquid lard, and then turned over before the lard solidifies to help seal the lid.

Cooking soap – We used lots of soap bars that Grandma made. Sad to say, we never saw her actually making that soap. Handling the lye part of the process can be a little dangerous so don't trying making soap on your own even if it means skipping your standard Saturday night bath. A basic sample recipe would be 22 oz of lard, 3 oz of lye, and 8 oz of water. Heat, stir, and pour into molds or a slab to be cut into bars later.

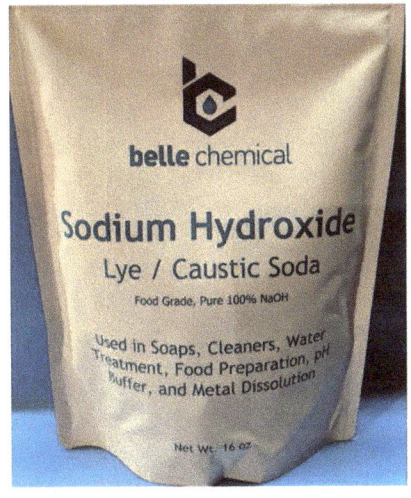

I assume Grandma bought her lye from a grocery store rather than making it herself from wood ashes like maybe your great great great great grandma Margaret Basler Reiss did on the home farm a 100 years earlier.

Will, Kayla, Ava, and Blake, I have many radical memories of visiting our Reiss grandparents on the family farm. We are truly blessed that Grandma put ten years of her memories in daily diaries that her grandson (aka Granddad) eventually put into print as two public books. Those diaries have led to half a dozen Granddad's Mondays stories and there may still be more to come.

Numerous visits to the home farm and Grandma's words from 75 years ago have significantly reinforced and defined our job descriptions as your grandparents. Both Grand DD and I are now blessed with time, resources, and almost enough energy to expose you four to the wonders of nature, history, travel, and society so you can broaden your experiences and learn to think way way way outside the box.

Love, Granddad

PS: I had saved the Family Circus cartoon on the left on 2/24/2020 to use it on a future story like this one. I also saved the cartoon on the right on 11/4/2020 to use it on another future story. Then on 11/10/2020, I noticed these cartoons are essentially identical except for colors and captions which are both pretty clever. Looks to me like Jeff Keane plagiarized his own stuff. Shame shame!!!

"Being a grandma must've been boring before us kids came along."

"Really, Grandma? I haven't noticed the world changing."

Grandma's Apron

Dear Will, Kayla, Ava, and Grant Jr.,   December 8, 2014

This is one of my favorite subjects. I sat down to write this story and was hoping to find a poem that would be a good start. This is the first poem I found. It was so great and so perfectly matched my memories of my grandma, that I stopped looking and pretty much stopped writing. Here it is:

I don't think our kids know what an apron is.

The principal use of Grandma's apron was to protect the dress underneath,
because she only had a few,
it was easier to wash aprons than dresses and they used less material,
but along with that, it served as a potholder for removing hot pans from the oven.

It was wonderful for drying children's tears,
and on occasion was even used for cleaning out dirty ears...

From the chicken coop, the apron was used for carrying eggs,
fussy chicks, and sometimes half-hatched eggs to be finished in the warming oven.

When company came, those aprons were ideal hiding places for shy kids.

And when the weather was cold grandma wrapped it around her arms.

Those big old aprons wiped many a perspiring brow, bent over the hot wood stove.

Chips and kindling wood were brought into the kitchen in that apron.

From the garden, it carried all sorts of vegetables.

After the peas had been shelled, it carried out the hulls.

In the fall, the apron was used to bring in apples that had fallen from the trees.

When unexpected company drove up the road,
it was surprising how much furniture that old apron could dust in a matter of seconds.

When dinner was ready, Grandma walked out onto the porch, waved her apron,
and the men-folk knew it was time to come in from the fields to dinner.

It will be a long time before someone invents something that will replace
that 'old-time apron' that served so many purposes.

Grandma used to set her hot baked apple pies on the window sill to cool.

Her granddaughters set theirs on the window sill to thaw.

They would go crazy now trying to figure out how many germs were on that apron. <mark>I never caught anything from an apron...But Love.</mark>

Here is my Grandma Katie in 1956 with her two-year old grand niece, Lynette Lang. It's no surprise that Lynette grew up to be the current <mark>state president of the Illinois Grange</mark>. Her Aunt Katie deserves some of that credit. Notice Grandma's apron.

Below is Grandma in 1951 at Hoelscher's sawmill on the northeast corner of her farm. She is with grandsons George and Richard. They are about a mile from the homestead. Notice Grandma's apron.

Here's an interesting article about aprons and a farm wife named Esther Duncan which appeared in the 9/1/2006 Danville, Illinois newspaper called "Commercial News." The author visited the Farm Progress Show in Amana, Iowa, which is something Grand DD and I will do in a few more years with all you young farmers.

AMANA, Iowa — While most farmers spent the 2006 Farm Progress Show examining new seed varieties and test driving the latest in farming machinery, Esther Duncan of Veedersburg, Ind., drew many of their wives to the arts and crafts tent.

Among dozens of booths boasting jewelry, cosmetics, and country crafts, Duncan, a seasoned Farm Progress exhibitor, showcased and sold her specialty: replicas of farm women's old aprons.

"I'm not trying to bring the apron back, it's more of a nostalgia trip," she explained of her passion for the garment that once was a staple on every farm.

Duncan has spent countless hours researching the history of aprons and listened to farm women everywhere tell the stories of their aprons.

"I'm more interested in the person who wore the apron than the apron itself. I want to hear the apron talk when I look at it, and how the apron was worn — the rips and tears in it — gives it a voice," she said.

It all started in 1996, when Duncan replicated her mother's old apron and told stories about it at a family reunion.

After that, people began contacting her about copying their old aprons and she started to give talks about the garment's history. The phone never stopped ringing and today she travels to farm shows all over the country with her business Farm Woman's Apron.

Duncan, whom some have branded "the apron lady," is not only driven by her company's success, but also by the resolve to rectify the fact that a woman's work on the farm rarely was recognized, even though the success of the farm depended on it.

In her booth at the Farm Progress Show hung a sign declaring that "Women's handwork is no longer considered women's work. Women's work shall be classified into a new category called ART," which is something Duncan feels strongly about.

Wanda Weber of Cedar Rapids, Iowa, visited Duncan's booth while her husband watched field demonstrations with corn planters and received a history lesson while admiring Duncan's work.

"It was really interesting," she said. Weber especially liked Duncan's farm daughter's apron line. "If I'd had a little granddaughter I would've bought that," she said and pointed at a small orange-and-white checkered apron."

The times when every farm woman owned at least three aprons — one for every-day use, one to wear when she had company and one for Sundays — may be long gone, or as Duncan jokingly puts it, "When women burned their bras, they burned their aprons as well," but she thinks the apron still has a place in modern society.

"Today, most women never wear an apron, but they want to be country chic and hang it in their kitchen. I think aprons are very collectible today and people follow that trend."

Will, Kayla, Ava, and Grant Jr., it looks like I'm not alone in appreciating the traditional farm apron or the wonderful women who wore them. There is great significance and history in farm aprons that you don't see much of today. The memories of Grandma's aprons have stuck with me for over 60 years.

Love, Granddad

Grandma's Custard Fruit Pies

Dear Will, Kayla, and Ava,   July 28, 2014

By now you know that my grandma Katie Reiss was an outstanding cook. My previous stories have mentioned her scrambled eggs and sausage, morel mushrooms, and even her store-bought Cheerios. Well, this story is about her very healthy fruit pies made with apples, cherries, plums, strawberries, gooseberries, blackberries, dewberries, or raspberries which also included custard filling. I don't know what happened to her recipe file, if she even had one, so I looked on Google for custard pie filling which made her pies both tasty and healthy. Here's what I found:

GRANDMA'S PLAIN CUSTARD PIE FILLING

1 c. white sugar
1/2 tsp. butter
1 tsp. vanilla
1/4 tsp. nutmeg
1 tbsp. white flour
4 lg. eggs
2 c. scalded milk
Heat milk in a saucepan to just scalding (do not boil). In bowl combine the sugar, flour and butter. Beat until well mixed. Add vanilla and eggs and beat hard for 3 minutes. While beating, add milk very slowly.

GRANDMA NORMA'S CUSTARD PIE FILLING

4 eggs, beaten
2/3 c. sugar
1/2 tsp. salt
1/2 tsp. nutmeg
2 2/3 c. scalding hot milk
1 tsp. vanilla
Mix in order given and pour into unbaked crust. Bake at 450 degrees for 15 minutes. Reduce to 350 degrees for 10 more minutes. Test for doneness with table knife - should come out clean when done.

AUNT HATTIE'S CUSTARD PIE FILLING

3 c. milk
4 eggs
1/2 c. sugar
1 tsp. vanilla
Heat milk to scalding, beat eggs, add sugar and vanilla. Pour hot milk over mixture. Pour in pie shell. Sprinkle with nutmeg.

These ladies aren't Reiss relatives but it's obvious they wanted to bake healthy pies for their own grandchildren. Notice that all their ingredients are good for youngsters and oldsters except perhaps the sugar content and even that is reduced as you go down the page.

Here are a few pictures of fruit pies with custard filling. Notice that pouring in the custard is the last step before baking so you can pour shallow so the fruit is on top or you can pour deep so the custard is on top. You can mix fruits together like the lower right which is a combination of apples, strawberries, and blueberries. Notice also that the cast iron skillet pie in the lower left which has no crust so it's probably the healthiest of them all. If you baked that skillet pie over a campfire, you could toss the emptied skillet back into the hot embers upside down which slowly converts the pie crumbs to a light grey dust that brushes off. No scrubbing or washing. That's the way the Boy Scouts do dishes but it only works on cast iron.

Will, Kayla, and Ava, we can make our custard fruit pies even more healthy by harvesting our own fruit or buying it at a farmers market rather than buying cans of small fruits at Krogers which probably contain a sugar syrup. If we bought fresh sweet Bing or Rainier cherries rather than traditional tart pie cherries, we could probably take all the sugar out of our custard filling. To further authenticate our pie-making process, you three could each choose different cherry pitters from my basement museum of antique kitchen contraptions. You could de-seed the cherries for our

pie but you might want to leave a seed or two as proof our cherries were not from a store-bought can. Just be sure to not bite down hard on a seed. I don't remember my grandma using any table mounted cherry pitter like the above left. Maybe she used a hand-held pitter or a small knife.

Will, Kayla, and Ava, I looked for poems about grandmas like mine and their fruit pies. The best poem by far came from the Peoria Poetry Club just down the road from us. That's further confirmation that the four of us need to pool our talents to hand make a very healthy custard fruit pie for our families. We could even use an iron skillet, probably with a lid, on the cast iron stove in our log cabin. It would be so healthy that it could be our entire lunch. Whaduyasay?

Love, Granddad

Grandma's Apple Pie

Of childhood recollections
Amid scenes that linger on,
Fondest thoughts (I need not lie)
Recall our Grandma's apple pie.
Black cast-iron coal stove
With radiant tended glow,
And heated baking oven
Warming just below.
Grandma in her flowery garb,
With apron dusted white with flour,
Porcelain mixing bowl with
Wooden spoon in this exciting hour!
Crisp Courtland apple slices,
Cinnamon-covered crumbly crust,
Pipe hot from the oven
With Grandma's smiling trust.
Patiently waiting in that Heaven-bound
Awesome line (and pray I'm not too late),
Amid God's blue celestial sky, to reach the Pearly Gate.
As St. Peter stands on high I'll humbly beg
For one more slice of Grandma's apple pie!

The Old Farm Pump by Franklin Reiss

Dear Will, Kayla, Ava, and Blake,   March 18, 2024

Cousins June and Jim McBrayer gave us this photo several years ago. It was taken in the mid-1960s by my dad's next older brother Franklin Reiss. He had it printed on canvas, framed, and then added a longhand message on the back. It was a gift in 1967 to his Uncle Bill and wife Rose. Uncle Will (as we called him) was born in 1890 on the Reiss Family Farm. He was the first of his generation to be born in the "modern" home built in 1889. All his older siblings were born in the adjacent log cabin built by my great great grandfather Adam Reiss in 1838. That 1889 home is also were my dad and his two older brothers were born.

This pump was in the pasture west of the old home and was there to water cows who drank from a nearby trough. You can see one of the two cedars rows in the background. That's why my grandfather named it the Cedar Row Farm.

Next is Uncle Frank's note on the backside of the frame. It's difficult to read so I retyped it below. Uncle Frank had three college degrees and was very proud of his photographic skills and his skills with written and spoken words. He was a professor at the University of Illinois.

Merry Christmas 1967 to Bill & Rose,

This nostalgic scene symbolizes simplicity, purity, and truth. It is nostalgic because it was taken in the pasture of the home farm, the locus of many memories for all of us.

Its simple lines and bygone technology bespeak an era almost gone from the American scene, an age in which simple jobs, homely virtues, and patient effort motivated men.

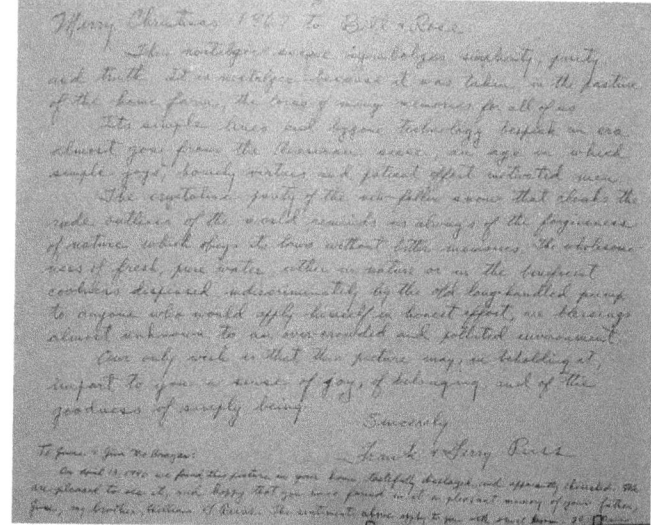

The crystalline purity of the new-fallen snow that cloaks the rude outlines of the world reminds us always of the forgiveness of nature which obeys its laws without bitter memories.

The wholesomeness of fresh, pure water, either in nature or in the beneficent coolness dispensed indiscriminately by the old long-handled pump to anyone who would apply himself in honest effort, are blessings almost unknown to an over-crowded and polluted environment.

Our only wish is that this picture may, in beholding it, impart to you a sense of joy, of belonging, and the goodness of simply being.

Sincerely,
Frank & Gerry Reiss

To June & Jim McBrayer:

On April 13, 1990 we found this picture in your home, tastefully displayed, and apparently cherished. We are pleased to see it, and happy that you have found in it a pleasant memory of your father, June, my brother, William G. Reiss. The sentiments above apply to you with equal love.

F. J. Reiss

Will, Kayla, Ava, and Blake, isn't this a wonderful gift with visual and written memories from 57 and 34 years ago. I'm honored to "save" this piece in the form of another Granddad's Mondays story. We don't know where the original will be in another 57 years!!!

Love, Granddad

The Old Barn is now a Garden

Dear Will, Kayla, Ava, and Blake,   May 31, 2021

Maybe you remember this barn photo from my Granddad's Mondays stories titled "Hoistin' Hay" on 6/8/2015 and from "The Old Barn Is Demolished in 2015" from 12/28/2015. My grandfather George "Pop" Reiss built this barn about 1920 and used it for storing hay in the upper level and for feeding livestock in the lower level.

Pop's generation and the next one have passed on. Barns became obsolete when farmers converted to jumbo hay bails that stay at the edge of their fields. So, the barn fell into disrepair and became dangerous. Updates and restoration could not be justified so it was demolished in 2015 and its footprint of foundation stones was left behind.

Our tenant then in the 1889 house was Beth Smith. She spent many hours rearranging some of those stones, adding a fence, and putting in a flower and veggie garden. We exchanged several emails on her wonderful job which included the pictures which follow.

beth smith <amishoakstore@gmail.com>
To: reiss_steve@yahoo.com
May 25, 2016 at 6:51 PM

Hi Stephen, although the barn is gone, the space is still contributing. Hope you enjoy the pictures. Maybe if you're in the area you can pick some things.

Stephen Reiss <reiss_steve@yahoo.com>
To: amishoakstore@gmail.com

May 25, 2016 at 8:03 PM

Hi, Beth. Thank you very very very much for recycling our old barn footprint into your garden. I'm sure our ancestors would be greatly pleased. I'm also sure the west half of that plot where the livestock were housed would be awesome soil. Be prepared for bumper crops.

I'm in Kazakhstan at the moment but do plan to visit the farm in August on my way to Memphis to spend a week building Habitat houses with Jimmy Carter.

Thanks again for the photos. I'm going to turn them into a story for our grandchildren and would like ongoing photos as your garden prospers. Steve

beth smith <amishoakstore@gmail.com>
To: reiss_steve@yahoo.com
Jun 9, 2016 at 8:32 PM

Here are some updated photos. Also, the stones that were buried and had to be cleared for the garden are now protecting the space around the summer kitchen. That space was open and all kinds of animals were living under there. Also included is a picture of the summer kitchen that is now a bedroom.

Happy and safe travels, Beth

Fast forward to January 2021. Beth is now working and living in St. Louis. Her son, his wife, and their baby are now living in the 1940 house. Her nephew is now living in the 1889 house with his girlfriend. Beth wants to locate a house trailer west of the garage and for us owners to share the cost of installing a septic system. Beth really really really likes the fresh air rural setting of our homestead. That's why she wants the trailer there for her occasional visits before eventually retiring when she and her husband would move to our farm fulltime.

Will, Kayla, Ava, and Blake, I have wonderful memories from 50 visits to our family farm starting in 1948. I was sorry to see the old barn disappear but that's the way things sometimes have to happen.

6-4
©2019 Bil Keane, Inc.
Dist. by King Features Synd.
www.familycircus.com
BIL and JEFF KEANE

"These vegetables will taste better than store ones 'cause we planted them ourselves. Right, Mommy?"

But the memories are still there and well documented in three public books, three family books, three stories to you grands, and lots of old photos. I'm thrilled that three generations of the Smith family may soon care for our homestead just like five generations of the Reiss family did before them.

Love, Granddad

Raising Sheep and Chickens on the Reiss Family Farm

Dear Will, Kayla, Ava, and Blake,   July 11, 2022

Here is a picture of your great great grandfather George Reiss with his hogs in 1905.
Notice the split rail fence behind him which separated the hogs in front from the sheep
and horses beyond. This picture is looking north from the log granary which is still there.
The tall barn was not there yet because George built it about 1920 and it was later
dismantled about 2017. The hogs look like a variety called Chester White including the
two darker ones which are reddish brown.

George W. Reiss in 1905 at the Reiss Family Farm

Here's another sheep picture from 1946. Notice their tails are not bobbed as is common
today.

Here are two 1956 pictures with the sheep shed on the left and the old chicken coup on the right. They were at the north edge of the homestead against the woods. My grandfather retired from farming in 1948 at age 75 having never owned a tractor. He did all of his farming with horses. My dad and I visited the family farm in 1948 when I was age 4. I stayed with my grandparents for a week while Dad traveled on to Sullivan, Indiana to meet his staff at Meadowlark Farms where he was taking a new job. He also looked around Sullivan for a new house. Anyway, I don't remember seeing any sheep at the family farm in 1948 so my grandfather "Pop" had exited that business by then.

Chickens were a major revenue crop for the family. Below is my grandfather's sister feeding the chickens in 1905. It's either Aunt Margaret – (Anna Margaretta Reiss born on 9/20/1875 who married George Dintelmann on 4/22/1908) or it's Aunt Katy – (Louisa Kathryn Reiss born on 9/22/1884 who married Philip Heinrich Petry on 6/2/1909).

Below is my grandmother Katie feeding chickens in 1946. The white chickens are Wyandottes, a docile, dual-purpose breed kept for their brown eggs and for meat. The dark chickens are **Rhode Island Reds** raised as a utility bird for meat and eggs, and also as a show bird. It is a popular choice for backyard flocks because of its egg laying

abilities and hardiness.

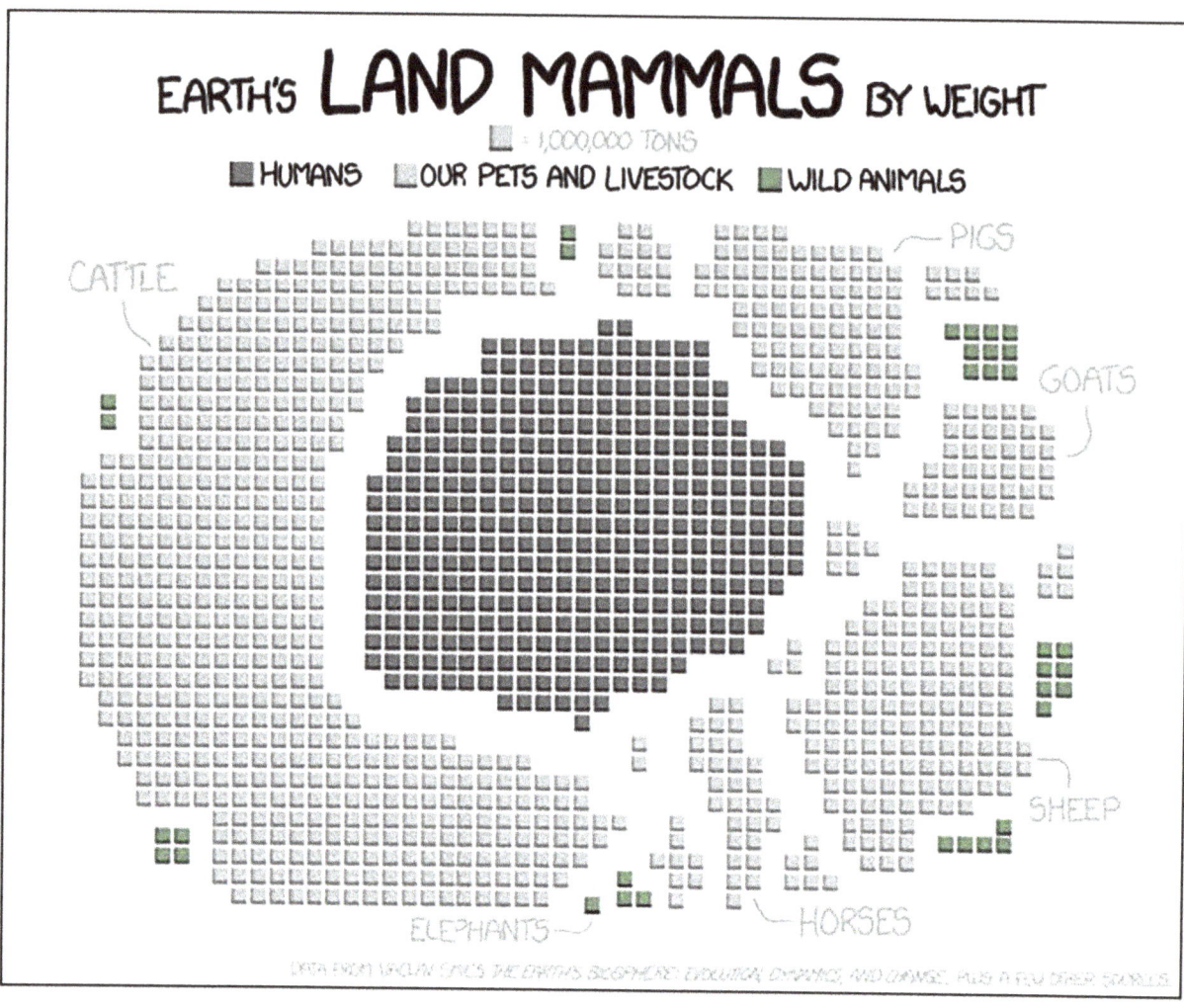

Will, Kayla, Ava, and Blake, here's a chart showing the Earth's land mammals by weight. People are in the middle. Chickens do not appear because they are not mammals. Let's do a little math to convert weight into headcount knowing that the average cow weighs 1660 pounds, human 137, pig 440, goat 100, sheep 230, horse 1200, and elephant 8000.

For just farm animals, I came up with 1,086 million sheep, 780 million goats, 409 million pigs, and 303 million cows. Never would I have guessed that sheep is the number one animal. Likewise, never would I have guessed that goats by themselves outnumber pigs and cows combined. We're so used to thinking of just US livestock that we don't realize that other countries and continents have far more livestock headcount than we do.

Anyway, enjoy eggs for breakfast, KFC for summer, and a warm wool scarf for the winters. You extended family was involved in producing all of that.

Love, Granddad

Reiss Clans in 1950 and 1982

Dear Will, Kayla, Ava, and Blake,   October 31, 2022

Our extended family gathered at the Reiss Family Farm south of Belleville every quarter for holidays in the 1950s and early 1960s. This may be the Fourth of July 1950. Back row left to right is Frank, Grandma, Gerry, Mom, Pop, Dad, Bill, and Anita. Front row is Richard, George, Ken, Mary Kay, Steve, and June Ann. Looks like stripes and suspenders were in style.

On the next page is fishing fun at the previous to the previous farm pond. We kids would get the biggest thrills over catching 4- and 5-inch catfish and bluegill. This pond was drained and recontoured with no trees about 1970. That second pond eventually went dry about 2010 so the dam was removed and that area converted back to farmland. All that remains is memories.

The second picture is the same folks but with two more families added. I think the tall bald man is Pop's nephew Edwin Dintelmann. He and Beulah had two daughters in the foreground.

Here's a photo from 1982 when three generations of the Frank/Gerry Reiss family visited our Lake of the Woods home. Left to right are Jesse, Frank, Adam, Diane, Steve, Grant, Becky, Richard, and Cala. Gerry took the picture. Richard and Cala were probably living in England at the time. Their two children were born there. Cala if from New Zealand.

Will, Kayla, Ava, and Blake, here's Frank/Gerry and the clan including Cala's mother then visited my sister in Sullivan in 1982. Left to right are Ron, Mom, Stephanie, Dad, Melissa, Frank, Becky, Mary Kay, Jesse, Gerry, Cala, and Mrs. Boyd.

Love, Granddad

Anticipating George (2/26/1942)

Dear Will, Kayla, Ava, and Blake,   February 20, 2023

Here's a letter my Grandmother Katie wrote to her family a few weeks before she headed to Urbana, IL to help with the arrival of another grandchild. He would be called George after her husband.

Our Dear Children,   January 27, 1942

It rained all night and is still raining. Well then, I'll go to a quilting today. Yesterday, Dad and I were at Belleville to get our check at the Farm Bureau office and I wanted to talk to Miss Hubbard but she had just left. So, she will write to me about going along with her or not (*to Urbana*).

But since then, Dad and I talked it over and I wonder if it would be better if I'd come a week later, say around the 7th or 8th of February as I want to be there when the baby comes and I can't hardly stay longer than 2 weeks. So, we think I'll be more help to you in that time. Write to me right away and tell me what I should do. Sunday we were at Aunt Katie's for dinner and in the evening, we went to Aunt Minnie's.

Yes, Franklin, we got the farm outlook and the farm economics book the other week and I read the article which you wrote, it's fine. My dear son, how can you do it? I'd be too dumb to even get a start on work like that. Son, we are so proud of you. Also, proud that you can teach at the University of Illinois. One thing more, we are proud of is that you got such a good and loving wife to go thru life with and to help you along with your duties. And now we are praying and hoping that everything goes well and that you will have luck and lots of enjoyment with the soon coming baby. You don't know yet what a wonderful feeling it is to have a sweet little baby in your home which you both can say it's all your own.

Dad and I often talk about our past years, how happy we were when we had our three little boys. How I'd coddle them in my arms, wrap them up in shawls, while Dad hitched the horses to the top buggy or surrey, sometimes it was the spring wagon. Grandmother and Grandfather also would get ready, each one holding one of the boys while I held the baby and off we went over the hills and thru the woods to Grandmother's house. And then too, everybody was so happy to see us come. Grandma and Grandpa Luetzelschwab always enjoyed having a lot of company, mostly their children and grandchildren and there were so many. But now that they are gone, it's not the same home anymore, no young life there anymore, so you know it's true when I say, there is nothing more enjoyable than a baby in a home.

Coming back to my three boys, I can still see them how they each pulled a wagon thru the deepest mud, built bridges, plowed with my table spoons, and so on. They were mud from head to foot at times. We had a laugh on Dad one Sunday morning. He looked the three boys over and said what's wrong? They look so pale. Are they sick? I had to laugh and said no, I just washed them once. I used to be in work up to my neck trying to help in the field as much as I could. So, they didn't get washed so often. But I still think each boy & girl should have a chance to play in the good Mother Earth dirt when they are small. After the mud puddle-ing years, the school-going years came. I'd bundle them up as best as I could and off they went facing the strong west wind, the rain, the snow, and cold. But never missed a day one year.

They all three made good records or good grades all the way thru grade school. Then came the high school that far away thru mud roads, but it all went, and you made us happy by bringing home honors of different kinds.

Then along came the time when you had attended the Farm and Home Week at Urbana with Mrs. Tillman and you wanted to go to college. I'll never forget that one night when you and Irwin went to drill practice at the Grange. Dad and I stayed home alone and I tried to talk Dad into letting you go to college. At first he didn't want to, but after talking it over awhile, he was satisfied to let you go the following year. And now we both are so happy we let you go thru college. We know you went thru a lot of hardships to get your education because we couldn't give you the money & you had to mostly work your own way thru. From three little boys we now have three fine young men and two fine young daughters and a sweet little granddaughter and soon another little boy or girl of which we will be very proud. Signing off,

Your Loving Mother and Dad

Will, Kayla, Ava, and Blake, isn't this an absolutely wonderful letter. Grandma Katie is one of my favoritest relatives. It's obvious that her husband Pop was totally pleased and satisfied with how she ran the family while he ran the farm. They were a tag team.

She mentions only two daughters-in-law because my dad Irwin didn't meet our mom Mary until 3/15/1942. They were married 7.5 months later on 11/8/1942 but Grandma and Pop were unable to travel from Illinois to California for that special event. Their funds were limited as Grandma mentions plus there was also a war going on.

I feel so blessed that Grandma wrote this very kind letter, that it was saved in Franklin's files, that cousin Jesse gave it to me, that it's now being read by you four great great grands, and that it will continue indefinitely in your 2023 Christmas books. The lesson here is to write, send, save, and share – WSSS.

Love, Granddad

Hoelscher's Sawmill

Dear Will, Kayla, Ava, and Blake,   July 14, 2025

My grandmother Katie Luetzelschwab Reiss was the fifth child of John Luetzelschwab who married Charlotte Hoelscher on May 26, 1881 in the village of Nameoki near

Granite City IL. The Luetzelschwab and Hoelscher farms were almost adjacent so those children grew up knowing each other. This set (bowl is original but pitcher is a replacement) was one of their wedding gifts. Charlotte re-gave it to her daughter Katie when she married George Reiss on 4/16/1911.

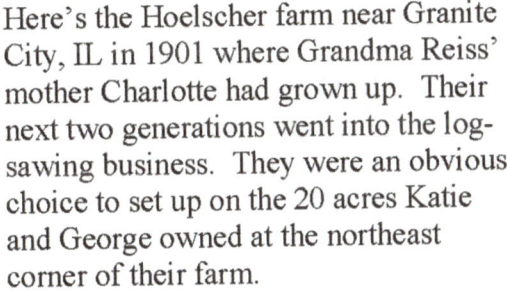

All eleven of their children reached adulthood which was unusual for those times. My grandfather George Reiss was also one of eleven children but only seven reached adulthood. Sons were John, Jacob, Herman, and Frank Luetzelschwab. Daughters were Mrs. Mary Weihl and Mrs. Caroline Gummerscheimer of Waterloo; Mrs. Minnie Sponeman and Mrs. Edna Lang of Millstadt Township; Mrs. Lena Becker of Belleville; Mrs. Katherine Reiss of Floraville; and Mrs. Lottie Sander of Columbia.

Here's the Hoelscher farm near Granite City, IL in 1901 where Grandma Reiss' mother Charlotte had grown up. Their next two generations went into the log-sawing business. They were an obvious choice to set up on the 20 acres Katie and George owned at the northeast corner of their farm.

Timber harvest and sawing are always done in the winter when the ground is frozen and no crops can be damaged by dragging logs to the mill. These pics were taken by Franklin Reiss in November 1945 with his young son Georgie watching. Frank added words on the backsides and then mailed them to his brother (my dad) Irwin in California.

Will, Kayla, Ava, and Blake, apparently, those sawyers built the small log shed from their trimmings for their weather or storage reasons which was visited by Frank's sons George and Richard about eight years later with our Grandma Katie. That photo is at the end and became the cover for our book about her 1944 – 1949 daily diary. I hope you four enjoy this family history as much as I do putting it together.

Love, Granddad

This is an old steam tractor that turns that flywheel which transfers rotational energy through a long loop belt like a monster rubber band. It then turns a circular sawblade which cuts oak logs into square cross sections. Sawyers then run those sections through the saw to make identical 5" square beams or slabs 1" thick by 8" inches or more wide by 10' or more long. They were very strong and very adequate for constructing barns, bridge decks, and other heavy projects.

3) An old fashioned choo-choo opined George, Run like helly but don't get anywhere. Power for Hoelscher's saw mill. Yep, its our old 192" friend (?) Joe Roth jr. putting some stickum on the drive wheel. Hoelscher is sawing logs out of their timber.

Man on the left looks like my
grandfather "Pop" Reiss.

7) Rolling the log (Georgie calls
it a limb) onto the carriage.
Man power, Joe jr and sr.
The background is looking
across the West Fork to
Roth's hills. I was standing
on the highest elevation of
the mound.

Notice the round saw blade protruding above the saw log. It rotated counterclockwise so it cuts downward into the log. We have one of those round blades that our artist friend decorated with memories from our previous yard. Great job! It's now a display item in our garage.

More slabs. That afternoon sun cast my shadow on this scene. Ah yes, these winter days the sun goes down behind those purple hills before 5:00 P.M., or is that against the law in California?

Here's the sawyers' log cabin. Maybe they had Grandma and Pop's grands in mind rather than making it for their own business needs. Now it's a diary book cover.

GRANGER, QUILTER, GRANDMA, MATRIARCH

Life on the Reiss Family Farm 1944 – 1948
St. Clair County, Illinois

BY STEPHEN W. REISS

Reiss Family Farm Events After Grandma's 1949 – 1953 Diary

Dear Will, Kayla, Ava, and Blake,   July 14, 2025

I'm doing a second edition of our book titled "Quilter, Granger, Grandma, Matriarch." It will show you four as co-authors and will include 45 Granddad's Mondays stories from 1940 - 1953. Here's Grandma's list of events after her second five-year diary.

1954 Feb 24   Franklin wrote the lease for Lavern & Lucille.

1954 June 10   Lavern & Lucille joined the Grange, got the first and second degrees.

1954   Josephs wheat crop made 870.30 bushels. We got $469.50 for our share.

1955 Feb 21   We got our deep freeze.

1955 Feb 24   We got the Maytag washer.

1955 May 4   We built Lavern's cistern.

1956 April 2   The Myers Company bulldozed.

1957   George planted the pine trees, the grass water way at two acres.

1958 April 3   Mr. Payne finished setting the furnace.

1958 May 6   We got our first Social Security check.

1958 June 11   June Ann graduation at Washington University in St. Louis.

1958 July 21   Mary's mother & father came to visit us.

1958 Sept 17   We paid our taxes, real estate $485.39, personal property $5.10.

Will, Kayla, Ava, and Blake, can you imagine getting your first deep freeze at age 65. That new washer was probably their first without a ringer to squeeze water out of clothes before hanging them on a clothesline to dry. That July 21, 1958 entry is six weeks after Easter when my California grandparents were driving back home after staying with us for six weeks in Sullivan, IN. Here's the Easter picture with Granddad Andrew, Grandma, Pop, and Grandma Daisy.

Love, Granddad

Becoming Your Family's Matriarch

Dear Will, Kayla, Ava, and Blake,   December 16, 2019

My favorite Granddad's Mondays story is about flying in Dad's B17 bomber. My next three favorites are about our three family matriarchs. Here's a summary:

- M1 – Margaret Basler Reiss Ebert (10/22/1818 –6/23/1902) married Adam Reiss at age 21, widowed at age 30 living with four children under age 11 in a 250 square-foot log cabin with dirt floor, married Conrad Ebert at age 31, had four more children but two died, survived second husband by 22 years.
- M2 – Anna Antonia Sybilla Feder Reiss (9/26/1844 – 5/14/1930) married Frank Joseph Reiss at age 21, had eleven children but only seven reached adulthood, no indoor plumbing or electricity, survived her husband by 8 years.
- M3 – Catherine Charlotte Luetzelschwab Reiss (3/25/1890 – 10/17/1986) married George William Reiss at age 21, all three sons reached adulthood and did well, no indoor plumbing until age 50 and no electricity until age 55, survived her husband by 22 years.

Here's from a blog I found on the Internet – Becoming your family's matriarch doesn't happen by accident. It's not a job that is passed down to you. You don't just grow into it. If you want to be your family's matriarch – the woman who leads them, who keeps them close, who everyone turns to for direction, then at some point, you have to decide that you are going to be that woman. You have to answer the question: Are you ready to be your family's next Matriarch? And then dedicate your life to fulfilling the role the best way you can.

Matriarchs are rare these days and getting more rare as time goes by. The days of a strong woman leading a family in a way that only a mother can do are fading away as more and more women change their focus from family to work place. Nowadays it is more common to find working moms, part-time housewives, and lots of woman who don't have the time or energy to devote to such an enormous responsibility. More than ever those same women need someone *else* to go to for guidance and reassurance. They just want to get through the day without collapsing from exhaustion.

A family matriarch is the foundation upon which her entire family is built. She is the constant. She is the one whose face can be depended on to be at every important event, and many of the seemingly unimportant ones too. She is the one who never forgets to send a birthday card–to her parents, siblings, children, grandchildren, in-laws, and friends. She makes everyone feel special. Valued. Important. She goes out of her way to ask how your life is. And she really listens because she believes you are significant.

She is the keeper of the family traditions. She hosts every holiday and expects as many of the family to be present as possible. She keeps them all close. She makes the traditional foods and hangs the traditional decorations. She tells the stories behind those traditions to her children and grandchildren to instill the importance of them well into the next generation. A sense of community, of belonging, springs from traditions carried down throughout the generations, and she knows it.

She is the keeper and teacher of the skills needed to make a house a home. She patiently shares those skills with her descendants and with the women who marry into the family as well. Cooking, sewing, knitting, quilting, gardening, canning, whatever her skills are, she teaches them to her children and grandchildren starting when they are very young.

When you are sick, she is the one to show up with soup, or an herbal remedy to take right alongside your over-the-counter medications. And she'll stay to be sure you take it. She seems to have an old remedy for everything, and most of them work!

Her house is the epitome of home, and you always feel welcome there. But you'd better be hungry before you show up because she's going to feed you before you leave. And that's okay because she makes the best foods. They all remind you of a comfortable, happy childhood.

Would *you* know what to do? If the world went crazy today, would *your* family gather around you? If that is what you want, it is never too late to become the woman you aspire to be. It is this that I strive for and it was with this purpose that I originally began the **Modern Day 50s Housewife** blog. I know there are women like me out there who aspire to be that woman. And I believe that when we support each other and share our skills and ideas, we can and will get there. So, I ask you again. Are you ready to be your family's next matriarch?

Will, Kayla, Ava, and Blake, the title for this story should also be **Becoming Your Family's Patriarch** because both roles as parents and grandparents are equally important. Traditionally, society has looked to women for homemaking, cooking, cleaning, clothing, and domestic issues and to men for job, home maintenance, and estate issues. I noticed that our three matriarchs above got married at age 21 and that all three married into the Reiss family. That probably made their challenges more difficult because they didn't have a 21-year head start like their husbands did. Their accomplishments through numerous hardships are absolutely amazing. You four will eventually have to figure out how you want to be remembered 75 years from now.

Love, Granddad

Epilogue

Quilting, grange, church, farming, family, and friends combined very well for Katie and George Reiss. She lived to age 96 and he to age 91. But now all their siblings, those spouses, their three sons, and those spouses have passed on to a greater reward. The Reiss Family Farm continues with ownership in the fifth and sixth generations. We celebrated 175 years of its existence with a family reunion on June 6, 2009. Katie's and George's DNA and legacy live on through 6 grandchildren, 11 great grandchildren, and 10 great great grandchildren.

Katie's Diary effectively provides a five-year window into life on the Reiss Family Farm.

Our website is stephenreissbooks.com

Stephen W. Reiss, born on June 12, 1944, is a seasoned professional with a rich career and personal history. He holds degrees in Electrical Engineering plus an MBA. He worked 40 years for Caterpillar Inc., retiring in 2006. He was awarded two patents and spent five years working in Asia – 3.5 years in Seoul, South Korea, and 1.5 years in Hong Kong with his young family.

Reiss is also a devoted family man. He married Diana Peterson in 1971. They have two sons, Adam plus Heather in Springfield with Will and Ava, and Grant plus Hany in Chicago with Kayla and Blake. He and Diane reside in Peoria, Illinois but also have a snowbird home in The Villages, Florida. His grandchildren are Will 15, Kayla 13, Ava 11, and Blake 10. Reiss has written over 1,600 Granddad's Mondays stories to his grands every Monday since Palm Sunday 2012. In addition to his Caterpillar career, Reiss is fanatical about Habitat for Humanity and met Jimmy Carter 13 times. He is the author of eight family history books. Reiss is blessed with energy and enthusiasm.